FOOD LOVERS' SERIES

Food Lovers' Guide to Connecticut

Third Edition

*Best Local Specialties,
Markets, Recipes, Restaurants,
and Events*

Patricia Brooks

gpp®

Guilford, Connecticut

Project editor: David Legere
Layout artist: Mary Ballachino
Text design: Nancy Freeborn
Maps: Rusty Nelson © Morris Book Publishing, LLC
Illustrations © Jill Butler; with additional illustrations by Carleen Moira Powell

Library of Congress Cataloging-in-Publication Data is available on file.

ISBN 978-0-7627-5280-5

Printed in the United States of America

Third Edition/First Printing

The prices and rates listed in this guidebook were confirmed at press time. We recommend, however, that you call establishments to obtain current information before traveling.

For my sons—Jim, Jonathan, and Christopher—for their willingness, from childhood, to be "tasters" and participants in my various gastronomic adventures, and also for my late husband, Lester, who has been a major player in everything gustatory I have ever done.

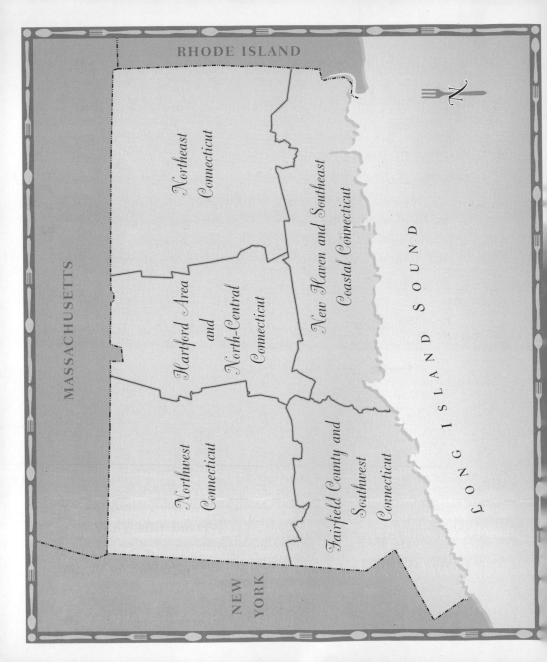

Contents

Northwest Connecticut

Hartford Area and North-Central Connecticut

New Haven and Southeast Coastal Connecticut

Northeast Connecticut

Preface

Time was—and within memory—Connecticut was considered a "white bread state." Ethnic meant Italian. Period. Even so, the pasta for sale in most groceries in Fairfield County, where I live, was limited pretty much to macaroni and spaghetti. If you wanted good bread, it meant a trip to Arthur Avenue in the Bronx. And creating an Asian meal involved a journey to New York's Chinatown for authentic ingredients. Even fresh herbs we consider commonplace today, like basil and cilantro, were impossible to find locally. A book like this one would have had so little material it would have been a four-page pamphlet.

That was then. What a difference a few decades make. Slowly, since the mid-1950s when I became a Nutmegger, Connecticut has evolved into a food lover's paradise. It happened little by little, not overnight. A national evolution in food experience and appreciation was influenced in Connecticut by two main factors: first, lots of foreign travel by our residents, tasting and enjoying foreign foods at the source; and second, the influx of immigrants from other countries and cultures, bringing their foods and recipes, opening restaurants and food shops.

Ethnicity today in restaurants throughout the state means Thai, Japanese, Lebanese, Asian fusion, Indian, Spanish, Portuguese, and even Persian, with all kinds of regional permutations, like South

Indian, Northern Italian, and regional Chinese. Just in my little community of a little over 20,000 residents (New Canaan), we have an Indian restaurant, a Japanese restaurant, a Chinese place, two Asian fusion stops, several Italian restaurants, a Mexican restaurant, two or more pizza parlors, and a French bistro. New Canaan is not unique; other Connecticut towns, which once were bereft of good places to eat, now boast dozens.

At the same time, gourmet food shops, cheese shops, chocolate shops, and ethnic markets have blossomed all over the state. Even the big chain supermarkets now stock Caribbean and Asian vegetables and spices. Lemongrass, napa cabbage, jicama, agave leaves, chayote squash, plantains, and bok choy have become staples.

My observations in this book are based on both personal and professional experience. Since 1977, I have been the Connecticut restaurant reviewer for *The New York Times*. This has involved sampling, analyzing, and reporting about food at more than 2,000 restaurants statewide—always anonymously. This experience has led to delightful discoveries as the restaurant scene has grown in sophistication and diversity. I have observed the arrival of notable French chefs and the expanding number of expert homegrown ones. I have observed and enjoyed the growth and range of farmers' markets and the increasing variety of crops that Connecticut family farms now produce. From my early roots in Minneapolis, I especially cherish the wondrous flavors of the fresh, natural foods I recall from childhood. Wine development has been a late-growth industry here, fascinating to observe. Microbreweries, even slower to appear, are a work in progress and also fun to observe.

Through the years, I have spent much time roaming the globe as a travel and food writer and guidebook author. Such travels have taken me from Aruba to Andorra to Ankara, from Zaragoza to Zamboanga, on food- and travel-article assignments for *Bon Appétit, Travel & Leisure,* and other national publications. My explorer's spirit has led me to remote locales to ferret out unusual foods and gastronomic exotica.

Possibly it was this spirit of discovery that has tempted me to seek offbeat sources of seafood, cheese, specialty food stores, and bakeries in Connecticut, all catering to an ever more knowledgeable clientele.

In tandem with all the food goodies available to buy, there are now many food events that the public—that means you and I—can participate in and enjoy, such as wine tastings and festivals in honor of oysters, apples, strawberries, and even garlic.

It has been a pleasure to discover, explore, sample, and take note of the many, many food-related phenomena and present them here. It is my hope that you will use this book to ferret out new food sources, whether shops, markets, or restaurants, and enjoy them. Connecticut is a relatively small state, and most of the sources included in this book are accessible within a short drive. Readers of earlier editions have told me they keep the book handy in their glove compartments, so when they are visiting other towns, they can refer to it as a quick resource. Other foodies have said they use the book as a guide for weekend excursions. Wine tours are especially popular. Enjoy.

Acknowledgments

It was evident from the get-go when researching this book that people in the food business are among the most generous on Earth—or at least the Earth in Connecticut. Every single person I talked to was willing and often eager to share sources and ideas and offer helpful suggestions. Major thanks go to my son Christopher Brooks, a fellow author and food-and-beer writer, who was extremely helpful about sharing his sources and ideas, to say nothing of his ever-wise editing of the finished manuscript. He has been an invaluable contributor to this book. The help of my late husband, Lester, an oenophile extraordinaire, was essential in the wine sections of the book and elsewhere. Thanks also to my good friend Georgia Bushman, whose timely suggestions and "late breaking news" about restaurant openings and closings averted some close calls in a culinary environment that changes frequently.

Also high on the list of helpers, whose contributions went "beyond the call," are the following food colleagues: Margaret Chatey, proprietor of Westford Hill Distillers in Ashford, whose generosity in recommending other producers and suppliers made my job easier and more exciting; Ina Bomze of Fabled Foods bread company in Deep River, a source of information about so many food shops and restaurants; James O'Shea, proprietor of West Street Grill in Litchfield, who volunteered with gusto some of his favorite sources; and Christopher Prosperi, chef-owner of Metro Bis restaurant in Simsbury, whose wide knowledge of and dedication to the best local food sources was kindly shared. And what can be said about Lee White, food writer and editor, that hasn't already been said over and over again? Her generosity, all-round food knowledge, and willingness to share information with friends easily make her a First Lady of Connecticut Foodery.

My thanks go also to David Legere, my project editor, who "rode herd" on the manuscript through the editorial and production process with good humor and to all the Globe Pequot staffers, artists, and production people who helped make this book possible.

I can't say enough about the many farmers I encountered at farmers' markets and their own farms who were willing to share their farm histories and experiences with me. Their commitment and hard work make living in Connecticut special for all of us fortunate enough to enjoy the fruits of their labor. Connecticut would be a different, less beautiful state without the rolling hills, pastures, and fields of its many family farms.

A special word of thanks also to Rick Macsuga, marketing representative, Connecticut Department of Agriculture and his colleagues Mark Zotti and Jane Slupecki. Their knowledge of farms, farm stands, and farmers' markets gave a huge boost to my research on the many exciting things happening with family farms in Connecticut today.

Thanks as well to the following individuals and establishments for graciously sharing their recipes, many of which were adapted for home cooks. These individuals and companies are not responsible for any inadvertent errors or omissions:

Adrienne's New England Clam Chowder and Lobster & Filet Mignon Wrapped in Phyllo: Adrienne Sussman, Adrienne restaurant

Authentic Belgian Hot Chocolate: Pierre Gilissen, Belgique Chocolatiers

Carole Peck's Puree of Chestnut Soup: Carole Peck, Good News Café

Catherine's Speculaas Belgian Cookies: Catherine Van der Maat Brooks, New Canaan

Chaiwalla's Strawberry-Rhubarb Cobbler: Mary O'Reilly, Chaiwalla

Chef Claire's Lentil Soup: Claire Criscuolo, Claire's Corner Copia

Chris Prosperi's Brussels Sprouts, Honey & Bacon and Metro Bis Beef, Corn and Pepper Salad: Christopher Prosperi, Metro Bis

Cilantro Couscous Salad: Kathleen Jonah Lenane, Bear Pond Farm

Debra Ponzek's Madeleines: Debra Ponzek, Aux Délices

Double Chocolate Raspberry Biscotti and Savory Apple Pizza: Margaret Chatey, Westford Hill Distillers

Eleanor's Linguine with Turkey Sausage: Eleanor O'Neill, New Canaan

Hopkins Inn's Mango Shrimp Salad: Chef Toby Fossland, Hopkins Inn

Ina Bomze's Cannelini Beans and Fabled Escarole and Eggplant, Pepper and Onion Spread: Ina Bomze's Fabled Foods

Jean Jones's Jumbo Pumpkin-Cranberry Cookies: Jean Jones, Jones Family Farm

Jean-Louis's Famous Potatoes au Gratin: Jean-Louis Gerin, Restaurant Jean-Louis

Lavender Blueberry Banana Bread: Fort Hills Farm

Riad Aamar's Baked Layered Moroccan Eggplant and Beef Ragu: Riad Aamar, Oliva Café

Sally Maraventano's Asparagi alla Parmigiano: Sally Maraventano, adapted from her *Festa del Giardino* cookbook

Simple Chicken Piccata: Debbie Harris of Cook's Kitchen, Guilford

Susan's Pancetta Herb Cheese Purse: Susan Goodman, Susan Goodman Catering

Sweet Maria's Chunky Monkey Cake: Maria Bruscino Sanchez, Sweet Maria's

Introduction

Connecticut's location between the monoliths of New York and Massachusetts sometimes causes it to be overlooked. Small it may be, but our state fairly bursts with gastronomic treasures, agricultural resources, ethnic diversity, and enterprising spirit. Connecticut Yankees have historically been great entrepreneurs and suppliers and purveyors of food—selling nutmeg from the West Indies, for example, which gave us the lasting nickname of "Nutmeggers." (A less kindly version has it that sharp-eyed "drummers" mixed wooden "nutmegs" in with the real ones they sold.) The food revolution that has been sweeping across America for the past few decades has taken hold with tenacity and exuberance in our state, making city after city, town after town, beehives of food production. Scores of new restaurants have opened and now thrive here. Even towns that were relative culinary wastelands, notably Darien and Fairfield, are now bursting with new restaurants and food activities. Gourmet food stores, bakeries, cheese shops, and special ethnic-food markets are now part of our state's topography. Recent years have brought new wineries, once a rarity in our state. They are a welcome stop on the food-and-beverage landscape.

Some of the resources in this book may be familiar; many others may not. It is a pleasure to introduce new ones to you. Even though I have been crisscrossing the state in a quest for new food sources for more than thirty years, I continue to marvel at the new food enterprises, specially food stores, and restaurants that continue to pop up, in the optimistic "can-do" spirit of Yankee ingenuity.

While I hope to bring new information to you, there is another purpose as well: to acquaint you with good fresh foods within easy reach so that you may exult, as I do, in the many natural resources of our state—the native clams, oysters, scallops, and other fresh seafood, the produce grown here and its many outlets, like farm stands selling fresh fruits and vegetables, local festivals featuring homemade food specialties, and local teachers expert in helping you learn to make specialties of all kinds. Also noteworthy is the return of old-fashioned farmers' markets, encouraged by the state's Department of Agriculture. These markets convene throughout the growing season, with their farm-to-consumer fresh produce and other farm products like honey, cheese, fresh eggs, maple syrup, and fruit jams, preserves, and pies. While we think of the United States as a major industrial society, we in Connecticut at the local "people" level are able each summer and autumn to reach back to revisit our country's roots, to relish the direct contact between the growers and consumers of wonderful, farm-fresh, natural foods.

This guide has been organized into five chapters, beginning with the Fairfield County area at the southwest edge of the state, radiating upward to the northwest, then to Hartford and the north-central area around it, south to New Haven and the southeast coast, finally ending in the northeast corner of the state. Each chapter includes a map of the area, enabling you to plan day trips for visiting and exploring.

Not all chapters are equal in length. Southwest Coastal Connecticut and the coastal area north of New Haven to New London are both population centers and have more than their share of good restaurants and food suppliers. But within each chapter, big or smaller, you will find the following categories:

Made or Grown Here

The large number of food producers in Connecticut may surprise you. Some are huge enterprises, like Munson's Chocolates; others are mere "cottage industries" of food products—individual producers who have come up with a superior salsa, cheesecake, or handmade chocolates. Some of these producers sell their specialties to wholesalers and/or retailers—in which case I have often cited several sources in the area where you may buy them—whereas many others sell directly to the consumer via e-mail, a Web site, or catalog. I have included prize-winning dessert makers, bakers, chocolatiers, and cheesemakers, among many other entrepreneurs.

Specialty Stores & Markets

This section of each chapter features a wide variety of specialty food stores, which range from ethnic-food vendors to gourmet delicatessens and fish markets. Included are stores selling cheese and chocolates, bangers and bouillabaisse, olive oils and oregano, teas and tamales—virtually every imaginable good thing to eat that can be packaged, marketed, and sold. Many of these shops are unheralded treasures, known only to locals—until now.

Farmers' Markets

In Connecticut at last count there are 125 farmers' markets operating throughout the state, most of them in the smaller towns. These offer shoppers a chance—one or two days a week—to buy seasonal, field-fresh fruits and vegetables directly from the grower. You won't find bananas, mangoes, or grapefruit here—only Connecticut-grown or home-produced products, whether eggs, honey, fresh produce, preserves, baked goods, meats or cheeses, maple syrup, fresh and dried flowers, ornamental gourds, Indian corn, and cockscomb. Most of the farmers' markets operate from late spring to early November, but for specific days of the week and times, check the individual chapters of this book. Even so, days and hours can change at the last minute, so the Department of Agriculture Web site is the most up-to-date source. A mere handful of farmers' markets—not the open-air ones—are open during the winter; they are duly noted.

Part of the fun of shopping at a farmers' market is the camaraderie that develops between sellers and regular buyers. Many of the farmer-growers travel to several market days in various Connecticut towns. Information about farmers' markets is available through the state Department of Agriculture.

Be aware that it is cash-only at most farmers' markets and farm stands, but occasionally a vendor will accept a check with proper ID.

Farm Stands

There are hundreds of small farms in Connecticut, and many have roadside stands where, in season, they sell their crops, freshly picked from the field. Some stands are literally that; others are ensconced in barns or outbuildings or are substantial structures in and of themselves. Many sell, in addition to their produce, fresh eggs; honey; maple syrup; home-baked pies, breads, and pastries; homemade preserves; and pickles. To sell their baked goods to the public, the farmers must have certified commercial kitchens. Although most of the farm stands we have listed keep regular seasonal hours, it is always prudent to check ahead of time.

Some farmers offer pick-your-own schedules, as various crops ripen—most often berries, apples, pears, peaches, tomatoes, pumpkins. Usually, the schedule is announced on the farm's voice mail, so call ahead. If you take advantage of such pick-your-own opportunities, be sure to carry with you sunscreen and water and wear old clothes, a hat, and comfortable shoes.

Food Happenings

Each year's calendar brings a surprising number of annual food events to Connecticut: festivals, fairs, and fund-raisers in which food is on center stage. This section in each chapter tells you about happenings throughout the year and where they take place, whether it is the Seaport Oyster Festival of Norwalk or the Dionysos Greek Festival in New Britain.

Learn to Cook

Cooking courses in Connecticut range from recreational classes and demonstrations to hands-on workshops. You will find everything from the basics of cooking to instruction in esoteric ethnic cuisines. A few cooking instructors offer guided tours abroad, which may be noted here.

Learn about Wine

Under this heading in various chapters, you will find information about wine tastings and sources helpful to novice and serious oenophiles alike.

Landmark Eateries

Connecticut now has an abundance of restaurants of every imaginable type—more than 12,000 of them, according to the Connecticut Restaurant Association. While this book is not a restaurant guide per se, I have included in each chapter some restaurants known for certain cuisines, specialties (like the Spanish tapas at Barcelona), or a notable ambience.

Considering the number and variety of restaurants in the state, our selection represents a relatively small helping of gastronomic gems. What our restaurant forkfuls have in common, in addition to memorable food, is character, personality, uniqueness—call it what you will—that adds to the pleasure of being there.

Nibbles

New in this edition is a category I call Nibbles. This consists of snack places, usually inexpensive, notable for a quick bite, not necessarily a full, fancy, or formal meal. Nibbles might also be food shops known for specific items or a particular special dish.

Brewpubs & Microbreweries

With the rise of microbreweries nationwide since the early 1980s, I have become fond of fresh-tasting craft beers and ales with real flavor and complexity. While Connecticut still lags behind much of the country in the number of its craft breweries, every region of the state boasts at least one beer producer. Whether a brewpub restaurant or microbrewpackaging plant, those companies are listed in this section of the appropriate chapters.

Wine Trail

Connecticut's wine industry has been a growth stock (no pun intended) in recent years, especially notable in the northwest, southeast, and northeast regions of the state. Established wineries are included in these specific sections, along with information about their tasting facilities and special events. Note that appendix B lists additional events held at various state wineries throughout the year.

Recipes, Etc.

Laced throughout the book are a few recipes harvested from various Connecticut sources. Some are from chefs and restaurateurs, others were provided by farm growers and vintners, still others by producers and specialty-shop owners, and a few from friends who are notable cooks.

Restaurant Price Key

$ = inexpensive; most entrees under $18

$$ = moderate; most entrees $18 to $24

$$$ = expensive; most entrees over $24

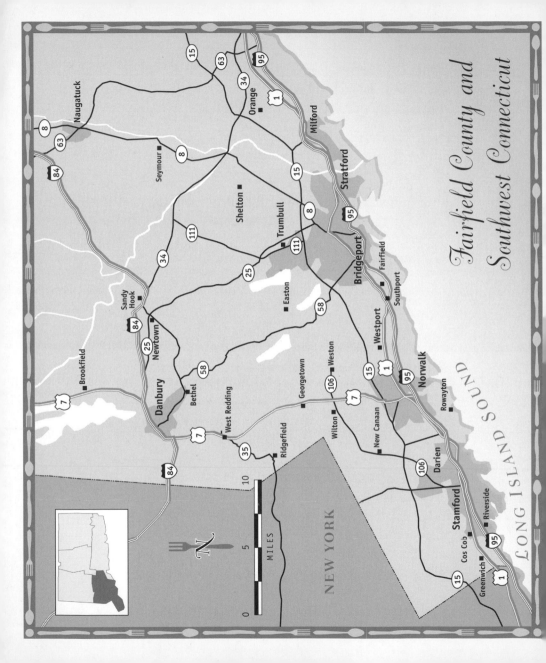

Fairfield County and Southwest Connecticut

Aside from Bridgeport, which is the state's largest city, the southwestern region consists mostly of small towns under the umbrella of Fairfield County. The county, one of the nation's richest, is often nicknamed "a New York City bedroom" because so many of the county towns are within an easy train commute of Manhattan and many workers in the city do indeed live in the county. While densely populated, the area is still, surprisingly, a terrain of woods, rivers, ponds, and wildlife preserves. Its Long Island Sound coastline has been dubbed the "Gold Coast" because of the many CEOs, moguls, hedge fund managers, and celebrities who live in expensive homes and super-McMansions on and near its shores, from Greenwich all the way up to Westport, Southport, and as far east as Stratford. Bedroom to New York it may be, but Fairfield County increasingly has a vibrant life of its own, as many national corporations and businesses have made their headquarters here, allowing their officers and top employees to work closer to home. Various ethnic groups have also migrated here as workers and burgeoning entrepreneurs.

This combination of affluence and diversity has changed the dining landscape, attracting established New York City restaurateurs and chefs. Some have opened their own restaurants; others have grabbed the reins (or range) at historic village inns and have brought new levels of culinary expertise and sparkle to the local dining scene. As a result, the number of authentic French restaurants, bistros, and cafes in this southwestern region exceeds that in any other part of the state. Gastronomic tastes have evolved from simple to sophisticated, with almost every imaginable type of ethnic restaurant now available. Indian, Japanese, Thai, Spanish, Chinese, Portuguese, Mexican, Peruvian, Colombian, Venezuelan, Central and South American, Greek, Lebanese, Persian, and, of course, the ubiquitous Italian are all here now. Towns formerly with a single decent restaurant—my own New Canaan (population 20,098) comes to mind—now have literally dozens, which range from good to excellent. Deluxe restaurants are on a par with those in major cities all over the United States. Comparisons are odious, of course, but in terms of quality dining, Fairfield County probably leads the state. Parallelling this welcome boom in restaurant diversity is the continuing growth of food-supply and specialty shops, food enterprises, ethnic markets, green markets,

elegant take-out services, catering businesses, and other gustatory innovations. Southwest Connecticut is no longer a pale imitation of Manhattan, but a bona fide and exciting source of fine food in and of itself. This "Gold Coast" now boasts a new, freshly burnished patina.

Made or Grown Here

Beldotti Bakeries, 605 Newfield Ave., Stamford; (203) 348-9029. Aside from the bakery, Beldotti sells its breads and cakes at the New Canaan farmers' market, where it does a thriving business all season long. Its walnut-raisin bread is really special, as is the sourdough and the many cakes and crispy "pig's ear" Danish pastries.

Beyond Bread, 216 Sound Beach Ave., Old Greenwich; (203) 637-2543. Anyone who cherishes the memory of Café du Bec Fin will be pleased to learn that master chef and superb baker Harvey Edwards is up to his old tricks: making wonderful breads and selling them retail from this small shop and wholesale to shops, markets, restaurants, and caterers. Harvey makes at least six breads (multigrain, sourdough, Tuscan, and black currant/walnut among them) daily, as well as croissants, muffins, Danish, and scones. He also makes and dispenses soups, pizzas, and sandwiches in his tiny shop. In warm weather, fans spill out to sidewalk tables to lunch and munch.

Billy's Bakery, 1885 Black Rock Turnpike, Fairfield; (203) 337-5349. This amazing hubbub of a place produces more than twenty-four different breads (not all the same day), as well as sweet rolls, croissants, scones, coffee cakes, cookies, biscotti, a dozen different tarts, and cakes. Named for its owner, Bill Hollis, Billy's boils and bakes a dozen different bagel types and makes ten different cream cheese spreads, from veggie mild to hot-and-spicy. Billy's also dispenses a selection of sandwiches, soups, and entrees to-go. And for Fido, there are house-made biscuits at a pittance apiece.

Briar Patch Enterprises, 322 New Haven Ave., Milford; (203) 876-8923. Nancy Follini and Joseph Gilbert have dug clams for years. Since 1982 their wholesale business of harvesting the juiciest, tastiest littleneck clams and bluepoint oysters, both from  Long Island Sound, and sea scallops farther out, has flourished. Local and area restaurants and fish markets gobble up almost their entire "crop."

Bridgewater Chocolate, 559 Federal Rd., Brookfield; (800) 888-8742; www.bridgewaterchocolate.com. Swedish-born chocolatier Erik Landegren moved from Bridgewater to larger Brookfield quarters, which has now doubled in size. There, the company produces American-style handmade chocolates from pure, premium ingredients. Bridgewater has won many awards from the Connecticut Specialty Foods Association, for best confection, best overall food product, and best packaging. The line includes chocolates, toffees, truffles, mints, caramels, turtles, chocolate-dipped fruits, and chocolate bark, all handsomely packaged, as well as a new line of sugar-free truffles and chocolate bars. All are for sale at the factory; at Bridgewater's store, 12 Lasalle Rd., West Hartford; (860) 570-0707; at gourmet shops (including Villarina's Pasta and More in Southbury and Newtown, The Pantry in Washington Depot, and Carol Peck's Good News Café in Woodbury); and via the company's Web site and catalog.

Cocoa Michelle, 190 Main St., Westport; (203) 221-0002; info@cocoamichelle.com. This petite chocolate shop sparkles like a jewel. In fact the artisanal candies are displayed in cases resembling jewelry store treasures. In the rear is a European-style coffee bar and overstuffed armchairs to sip and nibble any of twelve chocolate flavors made daily on the premises. A second shop is at 54 Railroad Place, Westport; (203) 221-0020; www.cocoamichelle.com.

Deborah Ann's Sweet Shoppe, 381 Main St., Ridgefield; (203) 438-0065; www.deborahanns.com. Chocolates made by two New York lawyers? Unlikely, right? Wrong! That's what Deborah Ann and Mike Grissmer's candy shop is all about. The Grissmers sought a change of scene and jobs that would make people happy. What's happier than chocolates? The Grissmers' all-white, tin-ceilinged shop, with its intoxicating aromas, reminds me of the movie *Chocolat*. While the main candy production has shifted to Brookfield, you can sit at one of three tables and sip hot chocolate, tea, or coffee while watching the hand-molding done in the shop. Or just sample some of the truffles, turtles, buttercrunch, caramels, and other delights. Besides the seventy-plus varieties the Grissmers make, they also tempt the inner kid in us with glass jars of hard candies (Jelly Bellies, Gummi Bears, and the like) displayed in the Candy Bar Creations counter in the rear. You can even design your own chocolate bars here. Or buy Mr. Shane's delicious, locally produced, hand-scooped ice cream.

Dr. Mike's, 158 Greenwood Ave., Bethel; (203) 792-4388. Don't let appearance fool you. Inside this modest-looking ice-cream parlor, tucked into the rear of an old frame house, lurks some of the richest, tastiest ice cream in Connecticut. Since 1975, Robert Allison has been churning out as many as fifty flavors, with a butterfat content of 16 percent. At any time there are eight flavors—four regulars (vanilla, rich chocolate, strawberry, and chocolate-lace-and-cream) and four daily specials. In warm months thirty different flavors rotate during a given week. Most popular are rich chocolate and chocolate-lace-and-cream, which use 22 to 24 percent cocoa butter and Bensdorf chocolate. There are several tables and a handful of places to sit on the porch. The parking lot holds sixty cars, which gives you an idea of Dr. Mike's popularity. A second Dr. Mike's (444 Main St., Monroe; 203-452-0499) is equally small, also with ample parking. And who, you might ask, is Dr. Mike? Dr. Michael Burnham was the original Dr. Mike. His daughter Mary started the business years ago, then sold it.

Ferris Acres Creamery, 144 Sugar St. (Route 302), Newtown; (203) 426-8803; www.ferrisacrescreamery.com. In 2004 Shirley Ferris opened this ice-cream shop and farm store, selling farm-made, hard-packed ice cream directly from the sixty-five cows (mostly Holsteins) that her husband Charles and their two sons raise on the eighty-acre farm the Ferris family has owned since 1864. From a repertoire of forty flavors (with thirty available daily), several are Shirley's own inventions: Raspberry Swirl Chip (vanilla base, raspberry swirls, dark chocolate chips); Cowtrax (vanilla base, peanut butter swirls, caramel, and tiny chocolate chunks); Elvis's Dream (vanilla base, peanut butter, banana, hunks of dark chocolate); and Bada Bing (chocolate base, Bing cherries, and big chocolate chunks). The shop's manager is Shirley's daughter-in-law Terry. It is open from noon to 9:00 p.m. Sunday through Thursday, until 10:00 p.m. Friday and Saturday, early April to mid-November. Also available: milk shakes, soft ice cream, frozen yogurt, and ice-cream cakes and pies. Shirley says modestly, "Part of the appeal is the farm setting. You can watch the cows close-up as you sit at a picnic table eating your ice cream."

Gelatissimo, 26 Forest St., New Canaan; (203) 966-5000; www .gelatissimo.net. With its ice-cream-colored interior (pistachio walls, mango counters, and lemon cabinets), this place is so clean and crisp, it almost sparkles. Gelatissimo, which opened its doors in late 2005, is the place for twenty-two flavors of rich Italian gelato. This tiny shop has four little tables where you may eat your gelato, as well as several wooden benches outside for warmer-weather slurping. Andrea and Nuccia Mazzonetto, a husband-wife team, make gelato fresh daily; chocolate hazelnut, nutty pistachio, and cappuccino are my favorites—so far.

Hauser Chocolatier, 137 Greenwood Ave., Bethel; (203) 794-1861; hauserchocolates.com. Ruedi Hauser Sr. was making chocolates as a teenager in his native Switzerland, long before he immigrated to the United States. In 1983 Ruedi and his wife, Lucille, started producing their handmade chocolate truffles in Bethel. The line now includes twenty-four to thirty different types of chocolates, chocolate dessert sauces, chocolate-covered nuts and coffee beans, and sugar-free chocolate and cocoa. The Hausers also create beautifully boxed assortments for corporate gifts, weddings, and special occasions like Valentine's Day. Hauser chocolates are sold at retail outlets throughout the United States as well as through their Web site and catalog. Although the main factory has moved to Rhode Island, the fudge and solid chocolates are still made in Bethel, right behind the Greenwood Avenue shop, with its vintage pressed-tin ceiling. The Chocolate Lace line is now part of Hauser.

Knipschildt Chocolatier, 12 South Main St., Norwalk; (203) 838-3131; www.knipschildt.com. Knipschildt chocolate truffles, rated among the world's top three by *Gourmet* magazine, are so ambrosial, each bite lingers on the tongue. Knipschildt chocolates in twenty-four flavors—with female names, like Madeline, Hannah, and Helena—are made with Valrhona and Michel Cluizel French chocolate and a high amount of cocoa butter; they are 100 percent natural, free of additives and preservatives. Since 1999 the company has been selling its unusual chocolates (many have spicy as well as the predictable sweet components) to upmarket stores like Darien Cheese & Fine Foods and Dean & DeLuca. Knipschildt also produces five dessert sauces and four intensely flavored, elegantly bottled fruit syrups, which make great gifts. A cozy cafe is attached to the factory (see below under Landmark Eateries).

Mel's Hellish Relish, 356 Round Hill Rd., Fairfield; (203) 259-7065; www.hellishrelish.com. Mel Gancsos launched his incendiary business in 2003, and it's been heating up ever since. There are now three fiery relishes available, all in twelve-ounce jars: Medium, Hot, and Extra Hot, as well as Mel's Sweet Inferno Pickles. They are sold via his Web site and to small groceries all over the state, including Lyman Orchards.

Michele's Pies, 666 Main Ave., Norwalk; (203) 354-7144. Michele Albano has brought a touch of rustic Vermont to her pie-baking business. Her shop has finely

lacquered tables and stools of cut logs, and hand-carved wood panels that highlight moose, deer, and a bear devouring pies. Pies are what Michele is all about. She usually makes twenty varieties a day, all from fresh ingredients. The fresh fruit pies are especially abundant in summer. There are always plenty of choices, including the ever-popular chocolate-pecan-bourbon. Name your favorite; Michele probably bakes it. She also makes entrees using her famous dough, from chicken potpies to various quiches.

Newman's Own, 246 Post Rd. East, Westport; (203) 222-0136; www.newmansown.com. Actor Paul Newman is gone, sadly, but his name lives on—and not just in the movies. He and author A. E. Hotchner started Newman's Own in 1982 as something of a lark (the Web site says "Fine foods since February" in Newman's wry style). It took off immediately with an initial high-quality salad dressing that featured Paul's smiling face. The company has grown phenomenally, and the natural-foods line now includes tomato-and-roasted-garlic pasta sauce, three flavors of Old-Style Picture Show Microwave Popcorn, steak sauce, fruit salsas, lemonades, limeades, and red-wine-and-vinegar salad dressing. Taking the company motto to heart—"Shameless Exploitation in Pursuit of the Common Good"—all Newman's profits after taxes, more than $175 million since 1982, go to a variety of charities. Newman's Own products, available nationally as well as via the company Web site, are recognizable by their clever labels, showing Paul in a variety of hats and outfits that are tailored to each product.

New Pond Farm, 101 Marchant Rd., West Redding; (203) 938-2635; www.newpond farm.org. Twenty cows graze over many of 102 pastoral acres on this hal- cyon land. The result is the production of more than a dozen hard cheeses (which include Gruyère, Gouda, Colby, cheddar, havarti, blue, and Jarlsberg) and yogurt, all made by farm manager Chris Casiello. Most of the cheeses, except the Camembert, are from raw milk and age at great length. General Putnam, which resembles English cheddar, takes at least six months to mature; the Gouda and Gruyère age for up to twenty months. The farm is a licensed milk producer; eight cows produce hormone-free, pasteurized but unhomogenized milk. That means rich cream and yogurt. Eggs and beef are also for sale.

Red Bee Honey, 77 Lyon Plains Rd., Weston; (203) 226-4535; www.redbee.com. Beekeeper Marina Marchese is rarely bee-reft of honey bees. Her raw, unpasteurized, natural honey comes in ten different varietals, available by jar, bottle, case, pail, and gift set, as well as by honeycomb, sold by phone and e-mail and through the Web site. She also sells varietals from other producers, which include clover, wildflower, buckwheat, alfalfa, goldenrod, poplar, raspberry, blueberry, and orange blossom. Red Bee is also sold in restaurants (like Grants and Bricco in West Hartford) and specialty shops (Aux Délices in Greenwich, Mirabelle Cheese in Westport, and

On the Half Shell—Raw Bar Heaven along the Southwestern Shore

Less than a century ago, Norwalk was known as "the oyster capital of the nation," and hillocks of shucked shells lined the Norwalk River on Water Street. Though no longer the industry it once was, the bivalves are still found at six or more Norwalk oyster farms, and the bluepoints can be savored along the entire Connecticut coast. In these two intriguing seafood restaurants, you will find varieties of tasty oysters fresh from local and other chilly waters east and west.

Harbor Lights, 82 Seaview Ave., Norwalk; (203) 866-3364; www.harborlightsrestaurant-ct .com; $$. Finding a good seafood restaurant that's actually on the water isn't as easy as you might think, considering Connecticut's long shoreline. But here, voilà! On a glass-enclosed deck (windows open in warm weather) overlooking

others). Marina also has a new book, *Honey Bee,* with more about bees than you ever thought you'd know.

Wave Hill Bakery, 196 Danbury Rd. (Route 7), Wilton; (203) 762-9595; wavehillbreads@aol.com. Opened in late 2005, this small artisanal bakery has caught on like the proverbial wave (it is

Norwalk harbor, you can dine on the freshest seafood, imaginatively prepared, often with a Greek twist. Shrimp and scallops Mykonos, Mediterranean sea bass, and salmon osso bucco are a few of the briny treats. Octopus Mediterranean is really special—as tender as I've ever had it. Also owned by the same Greek Gavrielidis family is **Rouge Winebar,** 88 Washington St., South Norwalk; (203) 354-4781, which is another very good restaurant.

Elm Street Oyster House, 11 West Elm St., Greenwich; (203) 629-5795; www.elmstreetoysterhouse.com; $$. Former luncheonette space has been converted to an attractive, modern, all-white cafe with sea-blue trim and a separate barroom with a long, long bar. The mostly seafood menu is especially strong on oysters, and the raw bar features six different types a day. Dips include horseradish, standard cocktail sauce, and a tangy mignonette of shallots, red-wine vinegar, and cracked black peppercorns. Pan-fried oysters are also wonderful here, as are the littleneck clams, steamed mussels, poached salmon, grilled shrimp, and pan-fried catfish. Check out the owners' newest venture, **Ten Twenty Post,** under Landmark Eateries section.

named for the garden in Riverdale where the proprietors were married). Spouses Mitch Rapoport and Margaret Sapir make seventy-five loaves of three-grain pain de campagne each day, Thursday through Monday. It is much prized, both at the bakery and at area stores like Walter Stewart's Market in New Canaan and Mrs. Green's Natural Market in Stamford. I can't get enough of it.

Abbondanza, 30 Charles St., Westport; (203) 454-0840; www .abbondanza.com. The large open space housing Abbondanza ("abundance" in Italian) has five parts: takeout foods (salads, pastas, desserts), shop (gourmet products), espresso bar, catering, and restaurant. The shop sells imported pastas, Provençal jams, Esprit du Sel gray sea salt, L'Estorvell caperberries, chocolates, and other sundries. Bonda, the upscale restaurant ($$$) with Mediterranean/New American food, is open for dinner, Friday and Saturday only.

Asia Bazaar, 131 Cove St., Stamford; (203) 961-1514. Packed into a cluttered, distinctly utilitarian corner store is a huge variety of Indian products. If you are serious about preparing authentic Indian food, Asia Bazaar is a valuable resource for all kinds of rice in bulk (basmati, long, brown, and jasmine, among others), Indian teas, a variety of beans and lentils, cardamom seeds, coriander, cloves, garam masala and other Indian spices, hot peppers, different kinds of flours, fresh produce, Indian soft drinks, spicy snack foods, and much, much more. An Indian nostalgic for home can even find Bollywood videos here.

Aux Délices, 1075 East Putnam Ave., Riverside; (203) 698-1066; www.auxdelicesfoods.com. When Debra Ponzek, former executive chef at Montrachet in New York City, opened this stylish gourmet take-out shop in late 1995, she raised the bar for local takeout and catering, making home entertaining a gourmet experience. Her Provençal-influenced menu changes weekly and can be faxed for ordering ahead. There are usually ten to twelve entree choices, more than a dozen side dishes, and at least twelve desserts from which to choose. Sample entrees might be peach-and-shallot-stuffed pork loin, pesto mushroom lasagna, or crab cakes with roasted yellow-pepper sauce. A few burnished copper-topped tables in the tiny shop are handy for noshing on soups, sandwiches, salads, and coffee while waiting for your order. The shop also sells directly and via mail order a number of blue-chip delicacies like aged balsamic vinegars, chocolate truffles, Aux Délices spiced nuts, biscotti, biscuits, almond macaroons, crispy crepes, and butter cookies. Gift baskets and homemade cakes and tarts are available for overnight home delivery. Three other Aux Délices shops are now open: at 3 West Elm St., Greenwich, (203) 622-6644; in Goodwives Shopping Center, Darien, (203) 662-1136; and in the Hyatt Hotel, 1700 East Putnam Ave., Stamford, (203) 344-1933.

Darien Cheese & Fine Foods, Goodwives Shopping Center, 25 Old Kings Hwy. North, Darien; (203) 655-4344; www.dariencheese.com.

Neat, compact, and immaculate, Ken and Tori Skovron's alluring shop is so full of tempting edibles that I want to scoop up everything in sight: dozens of olive types in fastidious crocks, and a heaping, expanded charcuterie selection. But it's cheese that rules supreme here. Ken has thirty-six years of cheese experience and it shows. Anything you've wanted to know about cheese, he can tell you—how to cut it, at what temperature to keep it, how to store it, and what kind to buy for every occasion. He has at least 200 cheeses at any given time (including whole wheels), both imported (from all over the world, sometimes from tiny mountain villages where the annual output is minuscule) and domestic (including Connecticut's own). Shelves along one wall contain dessert sauces, rarefied chocolate truffles, jams, biscuits, and teas. In the rear are bins of coffee and accessories like cheese knives and trays, salad bowls, baskets, and other handcrafts.

Fairfield Meat Emporium, 949 King's Hwy. East, Fairfield; (203) 696-2322. While this Hungarian market features meat and is famous for its house-made cold cuts, it has much, much more to show and sell, like all kinds of Hungarian goodies, from stuffed cabbage and paprikash to Hungarian Trappist and kashkaval cheeses, stews, soups, and strudels. All the cooked foods are made on the premises. That includes hot dogs, head cheese, and numerous sausages.

Fratelli Market, 17 Cedar Heights Rd., Stamford; (203) 322-1632; www.fratellimarketct.com. *Basta pasta!* Enough, you might say after seeing the many varieties of pasta in this unusual Italian market. There are more than thirty types of ravioli alone. The pasta and diverse sauces are made in Brooklyn and then fresh-frozen and shipped. While pasta is the star performer here, Fratelli also sells fifty different sandwiches and panini, various antipasti, and some aged cheeses, enough for a takeout or eat-in lunch at one of six tables on the premises.

Fuji Mart, 1212 East Putnam Ave., Riverside; (203) 698-2105. This tidy market is a rarity in Connecticut: a grocery dedicated almost exclusively to Japanese food products. Salmon, horse mackerel, yellowtail, and other fresh fish; sushi-ready maguro, tako, hirame, octopus, sea urchin, and other raw favorites; daikon, tofu, and other fresh vegetables; a variety of seaweeds, teas, rice, rice vinegars, canned, dried, and frozen goods—all these and much more are here. Fuji Mart is on the ground-floor, left-hand corner of a glass low-rise office building, just off exit 5 of I-95. Drive slowly or you'll miss it. Closed Monday.

Gold's Delicatessen, Compo Shopping Center, 421 Post Rd. East, Westport; (203) 227-0101; www.goldsdelicatessen.com; $. This large Jewish deli has been a local institution since it opened its doors in 1958. Julius Gold sold it in 2003, but it's *still* popular for its many kosher foods and also as an informal place for lunch (which can be a zoo of hyper-activity), seating seventy-two, with more than thirty types of sandwiches daily. Among the deli gems for takeout are roast beef, brisket, and other meats, various cheeses, smoked fish (kippered salmon, Nova, belly lox, sable, sturgeon), pickled herring, turkey roasted daily, salads (like whitefish, egg, chicken, and tuna), house-made soups, and super breads (some from Fabled Foods in Deep River).

Kaas & Co., 83 Washington St., Norwalk; (203) 838-6161; www .kaasnco.com. Also known as "A Taste of Holland," Jan Schenkels's spic-and-span shop has specialized in foods and decorative items (Dutch tiles, plates, jars, tea towels) from the Netherlands and Indonesia since 1990. Homesick Netherlanders come from as far as Pennsylvania and New Jersey for the Dutch cookies, jams, Droste cocoa, Pickwick teas, de Ruijter chocolates, Indonesian spices, honeycakes, speculaasbrokken, marzipan cakes, candies, and eighty-five types of Dutch licorice, as well as mixes and crackers. In the deli cases are Dutch cheeses—low-fat, regular, and aged Gouda, Leyden, Old Amsterdam, baby Edam, aged farmer cheese, raw milk cheese, Friese Nagel, cumin cheese, and Rookvlees—as well as herring and mackerel. Kaas & Co. even sells mettwurst, a smoked sausage shipped from a Dutch butcher in Michigan.

Mirabelle Cheese Shop, 190 Main St., Westport; (203) 227-0047; info@mirabellecheeseshop.com. Damon and Andrea Itin have some one hundred different cheeses in their neat little off-the-main-path shop. Most of the cheeses are European, but they also carry domestic varieties from Connecticut, New York, California,

Vermont, and other states, as well as fifteen charcuterie items and other gourmet foods.

The Olive Market, 19 Main St., Georgetown; (203) 544-8134; $$. Deli cases bulge with one hundred tempting cheeses, mostly from France, Italy, and Spain; ten large vats hold olives from there and also from Greece. Shelves are lined with imported goodies, including more than twenty types of olive oil. Breads, muffins, and biscotti are made daily on the premises. This well-stocked store also serves breakfast, light lunch (soup, pizza, panini, and chivito, a Uruguayan steak sandwich), and brunch on weekends, plus fixed-price tapas dinners three nights a week. The market now has a gift shop, The Olive Home, right next store.

Oriental Food Market, 109 New Canaan Ave., Norwalk; (203) 847-0070. This all-inclusive, if cluttered and a mite untidy, source for Asian foods is especially strong on Chinese, Japanese, and Philippine products—fresh (bok choy, snowpeas, sweet pickles, tofu, Japanese pumpkins) and frozen (dim sum dumplings, Filipino pampango lumpia, Chinese sweet sausage). Shelves are crammed with soy sauces (including tangy soy calamansi from the Philippines), rice vinegars, various oils, roasted sesame seeds, kimchi mix, pickled vegetables, teas, mung beans, dried mushrooms, and sugar palm, with many available in large sizes (like twenty-pound sacks of rice). Nonfood supplies include electric rice cookers and Chinese tableware. There's even a tiny Chinese take-out/eat-in section near the door. Cash only.

Penzey's Spices, 197 Westport Ave., Norwalk; (203) 849-9085; www.penzeys.com. Being inside this well-kept store on the Post Road is like entering spice heaven. There are some 260 spices to choose among, including thirteen varieties of chili peppers, nine blends of curry powders, and eight types of cinnamon, to say nothing of such exotica as annatto (used in Carribbean, Mexican, and Latin American cooking) and charnushka (smoky seeds topping Jewish rye bread). A knowledge-able staff will help you choose among various paprikas (such as smoky Spanish and Hungarian sweet kulonleges), peppers, cardamoms (like the intense green favored in India or the subtler white used in Scandinavian baking), and spices blended for various types of dishes (seafood, salads, chili, Asian recipes). Roaming among rustic shelves made from packing cases is a savory experience any home cook can relish.

Scandia Food & Gifts, 30 High St., Norwalk; (203) 838-2087; www.scandiafood.com. I would expect an emporium of Scandinavian foods to be bright and cheerful, and Scandia certainly is, with neat displays of cookies, flatbreads, crackers, crisps, breads, pastries (like cardamom braids filled with almond paste), pudding and juice mixes, lingonberries and other preserves, refrigerated cases with frozen fish (including lutefisk), tubes of salmon and herring paste, smoked herring and mackerel, and cod-roe caviar. Scandinavian cheeses include gräddost, Danbo, Herrgårdsost, Greve/Emmentaler, Norvegia, Jarlsberg, prästost, Västerbotten, and gjetost, as well as mushroom, shrimp, and ham cheese spreads. There are even Swedish meatballs and sausages, made in this country the traditional way. The shop now has a small cafe in one corner, seating a mere fifteen (space outdoors for twenty in warm weather), which some patrons say reminds them of "grandma's kitchen." At tables you can nibble open-faced sandwiches and pastries and sip Swedish coffee. The cafe is open Wednesday through Saturday. A large adjoining room displays sweaters, clothes, dolls, calendars, books, copperware, party supplies, Christmas ornaments, candleholders, candles, and other gifts and accessories from Sweden, Norway, Denmark, and Finland. Those nostalgic for a touch of the homeland come to Scandia from Long Island and as far away as Massachusetts.

Simpson & Vail, 3 Quarry Rd., Brookfield; (203) 775-0240 or (800) 282-TEAS; www.svtea.com. This restful haven—owned by Jim Harron, whose family has had the business since 1978—is tucked into a rock quarry. The company, begun in 1929, is believed to be the second oldest tea company in the United States and is ideal for sampling a huge variety of teas: green, black, white, aromatic, blended, organic, flavored, herbal, decaffeinated, even yoga teas. You can buy many tea accompaniments here: shortbreads, cookies, scone mixes, jams, honey, and Devon creams, as well as coffees,

TRADING UP

All but one of the six Trader Joe's in Connecticut are in the southwest part of the state. (The exception is in West Hartford.) Trader Joe's isn't a typical chain—if it were, you wouldn't find it in this book. Devotees travel across the state to load up on the many unusual items at these unusual stores, whose prices are often well below those of the ordinary food chain. TJ's, as its fans call it, specializes in organic, vegetarian, kosher, fat-free, sugar-free, gluten-free, salt-free, and all kinds of sybaritic foods, some of which you can't find elsewhere. Great buys are imported cheeses, crackers and breads, pita breads, nuts and dried fruits, dried pastas, jams and preserves, salsas and sauces, pesto, chocolates, candies, and cookie assortments. Natural cereals, fresh soy milk and other soy products, organic fruits and vegetables, olive oils and specialty vinegars, smoked salmon, organic fresh chickens, wasabi peas, soy nuts, and other snack items are among scores of products sold here, many with the Trader Joe's label. Vitamins, herbal soaps, and shampoos are also available. The frozen cakes and pies are exceptional; even the non-frozen baked goods are tasty. Every week new, irresistible products arrive to tempt us devout patrons.

Trader Joe's

www.traderjoes.com

436 Post Rd.
Darien
(203) 656-1414

2258 Black Rock
Turnpike
Fairfield
(203) 330-8301

560 Boston Post Rd.
Orange
(203) 795-5505

400 Post Rd. East
Westport
(203) 226-8966

113 Mill Plain Rd.
Danbury
(203) 739-00983

1489 New Britain
Ave.
West Hartford
(806) 561-4771

salsas, and other specialty foods. Also for sale: teapots, cozies, strainers, stoneware mugs, and other tea accessories. On a warm day, pack a lunch and sample your tea in S&V's gazebo. There are regular tastings of four teas most Saturdays from 10:00 a.m. to 4:00 p.m. Check the Web site for details.

Spic and Span Market, 329 Pequot Ave., Southport; (203) 259-1689; www.spicandspanmarket.com. Gregory Peck—no, not that one—runs the market. As for the name Spic and Span, it sounds more like a cleanser than the upscale market it is, from its knotty pine walls and pressed tin ceiling (that suggest a country store) to the diverse and eclectic food items it carries. There are sixteen different whole bean coffee varieties, an array of bottled hot sauces and marinades, a butcher counter featuring cut-to-order Angus steaks, boneless pork chops, and other prime meats, and takeout foods such as capon in brandy sauce, beef Stroganoff, and eggplant Parmesan. That's for starters.

Steve's Market, 69 Main St., Norwalk; (203) 853-4020. Compact and tidy, Steve's modest store is Greek to me—a great source of many things Hellenic: Kefalotyri and Manouri cheeses, taramasalata, frozen spanikopita and baklava, large pita breads, Greek cookies, whole squid—and that's just the alpha of it. Shelves are lined with jars of Kalamata olives and capers, rose and quince jams, sesame snacks, bulghur wheat, rice, biscuits, and all kinds of other tasty items.

Versailles, 315 Greenwich Ave., Greenwich; (203) 661-6634; $$. Sometimes it seems as though the cake at every wedding or special event I attend in Fairfield County comes from Versailles. No, not the royal estate in France, but a small patisserie, where Maurice Versailles has for decades been specializing in superb cakes, tarts, and breads, which are clearly worthy of being served in any palace. The Versailles repertoire includes French classics like Opera, Casino, Madeleine, Clairefontaine, Strawberry Montmartre, and Pont Neuf, along with individual delights like Paris-brest, St. Honoré, and assorted fruit tarts. A small cafe in the rear is popular for breakfast and lunch, with salads, quiches, fish dishes, and those yummy pastries.

Zumbach's Gourmet Coffee, 77 Pine St., New Canaan; (203) 966-2704. Near the railroad tracks is a teeny shop with just three tables. There Zumbach's dispenses morning coffee to scores of regulars—businessmen, housewives, and local politicos. But Doug Zumbach's main business is bulk: some fifty different types from twenty countries, with about 250 pounds of beans being roasted every single day. Zumbach's also wholesales to restaurants, caterers, country clubs, and corporations. Cash only.

For the most up-to-date farmers' market locations, days, and times, call the Connecticut Department of Agriculture at (860) 713-2503 or visit the Web site at www.state.ct.us/doag/ or e-mail ctdeptag@po.state.ct.us.

Bethel Farmers' Market, 67 Stoney Hill Rd., Bethel. Saturday from 9:00 a.m. to 1:00 p.m., mid-July through October.

Bridgeport Court House Farmers' Market, Baldwin Plaza, corner of Broad St. and Franklin Ave., Bridgeport. Tuesday from 1:00 p.m. to 6:00 p.m., July through October.

Danbury City Center Farmers' Market, Main St. at Kennedy Park, Danbury. Friday from 11:00 a.m. to 4:00 p.m., early July through October.

Darien Farmers' Market, Mechanic St., behind fire house, Darien. Wednesday from 11:00 a.m. to 6:00 p.m., mid-May through mid-December.

Fairfield Farmers' Market, Greenfield Hills, 1950 Bronson Rd., Fairfield. Saturday from 1:00 to 4:00 p.m., early June through late October.

Fairfield Brick Wall Farmers' Market, 1189 Post Rd., Fairfield. Saturday from 9:00 a.m. to 2:00 p.m., all winter.

Georgetown Farmers' Market, intersection of Main St. and Route 57, Georgetown. Sunday from 10:00 a.m. to 2:00 p.m., late May through October.

Greenwich Farmers' Market, commuter parking lot, exit 3 off I-95, Arch St. and Horse Neck Ln., Greenwich. Saturday from 9:30 a.m. to 1:00 p.m., mid-May through mid-December.

Milford Farmers' Market at Walnut Beach, East Broadway, Milford. Monday from 3:00 to 6:00 p.m., early July through October.

Monroe Farmers' Market, Monroe Congregational Church, across from town green, 34 Church St., Monroe. Friday from 3:00 to 6:00 p.m., early July to mid-September.

Naugatuck Farmers' Market, on the Green, Church St., Naugatuck. Wednesday from 10:00 a.m. to 2:00 p.m. and Sunday from 9:00 a.m. to 1:00 p.m., early July through October.

New Canaan Farmers' Market, Center School parking lot, South Ave. and Maple St., New Canaan. Saturday from 10:00 a.m. to 2:00 p.m., early June to late November.

Norwalk Farmers' Market, Flax Hill Rd., South Norwalk. Friday from noon to 5:00 p.m., early July through October.

Ridgefield Farmers' Market, 88–90 Danbury Rd. (Route 35), Ridgefield. Friday from 3:00 to 7:00 p.m., June through October.

Sandy Hook CV Farmers' Market, corner of Glen Rd. and Route 34, Sandy Hook. Sunday from 9:00 a.m. to 1:00 p.m., early June to early October.

Sandy Hook Organic Farmers' Market, St. John's Episcopal Church, 5 Washington Ave., Sandy Hook. Tuesday from 2:00 to 6:00 p.m., late June through second week of October.

Seymour Farmers' Market, Community/Senior Center front parking lot, Pine St., Seymour. Tuesday from noon to 6:00 p.m., early May through October.

Shelton Farmers' Market, corner of Cornell and Canal Sts., Shelton. Wednesday from 3:00 to 6:00 p.m., and Saturday from 9:00 a.m. to 1:00 p.m., mid-June through October.

Stamford Farmers' Market, Latham Park, Lower Prospect and Forest Streets, Stamford. Saturday from 10:00 a.m. to 2:00 p.m., early June to November.

Stamford Bartlett Arboretum & Gardens Farmers' Market, Bartlett Arboretum & Gardens, 151 Brookdale Rd., 1 mile north off exit 35, off Merritt Parkway, Stamford. Wednesday from 10:00 a.m. to 2:00 p.m., late June to early September.

Stamford High Ridge Farmers' Market, High Ridge Shopping Center, Stamford. Wednesday from 10:00 a.m. to 4:00 p.m., July through October.

Stratford Farmers' Market, Deluca Field, Main St., Stratford. Monday from 1:00 to 6:00 p.m., late June through October.

Trumbull Farmers' Market, Long Hill Green, Main St., Trumbull. Thursday from 2:00 to 6:00 p.m., mid-June through October.

Weston Farmers' Market, Route 57 at High Acre Rd., Weston. Saturday from 8:00 a.m. to noon, mid-June through mid-October.

Westport Farmers' Market, 26 Imperial Ave., municipal parking lot, Westport. Thursday from 10:00 a.m. to 2:00 p.m., mid-May to November.

Beardsley's Cider Mill & Orchard, 278 Leavenworth Rd. (Route 110), Shelton; (203) 926-1098; no1cidermill@yahoo.com; www.beardsleyscidermill.com. Dan is the third-generation Beardsley managing this 100-acre farm, and the apple of his eye is . . . apples. He has forty-two varieties of them in orchards spread over thirty acres, some planted in 1918 and still producing old-fashioned types like Baldwin, Wagner, Golden Russet, and Spitzenberg. On weekends from mid-September to Columbus Day, you can pick your own; and from mid-September through Christmas Eve you can stop by to see small batches of fresh apples being pressed into cider in Dan's cider mill. The farm store also sells peaches, pears, plums, and quince— as well as local honey, maple syrup, fruit butters, jams, jellies, cider vinegar, cider doughnuts, farm-baked cookies, and eleven kinds of pies. Call ahead for pick-your-own hours and availability.

Blue Jay Orchards, 125 Plumtrees Rd., Bethel; (203) 748-0119; www.bluejayorchards.com. At this 120-acre farm, the Pattersons invite you to pick your own apples from thirty varieties. Most popular is the Macoun, then the Mutsu (the big yellow Japanese hybrid sometimes called Crispin); there are McIntosh, Gala, Cortland, Granny Smith, Empire, and Winesap, too. Then browse the farm's Store & Gift Shop for apple pies, cider doughnuts, and fresh cider (August through October), pastries from the farm bakery, as well as maple syrup, honey, peaches, pears, and pumpkins. There are hayrides to the pumpkin patch in September and October. The Pattersons also have a luncheonette and the Sample Tasting Corner for trying the various types of apples. The store and cider mill are open daily, August to December, from 9:30 a.m. to 5:30 p.m.

Holbrook Farm, 45 Turkey Plain Rd. (Route 53), Bethel; (203)792-0561; www.holbrookfarm.net. On their twenty-acre farm, John and Lynn Holbrook raise organic vegetables, avoiding pesticides and chemical fertilizers. In their farm shop they sell eggs from their two hundred chickens, as well as garlic, carrots, various lettuces, mustard greens, kale, sugar snap peas, Swiss chard, and other vegetables. The shop also stocks Holbrooks' own peanut butter, fruit pies, bread and scones, along with products from other Connecticut farms, such as maple syrup, raw milk, gourmet oils and vinegars. Call ahead to learn what has just been harvested. Open Monday through Saturday, 10:00 a.m. to 6:00 p.m.

Jones Farm and Winery, 606 Walnut Tree Hill Rd., Shelton; (203) 929-8425; www.jonesfamilyfarms.com. Philip Jones began farming here in the 1850s, and six generations later the Joneses are still working the land. Terry and Jean Jones and their son Jamie are in charge now of 400 working acres in these rolling hills. Christmas trees have been a cash crop since 1947, but the farm also cultivates strawberries, blueberries, pumpkins, squash, and gourds. Hop aboard the Berry Ferry wagon to one of two locations—Strawberry Valley or Pumpkinseed Hill—for pick-your-own pleasures, from June through October, depending on crop conditions (call ahead for days

Jumbo Pumpkin-Cranberry Cookies

Jean Jones of Jones Farm and Winery in Shelton calls these cookies a favorite at Pumpkinseed Hill during the fall harvest season. I think you'll like them as I do anytime at all.

4 cups flour
2 cups rolled oats, uncooked
2 teaspoons baking soda
2 teaspoons pumpkin pie spice
1½ cups softened butter
1 cup granulated sugar

2 cups firmly packed brown sugar
1 egg
1 teaspoon vanilla extract
2 cups cooked, solid winter squash or pumpkin
1 cup dried cranberries

1. Preheat oven to 350°F. Combine flour, oats, soda, and spice. Set aside.
2. Cream butter; gradually add sugars, beating until light and fluffy. Add egg and vanilla.
3. Alternate additions of dry ingredients and squash/pumpkin; mix well after each addition. Stir in cranberries.
4. For each cookie, drop ¼ cup dough onto lightly greased cookie sheet and flatten. Cook in preheated oven for about 20 minutes or until cookies are firm and lightly browned.

Makes about 32 cookies.

Jones Farm and Winery
606 Walnut Tree Hill Rd., Shelton
(203) 292-8425
www.jonesfamilyfarm.com

and times). Jamie and his wife, Christiana, are in charge of the wine production (see below under Wine Trail).

Plasko's Farm, 670 Daniels Farm Rd., Trumbull; (203) 268-2716; www.plaskosfarm.com. In addition to the many different vegetables John Plasko's thirty-acre farm produces, he has six acres of orchards (apples, pears, peaches, and plums). A family farm for ninety-three years, Plasko's is also now known for its variety of fresh baked goods. Plasko's kitchen turns out twelve different soups (including gazpacho), two types of pesto (basil, sweet red pepper), seven different types of pies, fifteen organic breads (asiago, black olive, multigrain), and all kinds of tea breads, muffins, scones, cookies, and popular, award-winning apple cider doughnuts. Besides selling in ten farmers' markets in season, Plasko's wholesales its baked goods to markets like Walter Stewart's in New Canaan.

Shortt's Farm & Garden Center, 52-A Riverside Rd., Sandy Hook; (203) 426-9283; www.shorttsfarmandgarden.com. On a mere four acres, Jim and Sue Shortt produce a variety of organic vegetables and fruits. For sale at their farm store (and various farmers' markets) during the growing season are beets, Brussels sprouts, cauliflower, broccoli, beans, hot and mild peppers, six types of eggplants, summer and winter squash, bok choy, cucumbers for eating and pickling, six types of lettuces, heirloom and hybrid tomatoes, many other veggies, cantaloupes, watermelons, basil and other herbs, as well as fresh eggs, honey, and jams. The store is open April to November, but hours vary, depending on the season. Check ahead.

Silverman's Farm, Inc., 451 Sport Hill Rd., Easton; (203) 261-3306; www.silvermansfarm.com. You want apples? Peaches? Plums? They are all here in abundance (fourteen peach varieties, more than twenty apple types). You may pick your own from July to October. Call or check the Web site for hours. In addition, Irv Silverman's "animal farm" has goats, sheep, deer, pigs, emus, buffalo, llamas, exotic birds, and a pet-ting zoo. The farm market offers fresh produce (including twenty kinds of squash), flowers, eighteen different farm-made pies, preserved spiced fruits, jams, and even salsas. From August to October, there are tables for picnics on the grounds and, on fall weekends, tractor rides through the orchards to the pumpkin patch. Silverman's is open year-round.

Stone Gardens Farm, 83 Sawmill City Rd., Shelton; (203) 929-2003; www.stonegardensfarm.com. Since 1998 Fred and Stacia Monahan have been raising and selling all kinds of seasonal vegetables, flowers, plants, and Thanksgiving turkeys. You can also buy shares of beef from the Monahans. Their farm stand is open from May to Thanksgiving, 10:00 a.m. to 6:00 p.m. daily.

Treat Farm, 361 Old Tavern Rd., Orange; (203) 799-2453; treat.farm @snet.net; www.buyctgrown.com. Owner Jeff Wilson grows and sells field-fresh sweet corn, tomatoes, pumpkins, squash, peppers, and eggplants, plus various other veggies, all grown on his ninety-eight acres. His stand is open from mid-July through October and in December for Christmas trees, from 9:00 a.m. to 6:00 p.m. on Saturday and Sunday and from noon to 7:00 p.m. Monday through Friday.

Warrup's Farm, 11 John Read Rd., West Redding; (203) 938-9403; warrupsfarm@sbcglobal.net; www.warrupsfarm.com. Named for a local Indian, Warrup's has been in the Hill family since the 1700s. Proprietor now is Bill Hill, who works fifteen of his three hundred acres, growing organic lettuces, tomatoes, garlic, potatoes, other vegetables, and herbs. He sells them all at his roadside stand, along with fresh flowers and maple syrup. You may also pick your own vegetables and flowers starting in mid-August. Warrup's farm stand is open Tuesday through Sunday, 10:00 a.m. to 6:00 p.m. from mid-August through October. During maple-syrup season (the first three weekends in March), visitors to the sugarhouse can watch the entire syrup-making process, but be sure to call ahead for hours. Warrup's also sells at the Weston farmers' market each Saturday in season.

JANUARY–FEBRUARY

Annual Taste of Stamford, Sheraton Hotel, 2701 Summer St., Stamford; (203) 359-4761; www.stamfordchamber.com. In a three-hour period, from 5:30 to 8:30 p.m., on a single night in late February (check for the date), for a set price, you might wolf down the wares of some thirty area restaurants, bakeries, caterers, and others in the food industry, as well as samplings from various vineyards, beer importers, and specialty-coffee distributors. You'll be chewing for a worthy cause: The proceeds go to the Stamford Chamber of Commerce for program development efforts, including Kids Our Future Trust Fund.

Taste of Ridgefield, Ridgefield Community Center, 316 Main St., Ridgefield; (203) 438-4585. Sponsored by the Rotary Club, this annual fund-raiser (since 1999) is usually held in late January or early February (typically the Sunday before Super Bowl Sunday, but check ahead to be sure). This is a chance to critique specialties of between twenty-five and thirty Ridgefield eateries and be a do-gooder at the same time; 100 percent of the proceeds, usually some $30,000, goes to thirty-two local philanthropies. More than a "taste," the admission ticket permits unlimited samplings of appetizers, entrees, wine, and beer. Live jazz is performed through the day at two sessions: noon to 2:00 p.m. and 4:00 to 6:30 p.m. Each session is limited to 300 attendees due to fire-code restrictions.

APRIL–MAY

Fairfield County Eats!, Italian Center of Stamford, 1620 Newfield Ave., Stamford. An annual fund-raiser (since 1989), this corporate-sponsored event is held in early May. Contact is Linda Kavanagh at (203) 323-4185, e-mail at Linda@maxexposure.net. Many area restaurants, wineries, breweries, and specialty-food shops participate. A single entrance fee enables you to sample an extravaganza of delicious food. Proceeds benefit the Food Bank of Lower Fairfield County.

JUNE

Secrets of Great PBS Chefs, Norwalk. This special late-June event, held annually since 2001, is sponsored by and benefits the Public Broadcasting System. For specific date and locale, call the PBS Special Events Department at (800) 287-2788 or e-mail special events@CPTV.org, or check the Web site www.cptv.org. This high-powered, three-hour evening lets you rub elbows and lift forks with famous chefs who have appeared on PBS television. The chefs, who have included Rick Bayless, Joanne Weir, and Michael Colameco, provide a live demonstration and dinner at a set price.

AUGUST

Annual Milford Oyster Festival, Fowler Field & Town Green, Milford; (203) 878-5363; www.milfordoysterfestival.org. If it is the third Saturday in August, you must be in Milford, on the Green or along the harbor. Billed as the largest one-day event in New England, this festival began in 1974; 2009 marks the thirty-fifth year, and between 50,000 and 60,000 people now attend. Some seventy-five nonprofit organizations staff booths in the huge food court and elsewhere, where you can buy anything your palate desires from burgers and hot dogs to, yes, oysters, which come raw, fried, or stewed. Headline entertainers, canoe races, art and crafts exhibits (with over 200 vendors), schooner cruises, and a Classic Car & Motorcycle Hop are all part of the fun. Hours are from 10:00 a.m. to 6:00 p.m. Over fifty nonprofits benefit from this amazing event.

SEPTEMBER

Annual Norwalk Seaport Association Oyster Festival, Veterans Memorial Park, Seaview Avenue, East Norwalk; (203) 838-9444; www.seaport.org. Reserve the weekend after Labor Day: This "biggie" started small in 1978 and now draws as many as 50,000 to 60,000 visitors over a three-day period, usually held the second weekend of September. Oysters are definitely in the swim, with oyster boats and tall ships in the harbor, an "oyster pavilion" with displays commemorating the decades of oystering in Norwalk, an oyster-shucking contest, and the "Oyster Slurp-Off," in which you can demonstrate your oyster-downing prowess. Oysters star in the twenty food booths, too, along with clams, soft-shell crabs, lobster, shrimp, fish, calamari, jambalaya, pizza, Belgian waffles, and a host of international favorites, with proceeds to go to community groups, social services, and scholarship programs. Skydiving, marching bands, harbor cruises, tours of a World War II PT boat and others, entertainers on three stages, and arts-and-crafts exhibits keep the crowds entertained. Call for dates and hours or check the Web site.

Nibbles

Arcadia Cafe, 20 Arcadia Rd., Old Greenwich; (203) 637-8766; www.arcadiacoffee; $. In a high-ceilinged (with ceiling fans) former post office, you can enjoy breakfast (from 6:30 a.m. on weekdays, 7:00 a.m. weekends), an elevenses, lunch, afternoon snack, or early, informal supper. The fresh-baked muffins (as many as eleven flavors) are glorious, but wait. There are bagels, scones, pain au chocolat, a quiche of the day, smoked salmon plate, charcuterie platter, and croque monsieur and madame.

Baba Ghannouj, 172 White St., Danbury; (203) 205-0540; $. This unpretentious little Middle Eastern restaurant is a rarity in Connecticut, but if you want some fresh, house-made hummus, meat-filled safiha pastries, and chick pea patties, it can become a habit. My favorite item: mahamara, a velvety-smooth red pepper dip that goes well with toasted pita chips. Open 11:00 a.m. to 8:00 p.m. every day, but closed Sunday.

Burger Bar and Bistro, 58 North Main St., South Norwalk; (203) 853-2037; www .burgerbarsono.com; $. This little sleeper is a great pre- or post-movie stop if you're at the Sono movie complex. Tiny, but recently expanded somewhat, the funky place offers wonderful burgers with a choice of eighteen toppings. Try the Ultimate (with sweet onions, Gorgonzola, pancetta, and aged balsamic) or Tiajuana (with chorizo, green chili, and fried egg), among many options. Other zesty items: artichoke dip, Cuban spring rolls, and meat loaf. This is no ordinary burger-and-fries spot (the chef-owner is an experienced gourmet cook), though the prices are amazingly modest, with special low prices for the kiddies. Open daily.

Chocopologie Cafe, 12 South Main St., South Norwalk; (203) 854-4754; www.knipschildt.com; $. With its floor-to-ceiling windows fronting the street, this is an intimate little spot for an after-movie snack, a light lunch, or supper. It is also the display and sales room for Knipschildt chocolates, part of the space where the demonically good chocolates are made. If you sit on a stool along an inner wall, you can watch—as you nibble a quiche or devastating pastry—through a long window the candy-making process.

The cafe's hot chocolate, in gigantic cups, is among the best ever: rich, dark, intense. But what else would you expect at a first-rate chocolate factory? Open daily, irregular hours.

Tea for Two—or More. **The Drawing Room,** 5 Suburban Ave., Cos Cob; (203) 661-3406; www.thedrawingroom.cc; $. Simply but stylishly decorated, the limited space is comfortable whether you have a full formal fixed-price afternoon tea or just stop by morning or afternoon for a cuppa (tea, coffee, or hot chocolate) and to browse in the smart-looking boutique in the rear. The fifteen loose teas are house blends, richly aromatic. Tea sandwiches and sweets taste freshly made. The house-made scones, especially the cranberry-orange, are the best I've nibbled in years and are available for takeout. Open 8:00 a.m. to 5:00 p.m. Monday through Saturday; closed Sunday.

Pizza Supreme—that's what awaits you at **Fat Cat Pie Company,** 9-11 Wall St., Norwalk; (203) 523-0389; $$. Noisy and cacophonous, this large, glorified pizza parlor is a fun place to go before or after the movies. (It's just a short two-block walk from the Garden Cinema.) The pies are thin-crusted with some great toppings; and for the grown-ups the wine and beer lists are exemplary (the proprietors own a wine shop, so no wonder). Good salads and breads, artisanal cheeses and chocolates—what more do you need in a snack or light meal? Open daily from noon on. Next door is Fat

Cat's hyper-caffeinated offspring: **Fat Cat Joe,** 5 Wall St., Norwalk. This kitten dispenses coffee (natch!) and noshes for breakfast and lunch. This means coffee cakes, soups, salads, good breads, and sandwiches, open from breakfast time to late afternoon. Open 8:00 a.m. to 3:00 p.m.

Firehouse Deli, 22 Reef Rd., Fairfield; (203) 255-5527; $. As delis go, Firehouse is unusual. How many delis do you know that are ensconced in an old firehouse? That's just the beginning. This deli is known for its hefty, creative sandwiches, fifteen of which are featured on the blackboard daily—such as "Arthur Avenue" (salami, capicola, ham, provolone, lettuce, and tomato on a hoagie roll) or perhaps a "Redgate" (grilled chicken, bacon, Monterey Jack, avocado, and basil mayo on a hard roll). Take away or munch away in a greenhouse-like sunroom in the rear or at a picnic table in front in warm weather.

Patisserie Perfection—that's what **Isabelle et Vincent** offers at 1903 Post Rd. Fairfield; (203) 292-8022; www.isabelleetvincent .com; $$. This exquisite French pastry shop makes you want to buy at least one of every tart, éclair, cake, truffle, marron glacé, macaroon, and croissant in sight. Vincent Koenig is a seventh-generation pastry chef from France. It shows in every single gastronomic masterpiece, from his miniature quiches and petit fours to his croissants, Paris-brest, Arabica, and several dozen types of bite-size pralines. His wife, Isabelle, runs the shop, where it is possible to lunch (at one of three tables for two) on a Vincent-baked baguette and perhaps a Napoleon or other butter-rich pastry emerging from Vincent's kitchen. How sweet it all is.

La Sorpresa, 61 Cedar St., Norwalk; (203) 838-9809. This modest little shop-bakery reveals the ethnic diversity of Connecticut's southwestern region, which has recently attracted many immigrants from Latin America. Colombian-owned, the shop (whose exterior resembles a Spanish-style house with red tile roof) features freshly made sweet rolls, apple turnovers, crisp "pig's ears" pastries, breads, and rolls. A favorite is arepesa chocolo, a loose-textured corn cake, which, when warmed slightly, makes a tasty morning snack. A minuscule, no-frills restaurant is part of La Sorpresa, with a separate entrance and basic Colombian food at Depression-era prices.

Le Gourmet Store, 41 East Elm St., Greenwich; (203) 340-2780; www.restaurantjeanlouis .com. Chef Jean-Louis Gerin of Restaurant Jean-Louis has opened this delectible food-and-wine shop in partnership with Le Wine Shop, offering some choice wines and frequent wine tastings. There's a farmer's table seating twelve and a plat du jour and baguette du jour daily. There's also takeout; a frozen food section is packed with quiches, pastries, and other goodies. Breads are baked fresh daily, and the shop features imported vinegars, mustards, chocolates, and other tasty food items. Ask about the once-a-month fondue night.

Soulful is the word for the old-fashioned comfort food at **Miss Thelma's Restaurant,** 140 Fairfield Ave., Bridgeport; (203) 337-9957; $. Expect pork chops smothered in gravy, barbecued pork ribs, crispy fried chicken, fried catfish, sweet potato pie, and, on occasion, oxtail stew or chicken and dumplings. Nothing is fancy here, not the plastic cutlery nor Styrofoam plates, but the soul food is real, plentiful, and modestly priced. The weekend breakfast buffet, which lasts until noon, is a wonder unto itself. Closed Monday.

Myrna's Mediterranean Bistro, 866 East Main St., Stamford; (203) 325-8736; $, a modest Lebanese restaurant, sells excellent, not overly sweet baklava in five types: two pistachio, walnut, pine nut, and cashew. Call ahead to place an order.

At **Olé Molé,** 1030 High Ridge Rd., Stamford; (203) 461-9962; www.olemole.net; $, you have to see the limited space to believe it could be converted to a visually appealing dining area. Primarily a take-out place, there are merely four tables-for-two along one wall. Paper plates, cups, and plastic tableware do not hamper the enjoyment of the chunky guacamole, blue-corn calamari, blue-cornmeal-covered chicken wings, and other favorites. Salsas and moles are the stars, especially mole negro, slowly simmered with dried fruit, nuts, dried chiles, tomatoes, onions, cilantro, and various spices. Three olés and a cha-cha-cha for this tiny Mexican gem. Open daily. A second Olé Molé is now open at 1020 Post Rd., Darien; (203) 202-7051.

Rawley's, 1886 Post Rd., Fairfield; (203) 259-9023; $. People are as *dog*matic about best hot dogs as about best pizzas, and opinions do differ. My vote goes to this weathered shack for three reasons: 1) the way they cook their pork-and-beef wieners, starting them in a fryer, finishing them on the grill; 2) the toasted bun, which adds texture to the grilled dog (nothing turns me off faster than a flaccid, soft bun); 3) the "works"—bacon, mustard, sauerkraut, and raw onions—blanketed over the frank. You may have to wait five or ten minutes for your order and then eat at one of just a few counter stools. Rawley's also serves tuna melts, cheeseburgers, and other sandwiches to eat in or take out. But it's the doggone franks that are Best in Show. I'll Woof! to that.

Restaurant Jean-Louis, 61 Lewis St., Greenwich; (203) 622-8450; www.restaurantjeanlouis.com; $$$. Since it opened in 1985, this petite place has offered one of the state's premier dining experiences, thanks to the expertise of its chef-owner, Jean-Louis Gerin, a colleague of three-Michelin-star chef Guy Savoy. The restaurant seats a mere forty-five, and every detail is perfect, from the superb French food and flawless service to the fresh flowers, Christofoe silver and Bernardaud porcelain on the well-spaced tables. The food is "la nouvelle classique," lighter than haute cuisine, but based on classic styles, using stocks and reductions rather than the usual cholesterol-heavy ingredients. The results are full, natural flavors, as delicious and much healthier. Besides a la carte choices, there are two reasonable fixed-price options: ballade gourmande and tasting menus. French wines are a very big deal here, and Linda

Gerin, Jean-Louis's wife, is an experienced sommelier. Though elegant, Restaurant Jean-Louis is not pretentious. Once inside the doors, you feel you are in a French country inn rather than in downtown Greenwich. "A bientôt," as Jean-Louis might say. Closed all day Sunday and for lunch Saturday.

River Cat Grill, 148 Rowayton Ave., Rowayton; (203) 854-0860; www.rivercatgrill.com; $$. One of my favorite casual restaurants, River Cat Grill offers modern American food that is fresh, light, and creative, with salads, thin pizzas with offbeat toppings, burgers, sandwiches, pasta dishes, grilled meats, and fish. Cuban black-bean soup, ginger sesame-crusted salmon, and Moroccan lamb skewers are my favorites on a menu that changes often. Desserts are really seductive here, especially the warm Valrhona chocolate cake. As popular for lunch as for dinner, River Cat has live music Friday and Saturday evenings, when the bar and compact dining room really rock. In warm weather you might enjoy eating in the small fenced-in patio facing the road. Open daily, except closed Monday and for Tuesday lunch.

A deli-plus is what **Silvermine Market** (1032 Silvermine Rd., New Canaan; 203-966-4050; www.silverminemarket; $$) offers neighbors and passersby. Across a quiet country road from the Silvermine Guild Arts Center, the glorified grocery prepares delicious hot soups, generous

sandwiches, and several salads daily. There are a few tables on the cozy premises for noshing; Friday and Saturday nights dinner is served.

The SoNo Baking Company & Café, 101 Water St., South Norwalk; (203) 847-7666; www.sonobaking.com; $. This expert baking company whips up gorgeous cakes, pies, pastries, and eleven different types of bread daily. In addition, its little attached cafe offers a variety of tasty morsels—soups, sandwiches, and panini. Favorites of mine are the hearty, wholesome Canjiquinha Brazilian cornmeal soup, Cuban sandwich with pork loin, and virtually all the pastries and tarts.

Soup Alley Market Cafe, 239 Danbury Rd. (Route 7), Wilton; (203) 761-9885; fax (203) 761-9886. Summer or winter or anytime in between, Soup Alley has fifteen to twenty kettles simmering with hearty fresh-made soups. Some of my faves are the hot and spicy five-bean chili, a creamy corn chowder, spinach-chicken-artichoke Gorgonzola, and chipotle chicken chili. In addition are a few salads and nine or ten sandwich wraps. You grab a tray and select cafeteria-style and then eat in or have your order packed to-go. The menu changes daily and can be faxed ahead. Allison and Jeffrey Bernhard opened Soup Alley in 1998; they now have a second branch in South Norwalk at 45 North Main St.; (203) 866-7687.

The Stand Café and Juice Bar, 31 Wall St., Norwalk; (203) 956-5670; $. Juiced! That's what you'll get at this unique place that emphasizes freshly made juices and fruit smoothies from more than two dozen ingredients. There're also vegan and vegetarian dishes, wraps, sandwiches, salads, and sweets to-go or eat at one of five tables inside. Organic, wholesome, and unusual combinations are key words here.

Taco Loco Restaurant, 3170 Fairfield Ave., Bridgeport; (203) 335-8228; www.tacoloco.com; $. For a quick bite or full meal, this tidy little place on the Fairfield line makes its own Mexican specialties with a few surprises, such as crab cakes chipotle, cumin-accented spinach enchiladas, and a rich paella. Outdoor terrace seating in a residential neighborhood adds to the experience, as do the low prices for reliable, homey fare. Open daily for lunch and dinner.

If you want to play Columbus, a wonderful no-frills hole-in-the-wall discovery is **Valencia Luncheria,** 172 Main St., Norwalk; (203) 846-8009; $. This tiny luncheonette calls itself a "Venezuelan beach cafe." What sets it apart from many local restaurants are the Latin American specialties in generous portions at Depression-era prices. Many delights include arepas with a choice of fillings (black bean with white cheese is one of the best), ceviche, empanadas, chicken escabeche, sweet plantains, Valencian flan, and cinnamon rice pudding. There are twenty different juices and batidos (fresh fruit blended with milk). The trade-off is that there's no ambience to speak of, and a cash-only policy. Even so, Valencia's a true "discovery."

Whistle Stop Muffin Company (20 Portland Ave., Ridgefield; 203-544-8139; $) is the creation of Lolly Dunworth Turner. Her little cafe, ensconced cosily in the Branchville railroad station since 1982, turns out scores of mouthwatering fresh-baked muffins, scones, cakes, pies, and cookies for commuters and Route 7 passersby. Her newest offering, which flies out of the cafe, is chicken potpie.

Learn to Cook

Aux Délices, 23 Acosta St., Stamford; (203) 326-4540; www .auxdelices. In an all-modern 5,000-square-foot kitchen with stainless-steel tables, chef-owner Debra Ponzek conducts cooking classes for adults, children, and corporate groups, featuring classic French techniques, Provençal flavors, and innovative twists. Schedules of the cooking classes are posted in each of Ponzek's four Aux Délices shops.

Cucina Casalinga, 171 Drum Hill Rd., Wilton; (203) 762-0768; www.cucinacasalinga.com. Sally Maraventano has conducted cooking classes in her home since 1981, which includes a Tuscan

Debra Ponzek's Madeleines

Master chef and entrepreneur Debra Ponzek, whose three gourmet take-out shops now grace the Fairfield County landscape, happily shares her recipe for madeleines.

Vegetable spray
1 cup sugar
8 ounces butter, melted
1 cup flour

1 teaspoon baking powder
1 teaspoon vanilla
4 large eggs

1. Spray two madeleine pans with vegetable spray and set aside.
2. Preheat the oven to 350°F.
3. Combine the sugar and melted butter and stir together. Stir in the flour. Add the baking powder and the vanilla, stirring to combine. Add the eggs, one at a time.
4. Chill the batter for 1 to 2 hours.
5. Pour the batter into the madeleine molds, filling each halfway.
6. Bake for approximately 15 minutes, or until just firm to the touch. Cool and pop them out of the molds.
7. Keep in airtight container for 3 days.

Makes 3 dozen madeleines.

Aux Délices
23 Acosta St., Stamford
(203) 326-4540
www.auxdelices

wood-burning pizza oven in her kitchen. Sally's emphasis is on Italian regional cooking, especially Sicily, the home of her grand-father. Each class, which is sometimes conducted by a guest chef, stands alone, with a theme covering a complete meal, which the class enjoys afterward. Recent themes: A Taste of Venice and Comfort Foods. Check her Web site or call for the upcoming schedule. There are also classes for children ten to sixteen years old, corporations, and private parties. Additionally, Sally leads tours to the Italian markets of Arthur Avenue in the Bronx and conducts two annual culinary tours to Italy, where classes are taught by notable Italian chefs. The name of her cooking school means "homestyle cooking" in Italian—which is what Sally likes to emphasize.

Jean Jones Cooking Classes, Jones Family Farm and Winery, 606 Walnut Tree Hill Rd., Shelton; (203) 929-8425; www.jonesfamilyfarms.com. Experienced nutritionist and dietician Jean Jones is serious about healthy foods. Her hands-on classes emphasize healthy eating. Classes are conducted in a large barn building, rigged out with a new kitchen facility, across the yard from the tasting room on the Jones's 400-acre property. Class size is limited to fifteen. Call or check the Web site for class dates, times, and details.

Asparagi alla Parmigiana

Sally Maraventano's enthusiasm for Italian food is infectious. This recipe, from her cookbook **Festa del Giardino***, epitomizes, to me, Sally's zest for fresh, wholesome, natural ingredients. All that and it's a cinch to make, pretty to serve, and delicious to eat.*

2 pounds fresh asparagus spears, bottoms snapped off, spears scraped with a vegetable peeler and rinsed well	**6 tablespoons butter** **½ cup freshly grated Parmesan cheese or more to taste** **Fresh grated nutmeg**

1. Preheat oven to 400°F.
2. If you use an asparagus cooker, fill it halfway with lightly salted water and bring to a boil. Stand the asparagus spears upright in the pot, with spear tips up. Bring back to a boil, cover, and lower heat to a simmer. Cook until just fork tender, about 8 minutes. Note: If you don't have an asparagus cooker, use a large skillet and cook covered the same length of time.
3. Melt half the butter in a baking dish and place the asparagus lengthwise in the dish. Dot with the remaining butter and sprinkle with Parmesan and a few grindings of fresh nutmeg.
4. Bake for 7 minutes or until the top forms a light golden crust. Serve immediately.

Serves 6.

Cucina Casalinga
171 Drum Hill Rd., Wilton
(203) 762-0768
www.cucinacasalinga.com

Ronnie Fein School of Creative Cooking, 32 Heming Way, Stamford; (203) 322-7114. Since the 1970s, food writer Ronnie Fein has been teaching individually designed, one-on-one cooking workshops in her home. Sessions are limited to no more than four students and last three to three and a half hours. Usually five recipes are developed in the hands-on, single-day sessions.

Susan Goodman Catering, 327 Old Norwalk Rd., New Canaan; (203) 972-3793; www.susangoodman.com. A professional caterer, Susan Goodman teaches cooking classes on various aspects of cuisine at the Lapham Community Center, 663 South Ave., New Canaan; (203) 594-3620. For classes and schedule, call the Lapham Center.

Two Steps Downtown Grille, 5 Ives St., Danbury; (203) 794-0032. Seasonal cooking classes, held in the restaurant, are conducted by owners Tom Devine and Keith O'Marra. Usually there are five sessions, held Wednesday evenings, in each of which four dishes are prepared. Participants may partake of any or all sessions, with a price reduction for the series. Each session includes tasting all the prepared dishes, recipes, and wine. Though the classes are serious, there is a great deal of chatter, joshing, and wine imbibing, proof that you can have fun while learning.

Susan Goodman's
Pancetta Herb Cheese Purse

Susan Goodman Catering has been a household name in the catering business in New Canaan for years. From her repertoire of more than fifty creative hors d'oeuvre recipes, Susan feels the following is ideal for a last minute, easy-to-make cocktail party appetizer—quick, easy, and savory. The "purses" can be made early in the day and reheated.

½ pound pancetta, diced
1 cup shredded mozzarella
¼ cup grated Parmesan cheese
1 tablespoon finely chopped herbs, mixed together (thyme and sage work well together)
½ cup finely chopped green onion

1 can commercial refrigerated biscuits
1 egg, beaten
Poppy seeds, sesame seeds, or caraway seeds to garnish (optional)

1. Preheat oven to 375°F.
2. Sauté the pancetta. When cool, add the cheeses, herbs, and onion.
3. Cut each biscuit in half and flatten with palm of hand. Put a tablespoon of the mix in the center of each biscuit and fold it over into a half moon or triangular shape.
4. Seal the edge with some of the egg wash and place each biscuit 2 inches apart on a parchment-lined baking sheet. Brush with the egg wash and sprinkle with the seeds if you desire.
5. Bake about 12 minutes and serve hot.

Serves 4–6.

Susan Goodman Catering
327 Old Norwalk Rd., New Canaan
(203) 972-3793
www.susangoodman.com

Avenida, 339 Greenwich Ave., Greenwich; (203) 622-1400; www
.avenidamexican.com; $$. At last! An elegant Mexican restaurant
that isn't just a replay of Tex-Mex. Avenida gives even familiar
dishes a special twist. I'd call Avenida nueva cocina for its creative
cooking and flair in presentations. Among many gustatory gems
are the grape gazpacho, ceviche de atun moderna (marinated raw
tuna), and tostadita de cangrejo (crab). The food is far better than
the rather stark decor (black and white with a dash of lime), though
I like the way the front wall opens in summer like a garage door
to give diners a close-up of the Greenwich Avenue scene. Sunday
brunch Mexican style is something different—and delicious—and
not too spicy for the timid palate. Closed Monday.

Baang Café and Bar, 1191 East Putnam Ave., Riverside; (203)
637-2114; www.decarorestaurantgroup.com; $$$. The first to intro-
duce Asian fusion cooking to Connecticut, this unusual restaurant
opened in 1995 with a (yes) bang! Its eclectic decor (by New York
architect-designer David Rockwell) vibrates with colors and unusual
shapes, yet it plays second banana to the food, which is so fresh
it crackles, from the open kitchen directly to the table. East really
does meet West here, as Western cooking techniques combine with
Asian ingredients. My favorites are pan-fried pepper oysters, grilled
Shanghai beef, and gossamer-like crispy spinach deep-fried in soy
oil. Much copied is the sizzling calamari salad with ever-so-lightly

breaded squid, a hint of hot chile oil, and frisée and baby lettuces in a lime-miso vinaigrette. In peak hours the decibel level is high, but the fresh, creative food is worth enduring the cacophony. Open daily.

Basso Café, 124 New Canaan Ave., Norwalk; (203) 354-6566; www .bassobistrocafe.com; $$. Chef-owner Renato Donzelli was born in an Italian family and grew up in Venezuela. Culinarily he has the best of two worlds (which he skillfully offers guests at his teeny-tiny restaurant)—a happy blend of Mediterranean-cum-Italian dishes hyped with Latin-American ingredients and concepts. Tuscan grilled chicken and warm goat cheese-mushroom tarts complement beef empanadas on Renato's creative menu. Artful plate presentations and informal atmosphere combine with BYO necessity. (There's a liquor store just half a block away.) Closed Monday.

Bernard's, 20 West Lane, Ridgefield; (203) 438-8282; www.bernards ridgefield.com; $$$. This white clapboard inn was showing its age when Bernard and Sarah Bouissou arrived in 2000. They refurbished and raised its culinary level spectacularly. It is now lovely, from the outside plantings to the four airy, impeccably maintained dining rooms—a no-brainer choice for special-occasion dining. But Bernard's kitchen skills (from years at Le Cirque in New York, where Sarah was a chef, too) are so creative they make even a regular meal special. His contemporary French repertoire includes a galette of snails with wild mushrooms, roasted monkfish osso bucco wrapped in rosemary pancetta, and a signature foie gras trio. The lengthy wine list has been carefully selected, with many well-priced vintages as well as rarer ones. **Sarah's Wine Bar,** $$, upstairs, is a relaxed bistro with simpler food (and lower prices). Closed Monday.

Blue Lemon, 15 Myrtle Ave., Westport; (203) 226-2647; www .bluelemonrestaurant.com; $$. Expert but understated, this charming low-key restaurant is hidden in plain sight—just off the Post Road and a block from the Westport Country Playhouse. The menu is eclectic American-cum-global, offering dishes like steamed mussels, salmon carpaccio, braised "six hour" lamb shank, Vietnamese sea-

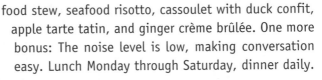

food stew, seafood risotto, cassoulet with duck confit, apple tarte tatin, and ginger crème brûlée. One more bonus: The noise level is low, making conversation easy. Lunch Monday through Saturday, dinner daily.

Brasitas, 954 East Main St., Stamford; (203) 323-3176; www.brasitas.com; $$. Brasitas is the sleeper every adventurous diner dreams of. In cozy, convivial surroundings, a creative Mexican chef com-bines the natural bounty of South America and the Caribbean (maize, plantain, yucca, mango, and the like) with sophisticated European techniques, coming up with gems like grilled pork chop in guava-ginger barbecue sauce and sautéed chicken breast in a tequila-honey-lemon-cilantro sauce. Inventive sauces bring new vitality to many Latin American standbys, and the plate presentations are knockouts. A second Brasitas is in Norwalk (430 Main Ave.; 203-354-7329). The menu and prices are the same, but I prefer the creativity of the Stamford original. Open daily for lunch and dinner.

Brendan's at The Elms Restaurant & Pub, 500 Main St. (Route 35), Ridgefield; (203) 438-9206; $$$. This historic inn dates back to 1799. In recent years New York celebrity chef Brendan Walsh has made it a marvel of modern New England cooking, "reinventing" the colonial Connecticut kitchen—with chowders, roasts, game (he has a way with venison), and puddings. Dine in the inn's newly renovated formal dining room or, if you're in the mood for something more casual, try the Pub—same menu at both.

Coromandel Cuisine of India, 25 Old King's Hwy. North, Darien; (203) 662-1213; www.coromandelcuisine.com; $$. In recent years Indian restaurants have sprouted all over the state, but Coromandel outdistances them all in its creative variety of south and north Indian dishes. Mirrors, murals, and colored lights create a festive ambience in limited space, while a quieter second room is only slightly more muted. Best value is the fixed-price buffet lunch—seven or eight hot dishes, breads, chutneys, salad, and several desserts. As if that isn't plenty, piping-hot naan bread and fresh-baked, mildly spiced tandoori chicken are delivered tableside by a waiter,

DOUBLE DINER DELIGHTS

City Limits Diner, 135 Harvard Ave., Stamford; (203) 348-7000; www.citylimitsdiner.com; $. With its art deco decor, oversize booths, and quadruple-lifesize coffee-cup-and-doughnut display, City Limits has a retro look. Surprisingly, it dates only from 2002 and offers a modern American menu. There are a few old-timey dishes, like Southern fried chicken, but many others have an Asian touch: steamed bass with fresh ginger and scallions in a wine-soy sauce and crispy crab wontons, for example. An in-house bakery does a variety of sweet rolls, muffins, doughnuts, pies, cakes, and tortes, as well as excellent breads. Reasonable prices make City Limits a fun place to drop by, especially for breakfast but also for lunch, snacks, or dinner.

The beer list is exceptional for a diner, with many microbrew selections from all over North America and Europe. Open 7:00 a.m. to 11:00 p.m. Sunday through Thursday, until midnight Friday and Saturday.

White's Diner, 280 Boston Ave., Bridgeport; (203) 366-7486; $. Open since 1935, this old-timer is the real deal, owned and run by the same couple—Greg and Linda Cerminara—for over thirty years. Featuring a cholesterol-be-darned menu of breakfast goodies, White's offers more than a dozen omelets, as well as hearty lunch choices, soups, goulash, and scores of sandwich combos, with almost everything assembled from scratch. A cross section of Bridgeport life parades daily through this long-standing local landmark, with its expansive counter, booths, and vintage photos of old Bridgeport. Open daily from 5:30 a.m. to 3:00 p.m.

as part of the fixed-price buffet largesse. The
a la carte dinner menu isn't pricey either,
with such pleasures as lamb chops, sizzling hot and well-seasoned Indian-style;
lasi gobi (spicy fried cauliflower); and a
delightful appetizer, shamm savera: tiny
spinach cups filled with farm cheese in a tangy
honey-edged tomato sauce. Whether you like your
Indian food mild, moderate, or incendiary, Jose and
Meena Pullopilly and staff are happy to oblige. Open daily.

A second location is at 68 Broad St., Stamford; (203) 964-1010;
$$. This version is larger, roomier, and well decked out in Indian
accoutrements. A second floor is available for parties. The regular
menu is similar to the original Coromandel's, and the warm welcome
from Matthew Poovathanical and staff is equally friendly. A third
Coromandel is at 185 Boston Post Rd., Orange; (203) 795-9055. A
new **Coromandel Bistro** is now open at 86 Washington St., South
Norwalk; (203) 852-1213. Here the clientele is younger and more
hip, as expected in SoNo.

Dressing Room, 27 Powers Court, Westport; (203) 226-1114; www
.dressingroomhomegrown.com; $$–$$$. A collaboration between
experienced chef Michel Nishan and the late Paul Newman gave
this faux rustic restaurant its cachet. A roaring fire in the stone
fireplace and the high-ceilinged, post-and-beam construction of
the main dining room add warmth and charm in cool weather. But
all the time there's Chef Nishan's dedication to fresh-grown, natural

Terrific Tuscan Trio

Hardly a week goes by that an Italian restaurant doesn't open up somewhere in the state. These are three of my northern Italian faves in Fairfield County:

Cava Wine Bar and Restaurant, 2 Forest St., New Canaan; (203) 966-6946; www.cavawinebar.com; $$$. In a well-lighted version of a wine cellar, complete with rough-textured stone wall, Cava serves scrumptious dishes like tortellini stuffed with roasted butternut  squash; risotto with duck confit and diced green Granny Smith apples; and wood-fire-roasted Long Island duck, all beautifully presented. The extensive wine list emphasizes regional vintages from Tuscany, Piedmont, and the Veneto. While dinner can be noisy, lunch is a quiet affair, good for conversation along with delicious pastas and salads. Open daily for dinner, Tuesday through Friday for lunch. The owners have recently opened another place in Fairfield: **55° Wine Bar and Restaurant,** 55 Miller St., Fairfield; (203) 256-0099; www.55winebar.com; $$$.

ingredients, mostly locally grown. They are manifest in such dishes as Berkshire pig, meat loaf, pan-roasted trout, and homey desserts like chocolate bread pudding and sticky toffee pudding. Closed Monday and at lunchtime Tuesday.

Strada 18, 18 Washington St., South Norwalk; (203) 853-4546; www.strada18.com; $$. In a long storefront made attractive by an exposed brick wall, simple decor, and good lighting, this relative newcomer is guided by David Raymer, co-owner and creative chef. His deft touch produces such pleasures as orecchiette with sausage, roasted chicken diavolo, lamb shank, house-made mozzarella, and desserts like strawberry-rhubarb crumble, flourless chocolate cake, and a remarkable black pepper biscotti. His sorbets (especially the white peach) and gelatos (even his experimental one made with Guinness) are inspired. Open daily for lunch and dinner.

Tuscany, 1084 Madison Ave., Bridgeport; (203) 331-9884; $$. This bustling, convivial storefront restaurant is full of surprises. First, in addition to the starters listed on the short menu, seven appetizers are brought to your table on a large tray for you to choose among. Then a second tray of nine uncooked, house-made pasta samples is presented, as your waiter describes the dish with which they will be served. The unusual visual presentation is only topped by the high quality of the food itself. The menu changes daily. Risotto with asparagus and shrimp, and grilled polenta with wild mushrooms and melted Gorgonzola are just two of many delightful dishes you may encounter. Closed Monday.

Eos Greek Cuisine, 490 Summer St., Stamford; (203) 569-6250; www.eosgreekcuisine.com; $$. Upscale authentic Greek restaurants are hard to find in Connecticut. Eos is one and it's a pure delight, from the bas relief of a wave along one white wall to the menu of Greek specialties. They range from delicious mezedes, or starters, to a gooey custardy dessert called galaktoboureko. I could make a meal of appetizers like spanakopita (phyllo spinach pie), loukaniko (grilled pork sausage), keftedes (Greek meatballs), and saganaki (grilled cheese flambéed). But then I'd miss the grilled salmon, moussaka, and char-grilled baby lamb chops. Open daily for lunch and dinner.

Greenwich Tavern, formerly **Palomino,** 1392 East Putnam Ave., Old Greenwich; (203) 698-9033; www.palominorestaurants.com; $$. Chef Rafael Palomino's latest venture is this spacious restaurant on the Post Road. A dramatic Americana mural covering one whole wall reinforces what is now a modern American menu, with such homey delights as rib-eye white bean chili, Mac 'n' cheese with white truffle oil, veal meat loaf, and braised Angus short ribs. Desserts are devastating: key lime pie, soufflés, and bourbon pecan tart. Señor Palomino has another restaurant in New Haven (Pacifico, 220 College St.; 203-772-4002) and two in Port Chester, over the line in New York state. Open daily.

Il Palio, 5 Corporate Dr., Shelton; (203) 944-0770; www.ilpalioct .com; $$. Il Palio's two expensively outfitted dining rooms, with fireplaces, exposed wood ceilings, and polished wood floors, are handsome backdrops for some expert, mostly Tuscan, cooking. Quaglia alla griglia (grilled quail stuffed with Tuscan beans and pancetta) is memorable, as are such dishes as osso bucco, medium-rare grilled tuna, and luscious desserts like riso dolce (pistachio-studded rice pudding), vanilla crème brulée, and tiramisu. Closed Sunday and for lunch Saturday.

Lao Sze Chuan, 1585 Boston Post Rd. (US 1), Milford; (203) 783-0558; www.laoszechuan.com; $$. Chinese restaurants are ubiquitous in Connecticut; good ones—not so much. That's why it's a pleasure to come upon this Sichuan gem hiding in plain sight on the Post Road. As is often the case in some of the better, more authentic Chinese restaurants, decor is secondary to the food. The regional Sichuan cooking is bona fide, visible in such dishes as sautéed lamb with cumin and onion, braised spicy tofu and pork, and lobster Sichuan. If you're feeling adventurous, give the braised pigs' ears a try. For most of us the fiery Sichuan cooking—in a dish like wild pepper chicken—is adventurous enough. Open daily.

Le Figaro Bistro de Paris, 372 Greenwich Ave., Greenwich; (203) 622-0018; www.lefigarocafe; $$$. On entering Le Figaro you might think you're in a time warp: a belle époque dining room with Tiffany-like glass tulip wall sconces, a bronze Moreaux sculpture holding center stage, art nouveau flourishes in the woodwork, framed covers of *Le Figaro* magazine on the walls, and staffers in black vests speaking French. Le Figaro isn't an ancient establishment; it just wants to appear that way, to accentuate its classic French bistro menu. On that you might find escargots de bourgogne, onion soup, confit of duck, quiche Lorraine, escalope of ris de veau, and desserts like chocolate-mocha mousse and expertly made fruit tartes. Open daily.

Little Thai Kitchen, 4 West Ave., Darien; (203) 662-0038; www .littlethaikitchen.com; $$. Small in size, huge in hot, spicy Thai flavors, this taste of Thailand in Darien is welcome to all lovers of Siamese food. Dishes like the clear hot soups, larb (ground beef dusted in toasted rice powder) salad, plar goong salad, sambal chicken, and various curries are spot-on. Brave the noise and concentrate on the delicious food. A quieter version of the same restaurant is in Greenwich at 21 St. Roch Ave.; (203) 622-2972. Open daily. **Little Buddha** (same owners), 2270 Summer St., Stamford; (203)356-9166, features Thai, Chinese and Asian fusion cooking.

Match, 98 Washington St., South Norwalk; (203) 852-1088; www .matchsono.com; $$. In warm weather the entire front wall of Match opens to the street, with the first row of tables putting you as much on display as the crowds passing along the sidewalk. No matter what the season, the food at Match is tremendously appealing, whether the pastas, the wood-fired chicken, seared tuna, or the luscious desserts. As is typical of SoNo, the atmosphere at Match is casual, but the food is always thoughtfully prepared. On weekends this area of SoNo is always a vibrant scene, and that liveliness can be contagious. Dinner only daily.

Matsuri, 390 Post Rd., Darien; (203) 655-4999; www.matsuri cuisine.com; $$. Amiable, efficient service is a hallmark of this newish, high-speed Japanese restaurant. Its star performers are sushi and sashimi, which are so fresh they fairly sparkle. There are other dishes, both traditional Japanese and Asian fusion ones like Vietnamese spring rolls, Indian pancake, and pan-seared Chilean sea bass. But with the nigiri, maki, and rolls so appealing, I tend to go to Matsuri for my occasional sushi "fix." Open daily for dinner; for lunch every day but Sunday.

Meigas, 10 Wall St., Norwalk; (203) 866-8800; www.meigasrestaurant.com; $$. This bewitching restaurant—whose name means "benign sorceress" in Galician—has new ownership and has reverted to a more traditional Spanish menu, abandoning much of the influence of Spain's whiz chef Ferran Adrià. Foams and infusions have had their run, and the classics are now making a welcome return. The menu emphasizes fresh seafood, game, and veal. An exceptional value is the fixed-price tapas menu for two—ten delightful dishes, quite ample for two, no entree necessary. A well-selected Spanish wine list really complements the food. On the ground floor of a restored trolley barn, Meigas resembles a Spanish country inn, with saffron-yellow walls, terra-cotta tile floors, well-spaced tables, and impeccable service. Bravo! Open daily.

Napa & Co., Stamford Marriott, 75 Broad St., Stamford; (203) 353-3319; www.napaandcompany.com; $$$. While located at the edge of the Marriott, Napa & Co. is not connected to the hotel. The space is relatively compact and can be noisy, but the natural, modern American food is worth it. There are engaging extra touches: a group of small plate dishes (like foraged-mushroom risotto or duck and foie gras meatballs) for tiny appetites; an excellent cheese plate with many choices of American and European cheeses; an intriguing selection of fresh-brewed teas (not bags). Co-owner Mary Schaffer is a knowledgeable sommelier; her 350-bottle wine selection is impeccable.  Specific wines are suggested for each entree, such as a Huia Gewürtztraminer from New Zealand paired with wild black sea bass (with artichoke-porcini marmalade and polenta). Open daily for all three meals; hours vary.

Ondine, 69 Pembroke Rd. (Route 37), Danbury; (203)746-4900; www.ondinerestaurant; $$. What makes Ondine special is chef-owner Dieter Thiel's first-rate French food in surroundings reminiscent of a French country inn, at very reasonable prices. Instead of ordering a la carte, consider Ondine's fixed-price menu: five courses (soup, salad, a choice from among ten appetizers, ten entrees, and ten desserts) and coffee or tea at a price some restaurants charge

Jean-Louis's Famous Potato au Gratin

The "secret" of this simple dish of Jean-Louis Gerin, chef-proprietor of Restaurant Jean-Louis in Greenwich, is in the cream/milk mix. He prefers it creamy, whereas many chefs are satisfied with a 50/50 ratio. He also uses the natural starch of the potato with no extra additives. In Jean-Louis's words: "There is a famous Riviera restaurant that recommends blanching the potato in milk, throwing the milk away, then adding powdered starch to the cream . . . oh la la! I have also heard some horror stories about egg in the gratin . . . Note that some recipes are just better when they have had time to rest. Potato au gratin is one of them! If you can, cook your gratin a day in advance. The next day, add a half-cup cream or so to the gratin, then reheat it slowly in a 275°–300° oven until the cream starts to boil."

1 tablespoon minced garlic
3¼ pounds baking potatoes
3½ cups heavy cream + ½–1 cup for reheating
1 cup whole milk
2½ teaspoons salt
1¼ teaspoons freshly ground white pepper
Dash nutmeg

1. Preheat oven to 350°F. Spread the minced garlic over the bottom of a large gratin or 3-quart baking pan (such as a Pyrex dish).
2. Peel the potatoes and rinse under cold water. Cut potatoes into slices between ⅛ and ¼ inch thick. Do NOT rinse these slices; it is their natural starch that will thicken the gratin. Spread the potato slices on top of the garlic in baking pan.
3. Heat cream and milk together in a medium pot until boiling. Add salt, white pepper, and nutmeg. Remember that with this step you are seasoning not just for the milk and cream mixture but for all of the potatoes as well, so don't worry if the mixture seems excessively salty! It will taste just right once it is baked.
4. Pour hot cream and milk mixture over the potato slices in the pan. Stir slices so that they are all just about submerged, then place pan in oven and bake until potatoes are tender and top is well-browned, about 1½ hours. Let rest at least 3 hours, or overnight if desired, then reheat as directed above.

Serves 10.

Restaurant Jean-Louis
61 Lewis St., Greenwich
(203) 622-8450
www.restaurantjeanlouis.com

for two courses alone. Such dishes as confit de canard, billi bi, black cod dusted with cumin, sea scallops poached in white wine, hazelnut soufflé, and tarte tatin complement tables dressed with fresh flowers, candles, Staffordshire china, and comfortable, padded plush chairs. In its handsomely appointed, two-tiered dining room, Ondine offers haute dining at bas prices. It's enough to make you hum the Marseillaise. Dinner only, but open all day Sunday. Closed Tuesday.

Rebeccas, 265 Glenville Rd., Greenwich; (203) 532-9270; www .rkateliers.com; $$$. Cool and minimalist in decor—some might say Spartan—Rebeccas is elegant without being rarefied. It's the work of Reza Khorshidi and Rebecca Kirhoffer, a husband-and-wife culinary team adept at turning less into more. Each dish speaks of the finest ingredients. Every detail is exquisite and nuanced, from, say, pan-seared duck foie gras with caramelized mangoes to grilled Dover sole in lemon sauce or roasted breast of wild Scottish pheasant, followed by pear tarte tatin or a selection of artisanal cheeses. Service is as seamless as the entire meal and the well-chosen wine list. Closed Sunday and Monday.

The Restaurant at Rowayton Seafood, Rowayton Avenue, Rowayton; (203) 866-4488; www.rowayton seafood.com; $$. In tight quarters facing the boats moored at Cavanaugh's Marina, this no-frills restaurant turns out some mighty fresh seafood. No

An Inn Place to Be

Roger Sherman Inn, 195 Oenoke Ridge, New Canaan; (203) 966-4541; www.rogershermaninn.com; $$$. While this landmark inn looks old-fashioned and traditional, the food, under new owners Joseph and Nes Joffre, is modern American (with a French accent) and exciting. It also looks beautiful. In any of five intimate dining rooms, you can enjoy such dishes as lobster ravioli, pan-seared Arctic char, wild mushroom fricassee, sweetbreads with lemon and capers, wild striped bass, and desserts like warm apple-cheddar bread pudding, Grand Marnier soufflé, or pear upside-down cake. Professional service and a decibel level conducive to conversation are further elements in what can be a superb dining experience. While the main dining room has a cheerful mien, with a wall of windows, historic paintings along two walls, and well-spaced tables, I'm partial to the smaller room down a few steps with its Tiffany windows and fireplace lined with Dutch tiles. Closed all day Monday and Saturday at lunchtime.

wonder! It is owned by an adjacent fresh seafood store of the same name. The raw bar features local bluepoint oysters and others from Maine and British Columbia. You might also spear the deep-fried Ipswich clams and oysters, steamed or broiled lobsters, or grilled or pan-roasted fish. The lobster rolls, copiously packed with fresh chunks of tender lobster, celery, and onions lashed together with mayonnaise, are popular at lunch. In warm weather the deck overlooking

Five Mile River is the place to be, but deck seating is first-come, first-served, no reservations. Open daily for lunch and dinner.

Solaia, 363 Greenwich Ave., Greenwich; (203) 622-6400; www .solaiaenoteca.com; $$$. You'll understand why Solaia subtitles its name "enoteca," as the entrance of this slightly-below-ground-level place is designed like a wine bar or enoteca. The restaurant, with its modern Italian menu and long banquette, is in the rear. The food is worth the short walk past the bar, particularly such dishes as pork saltimbocca, house-made ravioli, wild striped bass, hand-cut pappardelle, and every single appetizer on the menu. Quail with polenta and the chilled spring pea soup are especially wonderful. All desserts, too, are ambrosial. Open daily, but lunch only served Wednesday through Sunday.

Splash, 260 Compo Rd. South, Westport; (203) 454-7798; $$$. Splash, located at town-owned Longshore Country Club, has the same ownership as Baang in Riverside. Splash's Pacific Rim menu is different and the dining room, with its stylized 3-D "wave" wall mural, has an even higher decibel level. In warm weather it's best to arrive early enough to sit on the deck (no reservations taken for the deck) with a view of Long Island Sound. Otherwise you'll need a megaphone to be heard by your tablemates. Even so, the food is very good indeed—creative and original. Closed Monday.

Monster B's Bar & Grille, 489 Glenbrook Rd., Stamford; (203) 355-1032; www.monsterbsbarandgrille.com; $. Beer for what ales you? Try this congenial bar-cum-pub. While neither a brewpub nor a brewery, it's the thirty beers and ales on tap that make Monster B's worthy of your attention and worth including in this section. It's an awesome assortment—more than one hundred and fifty bottled beers from microbreweries in many states and countries around the globe. (Belgian choices number more than twenty brands.) There's pub grub too, of course, with assorted burgers, sandwiches, salads, a few entrees, and a locally famous chili. And in warm weather you can—and should—do your imbibing on the outdoor deck.

SBC Downtown Restaurant Brewery, 131 Summer St., Stamford; (203) 327-2337; www.sbcrestaurants.com; $$. This off-shoot of Southport Brewing Company opened its cavernous faux-industrial quarters in 2001. The stacks of barley-malt sacks and gleaming fermenters near the entrance suggest that SBC takes beer seriously. Co-owners William and Mark da Silva (brewer) and Dave Ruligliano (executive chef) had five years of success at Southport Brewing Company before expanding here. Slightly sweet, somewhat spicy Stamford Red is one of the more complex-tasting house beers. Request sample tastes of others (twenty-seven in all, with about eight available at any given time), such as Rippowam Lager, One Way IPA, and Bull's Head English pale ale. Chef Ruligliano presides over the menus at Southport's and all the SBC kitchens, with tasty hanger steak, crunchy "brew fries," and assorted pizzas as reliable menu items. Thursday is Karaoke Night, and Sunday evening is "family time" (with a magician). Hours are Monday to Thursday 11:30 a.m. to 1:00 a.m., Friday and Saturday until 2:00 a.m., and Sunday to 10:00 p.m. There are now three additional SBC locations, with the same brews, menus, hours, and entertainment: 850 West Main St., Branford, (203) 481-2739; 33 New Haven Ave., Milford, (203) 874-2337; 1950 Dixwell Ave., Hamden, (203) 288-4677.

Southport Brewing Co., 2600 Post Rd., Southport; (203) 256-BEER; www.SBCrestaurants.com; $$. A loyal clientele has been enjoying the brews and food here since it opened in 1997. Once past the copper-clad beer tanks by Southport Brewing's entrance, you are in a large restaurant-cum-brewery where a wide range of estery, ethereal ales are made. Your best bet is a sampler assortment. Fifteen beers on tap range from the refreshing Bones Light to nearly opaque, espresso-like Black Rock Stout and Fairfield Red, an award-winning deep amber. Seasonals include Old Blue Eyes blueberry ale, Mill Hill pilsener, and SouthToberfest. Southport's strengths are in the three P's: pints, pizzas, and porterhouse steaks. The kitchen was voted best brewery-restaurant in the state in several recent surveys. Early-evening and late-night happy hours on weekdays keep this convivial place humming, with schedule and hours the same as at all the SBC spin-offs (see SBC above).

Tigin Irish Pub, 175 Bedford St., Stamford; (203) 353-8444; www.tiginirishpub.com; $. Not a brewery and not a brewpub, Tigin oozes authenticity as a wonderful Irish pub, whose interior was actually brought over from the old country. Cozy rooms and alcoves, gas fireplaces, dartboard, even a traditional Irish snug, where women can drink facing, but sheltered from, the 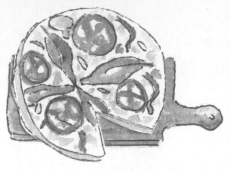 bar, are all part of Tigin's charm. Eight Irish brews on tap, nine more in bottles, plus eight Irish whiskeys and Fado Irish Coffee are all here. A hearty Irish breakfast is available from 11:30 a.m. all day, as well as a more varied menu than the usual pub grub. On the first Thursday of the month, The Irish Band entertains live. Soccer maniacs aren't the only fans of this old-fashioned snuggery pubbery. Open daily.

Wine Trail

Connecticut Wine Trail, www.ctwine.com, offers two trail plans that show where the state's wineries are located, the best roads to reach them, and important information about each (hours for tastings, tours, picnicking, nearby points of interest). In this area, DiGrazia, Jones, and McLaughlin are the wineries included in Connecticut Wine Trail, Trip 1, which can be printed out from the Web site listed above.

FUSION BUT NOT CONFUSIN':
A QUARTET OF TOP ASIAN FOOD PARLORS

Ching's Table, Main St., New Canaan; (203) 972-8550; www
.chingsrestaurant.com; $$. On a Friday night it seems as though
every family in New Canaan is dining at this small restaurant in the
center of town; the place is quieter during the week and at lunch.
Ching's strengths are the Thai and Chinese specialties, served piping
hot and consistently well prepared. My favorites are wild sticky rice
dim sum, tempura shrimp with a lemon dip (not like the Japanese
original but tasty in its own way), pad Thai, spicy Indonesian beef
sambal, sesame chicken, and Thai curry casserole. What gives Ching's
Table such appeal is the freshness of each dish, as well as the pleasing
presentation. The decor is low-key, with large windows, rattan
furnishings, and oriental artifacts. Open daily. Its new offspring, **Wild
Ginger,** is in Darien at 971 Post Rd. (203-656-2225), and another
Wild Ginger is in Ridgefield at 461 Main St. (203-431-4588). Still a
third, **Hunan Café,** is at 228 Town Green, Wilton; (203) 761-8998.
I still prefer Ching's.

Nuage Restaurant and Bar, Mill Pond Shopping Center, 203 East
Putnam Ave., Cos Cob; (203) 869-2339; www.nuagerestaurant.com;
$$–$$$. A marriage of French and Japanese, Nuage (as in New Age)
offers the best of two culinary traditions, with seafood the specialty in
this serene place. Nuage's decor is as subtle as its food, the latter being
exemplified by such lovely dishes as black cod with miso; monkfish
pâté with sesame miso, caviar, and scallion; and rock shrimp tempura
with a creamy-spicy sauce. Appetizers are so outstanding I usually
make a meal of them, ordering two instead of an entree. Prices at
Nuage can be rarefied, but so is the dining experience.

Tai Pan, 376 Post Rd. East, Westport; (203) 227-7400; www .taipanrestaurant.com; $$. At first you may wonder where you are. Is this a Yangtze riverboat or a jungle path? Why are you walking to your table over a bridge with a pond visible beneath the glass floor? And what's with that waterfall gushing over a fieldstone wall? Surprisingly, the funky decor works and won't distract you from the very good food, with origins all over Asia. Favorites include Indonesian dishes like salad gado-gado, rendang beef, prawns Bali style, and pork a la Bali, along with Panang curries and Szechuan Chinese specialties. There is a decent microbrewery beer list as well. Tai Pan does a sizable takeout business, with free delivery in the Westport-Weston area (if the order is a minimum of $15 for Westport, $30 for Weston). Open daily.

Tengda Asian Bistro, Goodwives Shopping Center, 25 Old Kings Hwy. North, Darien; (203) 656-1688; $$. The word *Tengda* means prosperity, which seems to suit this large, almost cavernous space. There's a good sushi bar in the rear, but I'm just as partial to the various Asian dishes on the menu, notably Thai crab cake, crispy calamari salad, spicy mango chicken, Tengda curried hot pot, and Asian spiced glazed duck breast. There are two other Tengdas in Fairfield County, but in my view the Darien one is the best. Open daily. The others: The original Tengda is at 1330 Post Rd. East, Westport; (203) 255-6115; the second, more a combo of Asian and European, is at 21 Field Point Rd., Greenwich; (203) 625-5338; still a third, a new one, is at 1676 Boston Post Rd., Milford; (203) 877-8888.

DiGrazia Vineyards, 131 Tower Rd., Brookfield; (203) 775-1616; www.digrazia.com. Paul and Barbara DiGrazia founded their winery in 1978 with four types of wine. At present they sell sixteen to nineteen different wines, based on homegrown French vinifera hybrid grapes, plus inventive combinations of fruit and flavors, and have garnered gold, silver, and bronze medals for their efforts. Their strong suits, in my view, are their dessert wines, such as Winterberry (grape, black currant, and raspberry), Autumn Spice (white grapes, pumpkin, and spice), and two popular new combinations: Wild Blue (blueberry and brandy) and Paragran (pear and pomegranate). The tasting room and gift shop are inside a low-slung contemporary building festooned with fresh garden flowers. Tours are daily Saturday and Sunday, 11:00 a.m. to 5:00 p.m., year-round. Group tours can be arranged with advance notice.

Jones Winery, 266 Israel Hill Rd., Shelton; (203) 929-8425; www.jonesfamilyfarms.com. Having studied viniculture at Cornell University, young Jamie Jones and his wife Christiana worked for more than five years to turn about five acres of the family's 400-acre farm into a viable winery. Jamie's grapes now yield some smooth wines. They include Heritage Barn Red, a dry European-style Ripton Red, and Woodlands White (the best seller), with a sweet crispness. For all-out wine-plus-fruit flavor, Jamie then adds (as appropriate) apples, pears, black currants, strawberries, blueberries, and/or raspberries in Dawn's First Blush, Harvest Time, Strawberry Splendor, Blueberry Bliss, and Raspberry Rhapsody. Call for the days and hours that the vineyard is open. There is a homey, rustic tasting room, which Christiana manages, at the end of a long room in an old barn, alongside a small shop selling wine-related gift items.

McLaughlin Vineyards, 14 Albert's Hill Rd., Sandy Hook; (203) 426-1533; mclauqhlinwine@snet.net; www.mclaughlinvineyards .com. Bruce McLaughlin is the president and winemaker of the fifteen-acre vineyard that is part of a beautiful 160-acre farm property his family bought in the 1940s. This Housatonic River valley estate produces 60 percent of the fruit for their chardonnay, merlot, cabernet sauvignon, and Riesling and has contracted for the rest. Blue Coyote, a blend of vidal and aurora, is the vineyard's most popular wine. Also pleasing is Snow Goose, a blend of whites. In February and March you can watch maple-syrup-making in the sugarhouse, ride the tractor, cross-country ski, and hike the trails. In summer, you might order in advance a catered picnic basket and lunch al fresco on the grounds. From the end of May through October, there are jazz and bluegrass concerts (call for details). New England food products—jams, salad dressings, McLaughlin's own maple syrup, local honey, and wines—are for sale in the country store, an adjunct of the tasting room. Open daily year-round, from 11:00 a.m. to 5:00 p.m., but closed Monday and Tuesday from February to June 1. Winery tours are by appointment only.

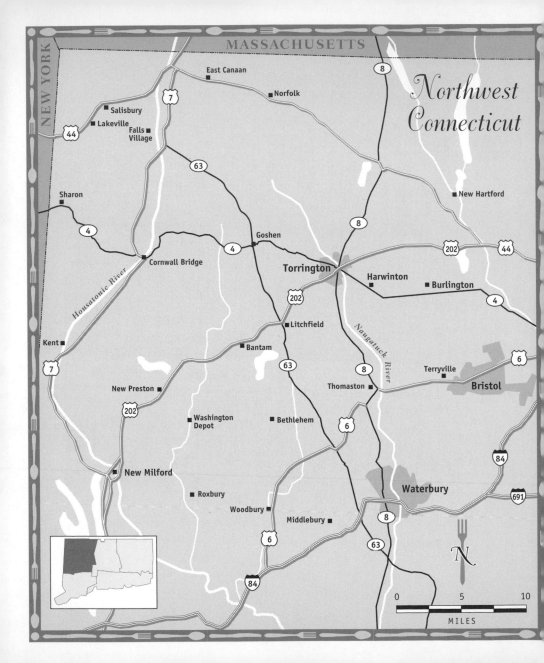

Northwest Connecticut

This corner of the state encompasses Litchfield County, long known as a weekend vacationland of the rich and famous—the likes of Meryl Streep, Kevin Bacon, other actors, fashionistas, and politicos—who come not to be seen but to escape being seen. It is no wonder that people in pressure-cooker jobs gravitate to this region. It is a beautiful area of undulating hills, placid lakes like Waramaug (which is surrounded by several delightful country inns, known for their excellent dining rooms), trout streams, the meandering Housatonic River, and wooded nature preserves, such as the White Memorial Foundation & Conservation Center, with its 35 miles of hiking and cross-country ski trails just outside Litchfield.

Litchfield is a treasure of another kind, with a much-admired village green and wide carriageways lined with imposing eighteenth-century clapboard houses. Don't be deceived: Litchfield may look drowsy, but it has one of the area's most sophisticated restaurants and a European gourmet food shop with home-baked German and Dutch breads and pastries. As in so much of this area, pastoral beauty is cosseted with urban comforts.

This is a land of secluded country estates and postcard-pretty villages like Salisbury, Lakeville, and Sharon, with steepled churches, scenic greens, and historic inns. The sleepy town of Woodbury is an antiquer's idea of heaven with its many antiques shops tucked into vintage houses along the town's mile-long main thoroughfare. The street also boasts several fine restaurants and one of the state's most complete natural food markets. Kent's main street is bordered by art galleries, craft shops and boutiques with clothing, ethnic jewelry, and artifacts, a bakery, a Belgian chocolatier, and other specialty food stores and cafes, as you might expect in such a bustling art center. No wonder New York visitors flock there on summer weekends.

The region is also a patchwork quilt of farmlands, with some local farms still worked by descendants of the families that started them in the 1700s. Through the generations they have raised cattle, sheep, and pigs; maple trees for sugar; and fruits and vegetables. Many still sell their produce, at old-fashioned roadside farm stands, often operating on the honor system. The woods and back roads offer wide-angle vistas of hillsides dappled with old orchards and new vineyards. A surprising number of independent food entrepreneurs—butchers, bakers, and candlestick makers; producers of smoked meats and game, cakes and candy, ice cream, chocolates, cheese—have their homes and plants here, in villages and hamlets tucked among wildflower meadows, woods, and fields. You will find them in these pages.

This tranquil area appeals to many people because of what it doesn't have: no superhighways, casinos, blinking neons, huge resort hotels, ubiquitous advertising signs, an excess of strip malls, fast-fooderies, chain hotels, or theme parks. These omissions are seen as positives by those who live or weekend here. They are a motley crew: high-powered New York executives, novelists, musicians, actors, nature lovers, sportsmen who fish, canoe, and go tubing on the Housatonic, balloonists soaring high above Mohawk Mountain, hikers of the Appalachian Trail or the summit of Mount Tom near Bantam or Bear Mountain (Connecticut's highest peak), just outside Salisbury. Whether sportsmen or stage stars, artists, diplomats, or CEOs, they all have chosen this north-by-northwest area for its restful pleasures, an important one of which is good food, which your taste buds will appreciate.

Made or Grown Here

Bantam Bread Company, 853 Bantam Rd. (Route 202), Bantam; (860) 567-2737. In the rear lower level of an old clapboard house is a little bakery where Niles Golvon (with helpers) makes and sells his fresh-from-the-oven breads. The aromas are so intoxicating I can rarely leave without a loaf of Kalamata-olive sourdough clutched in my hands. Other compelling choices include sunny flax sourdough, semolina, baker's white, caraway rye, French white, wheat-free whole spelt, Jewish rye, and holiday fruit-and-walnut. There are focaccias with four different toppings, five kinds of pound cake, ricotta cheesecake, and five cookie varieties as well. Certain breads are baked only on specific days of the week, like Irish soda bread on Thursday, sourdough raisin bread Thursday and Saturday, and challah on Friday. Niles's tarts—like the latticed fresh berry and fresh peach—are equally seductive, with wonderfully crisp and flaky crusts. In limited display space, jams, vinaigrettes, maple syrup, Bridgewater Chocolates, and imported pastas are also sold. Closed Monday and Tuesday.

Belgique Patisserie & Chocolatier, 1 Bridge St. (corner of Routes 7 and 341), Kent; (860) 927-3681. This charming shop, in a Victorian carriage house, is as beautiful as a European patisserie, which isn't surprising, as the owner, Pierre Gilissen, is Belgian. His handmade chocolate candies (traditional Belgian pralines, chocolates, and truffles), cakes, tortes, and pastries are in the elegant Belgian style and are made on the premises, without preservatives. Pierre uses the premier Belgian-made Callebaut because it is 100 percent cocoa butter, without any vegetable oils. Arlequin, Javanais, raspberry Bavaroise, chocolate hazelnut dacquoise, and fruit mousse are a few of his cakes, along with cookies, fruit tarts, breakfast pastries, and delicious Belgian hot chocolate. In warm weather Pierre and his wife, Susan, make refreshing ice creams in unusual flavors—toasted almond and fig, for example—

Authentic Belgian Hot Chocolate

When Belgian chef-chocolatier Pierre Gilissen provides a recipe for hot chocolate, it's time to listen up. You know it will be rich, authentic, and delicious.

2 cups whole milk
**8 ounces Callebaut semisweet
    chocolate (broken into bits)**
**5 ounces Callebaut bittersweet
    chocolate (broken into bits)**

1 cup heavy cream
¼ teaspoon vanilla
½ cup powdered sugar

1. Heat on stove enough whole milk to make as many cups of hot chocolate as needed (i.e., 1 cup per person). When milk is very hot (be careful not to scorch), add semisweet and bittersweet chocolate to melt in and stir. Add more chocolate if a richer, more chocolatey drink is preferred. Taste.

2. For more sweetness, add more semisweet chocolate or vice versa if hot chocolate is too sweet for your taste.

3. To make whipped cream, beat heavy cream in a bowl until thick. Add vanilla and sugar to taste. Add more sugar if greater sweetness is required. Dollop the whipped cream onto the hot chocolate and serve.

Makes two large cups

Belgique Patisserie & Chocolatier
**1 Bridge St. (corner of Routes 7 and 341), Kent
(860) 927-3681**

and sorbets, like lime and pear. Also for sale are imported Belgian treats: pralines, truffles, marzipan, pâtés de fruit, and Callebaut chocolate for baking.

The Daphne Baking Company, 1 Landmark Lane, P.O. Box 417, Kent; (860) 927-1818; www.daphnebaking.com. Baker Bo Bartlett has developed a line of six devastating tarts (chocolate, pumpkin, macadamia nut, chocolate raspberry, passion fruit, lemon), pastry shells to be filled, and an almond tea cake, all made naturally, with no trans fats, no artificial anything. She makes them, you serve them, your guests swoon (presumably) as they devour them. Bo's motto is "We do the work, you take the credit." You can buy her Daphne product line at upmarket shops all around the state. Among them: various Whole Foods markets and The Olive Market in Georgetown. You can also order the Daphne line directly on the Web.

Fascia's Chocolates, Inc., 2066 Thomaston Ave., Waterbury; (203) 753-0515 or toll-free (877) 807-1717; www.fasciaschocolates .com. Loyal fans swear by the mouthwatering, hand-dipped, homemade chocolates John Fascia and his family have been making since 1964. Fascia's produces over fifty types of chocolates and numerous combinations: boxed chocolates, gift baskets, molded holiday specialties (Santas, Easter bunnies, et al.), assorted chocolate truffles, cream centers, caramels, and toffees. Fascia's ships all over the United States, but if you're in the neighborhood, you might drop by the retail store attached to the factory. Popular favorites are the pecan turtles, gourmet truffles, and chocolates with double-dip cordial cherries. Among eight outlets, Orchid Florist, 1 Chase Ave., Waterbury, (203) 573-0690, has the full line and even delivers.

Gourmet Conveniences, 457 Bantam Rd., Litchfield; (860) 567-3529; www.sweetsunshine.com. In honor of their Louisiana-born father, Paul and Van Sarris developed a line of chili sauces, which they call "flavor before fire." There are now six all-natural Sweet Sunshine sauces (Warm, Hot, Jamaican Jerk, Atomic, Roasted Shallot & Garlic, and Sweet), sold at Whole Foods and other stores. Various sauces have won numerous awards in a number of food shows.

Lombardi's Bakery, 177 East Main St., Torrington; (860) 489-4766. This homegrown bakery has been a local fixture since 1978, turning out cookies by the platter and the piece, as well as fruitcakes, éclairs, Napoleons, tiramisus, and all kinds of pastries, including Hungarian kolache. My favorites are the heavenly, cloud-like almond macaroons. Breads are another Lombardi specialty, even fresh pizza dough. Closed Monday. Cash or checks only, no credit cards.

Matthews 1812 House, 250 Kent Rd. (Route 7), Cornwall Bridge; (860) 672-0149; www.matthews1812house.com. What began in

1979 in the kitchen of Deanna Matthews's 1812 farmhouse with a few brandied apricots and fruit-nut cakes is now a flourishing line of cakes, candies, cookies, and dessert sauces and toppings, sold via the company Web site and by catalog (165,000 printed each year) all around the United States and in a compact shop on the factory grounds. Fresh, all-natural ingredients are used, and everything is hand-baked. New products are added regularly, like the chocolate toffee almond cookies, apple brunch cake, and award-winning almond roll-up cookies. My current favorites are the marzipan cake and shortbread. A good way to get acquainted with the line is the 1812 Cake Sampler of four loaf cakes (country spice, chocolate-raspberry liqueur, chocolate rum, and lemon-rum sunshine) or Cookies Deluxe tin (fifty-three cookies, eight different types).

Nodine's Smokehouse, North St. (Route 63), Goshen; (860) 491-4009; www.nodinesmokehouse.com. You name it, Nodine's (pronounced no-dine) probably smokes it: sausages (venison, chorizo, kielbasa, beef, maple, chicken with sun-dried tomatoes and with green peppercorns), whole game (Cornish game hen, pheasant, turkey, goose, duck, chicken), fish (bluefish, mackerel, trout, salmon), meats (pork and beef), and various Cajun-spiced items (andouille sausage, tasso ham, bayou bacon), as well as New England cured ham, available in spiral cut and boneless. Then there are the smoked cheeses (cheddar, provolone, Gruyère, Swiss, Pepper Jack). In business since 1969, Johanne and Ronald Nodine and their son Calvin sell to shops and restaurants throughout Connecticut and in New York City. A modest shop (with the rather highfalutin' name

"Nodine's Gourmet Shop"), inside an old dairy barn on the ten-acre property, is crammed with smoked goods, New England–made crackers, jams, and jellies. People stop by for fresh-made soup, sandwiches with as many trimmings as a delicatessen, and giant homemade cookies (delicious!). The beef barbecue on sesame-seeded bun is really special. Smoking was originally done in the barn, but now it's done in Torrington. Factory tours can be arranged by calling (860) 489-3213. For ordering, the entire product line is listed on the company Web site and mail-order catalog.

Sweet Maria's, 159 Manor Ave., Waterbury; (203) 755-3804 or (888) 755-4099; www.sweet-marias.com. Since 1990 Maria Bruscino Sanchez has been fulfilling a childhood dream, whipping up delicious cakes and cookies in her own well-named bakery. As a teenager she worked in a neighborhood bakery. After college she moonlighted from her job in advertising to bake cakes at night. Now she has her own bakery in her old neighborhood, with the motto "More than just another pretty cake." Her huge repertoire includes layer, loaf, tea, carrot, amaretto apple, birthday and wedding cakes, cheesecakes, apricot/strawberry/pineapple mousse cakes, and special creations like Maria's Booze Crooze (yellow cake with rum, coconut, and pineapple).

Maria's frostings are just as creative: Cherry Nutter (cherry with buttercream), Chocolate Heath Bar Crunch, and Rocky Road (chocolate buttercream with chocolate chips, walnuts, and marshmallows), plus all the standard flavors. Custom cakes can be special-ordered. Maria's also sells, via Web site and mail order, loaf and Bundt cakes, biscotti in six flavors, fifteen different cookie types (including the award-winning pignoli and chocolate almond), and Maria's four cookbooks. The bakery has a petite cafe with five tables for on-the-spot nibbling.

Specialty Stores & Markets

Artisan Made-Northeast, 760 Main St. South, Southbury; (203) 262-9390; www.artisanmade-ne.com. In straightforward displays, this artisan-friendly shop, owned by Tom and Sally Camm, has been open since 2003. It features one hundred and twelve artisan cheeses, from Maine to Virginia (including Connecticut, of course), hand-crafted chocolates, all kinds of jams, jellies, sauces, condiments, sourdough breads, coffees, teas, gourmet sandwiches, and other all-natural products. Open Tuesday through Saturday 10:00 a.m. to 7:00 p.m., Sunday 12:00 p.m. to 5:00 p.m.

The Dutch Epicure Shop, 491 Bantam Rd. (Route 202), Litchfield; (860) 567-5586; www.dutchepicure.com. German-born pastry chef Wolfgang Joas and his Dutch wife, Betsy, emigrated to the United States in 1967 and took over a simple Dutch bakery. With their daughter, Wilma, they have made it a gallimaufry of Dutch and German treats, all baked by Wilma or Wolfgang: cakes, twenty-five types of cookies, breads, seasonal specialties like New Year's Eve berliner, Easter eggs filled with house-made truffles, Christmas stollen, Dutch chocolate letters, and German-style pretzels. This well-stocked shop also disperses eight different kinds of Gouda, Dutch hard goat cheese, other Dutch and European cheeses, sausages and meats (supplied by a German butcher in New Jersey), jams, jellies, Dutch licorice, condiments, stroopwafels, speculaas spice cookies, pannekoeken mixes, Indonesian sambals, spices, seasonings, ingredients for rijstafel, and Indian mixes and curries. A freezer bulges with house-made soups, casseroles, chicken potpies, quiches, and spätzle. Among nonfood items are Delftware, German soaps, and 4711 cologne. Closed Monday and Tuesday. Open Wednesday through Saturday from 9:00 a.m. to 5:00 p.m., Sunday until 2:00 p.m. If you can't make it to Litchfield, the Web site lists a number of Dutch Epicure mail-order products.

Harney and Sons Fine Teas, 1 Railroad Plaza, Millerton, New York (on Route 44); (518) 789-2121 (shop) or (800) 832-8463 (factory, for a catalog); www.harney.com. The Harneys have been selling tea since 1983. They outgrew their space in Salisbury and are now just across the state line in Millerton, 2 miles from Lakeville, in an 1879 smokehouse. Even though Harney's is now technically out of state, it has such strong Connecticut ties and identity I feel it *must* be included here. In addition to a wholesale, mail-order, and

Internet business, with teas shipped all over the world, this handsome shop/tasting room, with its wide pine floorboards, retails Harney teas and tea samplers, as well as tea-related items: teapots, cozies, tea strainers, and Harney's book about tea. Sample several of the 200-plus varieties of tea in smart black canisters with gold labels that line the shelves and cabinets. Among the selections are black, green, and white teas (including a delicate Winter White Earl Grey), organics, herbals, decaffeinated teas, floral and holiday teas, sachets, and art teas. Also for sale are English scone mixes, shortbreads, honey, and crispy Brittany crepes, among many upscale products. You don't have to be a teetotaler to enjoy a visit to Harney's, which now has a small restaurant that serves lunch as well as afternoon tea. Tours of the factory require an appointment. Shop hours: daily 10:00 a.m. to 5:00 p.m., but Sunday 11:00 a.m. to 4:00 p.m. Restaurant: daily 11:00 a.m. to 4:00 p.m. for lunch and tea, Sunday noon to 3:00 p.m.

Hunt Farm Trust, 44 Upland Rd., New Milford; (860) 355-0300 or (800) 353-SILO; www.hunthillfarmtrust.org. The largest section of this interesting store, which is part of Ruth and the late Skitch

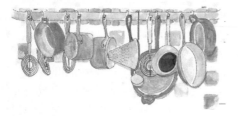

Henderson's Silo Farm, is devoted to high-end culinary tools, pots, pans, casseroles, cookware, glassware, utensils, linens, and other accoutrements. There is a section in which nonperishable Connecticut-made food products are sold, like

local honey, maple syrup, jams, raspberry-wasabi dipping mustard, olives, condiments, and the farm's own Silo Salt. Despite its remote location, the store (with a notable cooking school) has been going strong since 1972. Hours change with the seasons, so it is best to call ahead. The Skitch Henderson Museum, with mementoes of his career, is on the same premises.

The Kent Coffee and Chocolate Company, 8 Main St., Kent; (860) 927-1445 or (800) 927-4465; www.kentcoffee andchocolate.com. More than the life-size, over-stuffed black gorilla positioned near the entrance, the heady aromas of chocolate and coffee have lured passersby to this shop-cafe since it opened in 1991. We can't think of a better place to stop, between browsing at Kent's many art galleries, for a cup of coffee, tea, or cocoa. Many of Kent's chocolates are house-made—like the chocolate bark and chocolates in sixteen different flavors. Most popular are the hand-dipped truffles, pecan turtles, and chocolate-dipped pretzels. Kent's thick, old-fashioned fudge comes in six seductive flavors, including chocolate peanut butter, penuche, mudslide fudge, and Heath bar fudge. Coffee is a big deal here too, with Arabica beans imported from Sumatra, Kenya, Colombia, Costa Rica, Guatamala, and elsewhere, roasted in small batches for maximum flavor and aroma. Available by mail order or the Web site are over fifty coffee blends, one hundred teas, twenty-one chocolate assortments, fudge, and several nicely packaged gift items: maple syrup miniatures, King Ludwig's Bavarian nuts, and four types of tea jams. Join the gorilla and sit and sip, or, in summer, carry your iced coffee or frozen cappuccino outdoors to the Board of Directors bench and watch the passing scene. Open daily from 6:00 a.m. to 7:00 p.m.

La Molisana Italian Sausage, 305 Congress Ave., Waterbury; (203) 574-1272. When Tullio and Assunta Lupo opened their small store in 1998, they named it after Italy's Moliese region. Their mainstay then—and now—is sausage, a range of Italian sausages, including an unsual dry sausage, soppresseta, coppa, and garlic pork sausage. The Lupos sell other house-made foods as well— marinated mushrooms and eggplant, meatballs, provolone-stuffed peppers, house-seasoned olives, and two types of panini. Also for sale are various Italian cheeses, anchovies, pastas, cookies, coffee, and other Italian goods, as well as, occasionally, rabbit. Cash or checks only. Closed Sunday.

The Monastic Art Shop at the Abbey of Regina Laudis, 273 Flanders Rd., Bethlehem; (203) 266-7637; www.abbeyof reginalaudis. There is a small shop on the grounds of this cloistered convent, which is scenically snuggled into the hills, that boasts many products made by the Benedictine community. Sister Noella Marcellino was taught cheese-making by a French expert. She uses the milk of Dutch belted cows to produce boutique French-style cheeses and a sharp English-type cheddar, all of which are first rate. Also available in the shop are honey, herbs, vinegar, and hot mustards, along with such non-comestible products as woven and knitted scarves, stoles, and sweaters (all made from Abbey sheep wool); cards; books; religious art objects; and compact discs of Abbey chants. Closed Wednesday. Call ahead for hours.

New Morning Natural and Organic Foods, Middle Quarter Mall, Route 6, Woodbury; (203) 263-4868; www.newmorn.com. Shoppers partial to organic and natural foods may be awestruck, as I was on my first visit, by the magnitude of this family-owned supermarket. If it is missing anything, I can't think what it might be. Fresh fruits and vegetables, chicken, fish, cereals, breads, virtually every kind of packaged natural-food product along with herbs and spices, teas, soy and organic milk and cheeses, and packaged frozen meals (vegetarian and organic) are all here. There are bins with beans and lentils (including black turtle beans, adzuki, and black-eyed cowpeas), dried fruits, nuts (including five different types of cashews), seeds (flax, brown sesame, and Hungarian pumpkin among them), rice, couscous, hulled barley, quinoa, whole wheat, and organic coffees. Help yourself to fresh soup from three huge cauldrons in a small soup corner. A deli case displays takeout salads, salmon cakes, and other entrees, and there is a separate room with homeopathic medicines and vitamins. This store is definitely worth a detour. Open daily 8:00 a.m. to 7:00 p.m., Sunday from 10:00 a.m. to 5:00 p.m.

Nine Main Bakery & Deli, 9 Main St., New Preston; (860) 868-1879. Just off New Preston's town center, Nine Main is a welcome addition to this part of the Litchfield Hills landscape. The inspiration of owner Liz Johnson, the tidy shop, with its mere five tables, is so immaculate it glistens. Salads, sandwiches, and two soups are available daily. Cookies, scones, and muffins are oven-fresh from the kitchen. The muffins come in twenty-seven flavors—lemon raspberry, blueberry, banana, peanut butter, and butterscotch pecan among them. Cakes made to order are also available. There is a small selection of Connecticut-made preserves, chutneys, and salsas for sale, as well as artwork by local artists. Open daily: weekdays from 6:30 a.m. to 3:00 p.m., weekends from 7:30 a.m.

The Pantry, 5 Titus Rd., Washington Depot; (860) 868-0258; www.thepantryinc.com; $$. Since it opened in 1977, The Pantry has been a meeting place for locals, who congregate for lunch, coffee, sweets, and specialty food shopping. Michael and Nancy Ackerman bought the business in 1986 and have maintained admirable consistency in this delightful gourmet food shop–cafe. There is seating for thirty-five, surrounded by racks and shelves chockablock with packaged delicacies, herbs, spices, various olive oils, mustards, jams, and goodies like Bridgewater Chocolates, Chocolate Lace, marzipan, and truffles, as well as European pottery, baskets, Le Creuset pots, and other high-end culinary supplies. A refrigerated display case features English, French, and regional artisanal

U.S. cheeses. People come from miles away to enjoy the baked ham and other made-to-order sandwiches, fresh-baked breads, muffins, and mouthwatering pastries, all prepared on the premises. Lunch is served almost all day, from 11:00 a.m. to 5:00 p.m. Tuesday through Saturday. Closed Sunday and Monday.

Three Oaks Chocolatier, 583 Bantam Rd., Litchfield; (860) 567-0392; www.threeoakschocolatier.com. Since 2006 Wilfred Parilla has been making and selling small batches of handmade chocolates—truffles, turtles, toffee, caramels, marzipan, chocolate bark, white chocolates, and the like, made from fine Belgian chocolate. Open Tuesday, Wednesday, and Saturday from 10:00 a.m. to 5:00 p.m., Thursday and Friday until 6:00 p.m. Closed Sunday and Monday.

Farmers' Markets

For up-to-the-minute information about dates and times, call the Connecticut Department of Agriculture at (860) 713-2503, visit the Web site at www.state.ct.us/doag/, or e-mail ctdeptag@po.state .ct.us.

Bantam Farmers' Market, Bantam Borough Hall, Route 202, Bantam. Saturday from 8:30 a.m. to 1:00 p.m., the first week of June through mid-November.

Bristol Farmers' Market, Depot Sq., North Main St., Bristol. Wednesday from 3:00 to 6:00 p.m. and Saturday from 10:00 a.m. to 1:00 p.m., first week of July through October.

Burlington Farmers' Market, First Congregational Church of Burlington, Route 4, Burlington. Friday from 3:00 to 6:00 p.m., early July to October.

Cornwall Farmers' Market, near the Covered Bridge, 413 Route 128, West Cornwall. Saturday from 9:00 a.m. to 1:30 p.m., June to October.

Kent Farmers' Market, Kent Green, Kent. Saturday from 9:00 a.m. to noon, mid-May to October.

Litchfield Farmers' Market, Center School, 125 West St., Litchfield. Saturday from 10:00 a.m. to 1:00 p.m., mid-June to October.

Morris Farmers' Market, Morris Senior Center, Morris. Wednesday from 10:30 a.m. to noon, July 1 to October.

New Hartford Farmers' Market, Pine Meadow Green, Route 44 and Church St., New Hartford. Friday from 4:00 to 7:00 p.m., end of May to October.

New Milford Farmers' Market, Town Green, Main St., New Milford. Saturday from 9:00 a.m. to noon, mid-May through October.

Norfolk Farmers' Market, Route 44 at the corner of Shepard Rd. (just west of downtown), Norwalk. Saturday from 10:00 a.m. to 1:00 p.m., first weekend in June through October.

Riverton Farmers' Market, Riverton Center, Route 20, Riverton. Sunday from 11:00 a.m. to 2:00 p.m., late June to late September.

Southbury Farmers' Market, 501 Main St. South, Southbury. Thursday from 2:00 to 6:00 p.m., from first week of July to mid-October.

Thomaston Farmers' Market, Seth Thomas Park, South Main St., Thomaston. Thursday from 2:30 to 6:00 p.m., early July to October.

Torrington Farmers' Market, Downtown Shopping Center, 100 South Main St., Torrington. Tuesday from 3:00 to 6:00 p.m. and Saturday from 10:00 a.m. to 1:00 p.m., early June to October.

Washington Depot Farmers' Market, Washington Senior Center, 6 Bryan Hall Plaza, Washington Depot. Thursday from 10:30 a.m. to noon, first week of July to first week of October.

Waterbury Fulton Park Farmers' Market, Fulton Park Greenhouse, Waterbury. Every other Saturday from 9:00 a.m. to noon, early July through first week of September.

Waterbury-Mall Farmers' Market II, Brass City Mall, west parking lot, Waterbury. Thursday 2:00 to 5:00 p.m., mid-July through October.

Watertown Farmers' Market, Watertown Library parking lot, Watertown. Saturday from 9:00 a.m. to 1:00 p.m., mid-July to mid-September.

Woodbury Farmers' Market, Hollow Park, 43 Hollow Rd., Woodbury. Wednesday from 3:00 to 6:00 p.m., from mid-July through September.

Farm Stands

Averill Farm, 250 Calhoun St., Washington Depot; (860) 868-2777; www.averillfarm.com. The Averill family has farmed these 200 hilltop acres since 1746, with some of the buildings, the house (1830), and the barn dating back to the early 1800s. Sam and Susan Averill took over the farm in 1990, and now their son Tyson, the family's tenth generation, is helping out. They grow many apple varieties and twelve types of pears, most available for picking your own. The Averill farm stand also stocks honey, delcious fresh apple cider, doughnuts, maple syrup, pumpkins, Vermont cheeses, and cut flowers. Open Labor Day to Thanksgiving, daily from 9:30 a.m. to 5:30 p.m.

Eagle Wood Farms, 325 New Hartford Rd., Barkhamsted; (860) 738-1144; www.eaglewoodgourmetfood.com. Animals are the "crops" for sale at this unusual farm store (not a stand). David Finn, a cabinet maker in his spare time, raises various breeds of pigs, goats, and cows to produce hormone-free (but not certified organic) meats (including kielbasa, hot dogs, and knockwurst) ready-made for the barbecue grill. Special orders, such as suckling pig, should be placed at least two weeks in advance.

Ellsworth Hill Orchard & Berry Farm, 461 Cornwall Bridge Rd. (Route 4), Sharon; (860) 364-0025; www.ellsworthfarm.com. In addition to the 3,000 plum and apple trees (eighteen varieties including Macoun, Cortland, Empire, and Red Delicious), blueberries, strawberries, raspberries, and pumpkins that Michael Bozzi and his family cultivate on their seventy-acre farm, they also planted Australian pumpkins one year and came up with a pink one that made headlines nationally. June through November is pick-your-own time for berries, apples, peaches, pears, cherries, pumpkins, and gourds. In the big farm store near the road, you can buy Bozzi's cider, home-baked cider doughnuts, pies, muffins, and pastries, as well as all the fresh fruit in season. The Bozzis welcome visitors to roam their fields, explore the six-acre corn maze, and enjoy the woods and views of buildings that date back to the 1700s. Hayrides in September are another popular attraction. Open daily from 10:00 a.m. to 5:00 p.m., June through November.

Freund's Farm Market and Bakery, Route 44, East Canaan; (860) 824-0650. In a huge barn-red building next to a large greenhouse, Theresa and Matthew Freund sell fruit, corn, and other vegetables, maple syrup, honey, and cut flowers from the family farm, which includes a 240-cow dairy complex. In a full kitchen on the second floor, Theresa and helpers bake whole-grain breads and baguettes, pies, cakes, cookies, and doughnuts. Pies are a specialty, some two dozen types (even sugar-free), and Theresa's bite-size holiday cookies can be ordered in three-pound assortments on 12-inch dome platters. Also for sale are Theresa's own jellies, salsas, Cabot and McCam cheeses, and Guida ice cream. Freund's catering orders are especially heavy during the Christmas holidays. "This all started," Matthew says, "back when my mother sold her corn under a maple tree by the side of the road." Open daily from 9:00 a.m. to 6:00 p.m. in season. Closed January through March.

Lamothe's Sugar House, 89 Stone Rd., Burlington; (860) 675-5043; www.lamothesugarhouse.com. On 350 leased acres, this working farm has grown from seven taps for maple sugar to its current 4,400, making Lamothe's the largest producer in the state. From mid-February to the end of March on Saturday and Sunday, from 1:00 to 5:00 p.m. visitors can watch the maple-sugar-making process. The country store sells maple sugar products year-round, from soup to nuts, or rather from maple syrup to maple-sugar-coated nuts, as well as other gifts and  Connecticut-made products. They include maple candy, maple cream, maple-walnut caramels, maple sugar, even maple vinegar, barbecue sauce, honey, and jams. Lamothe's wholesales and mail-orders its products, too, which can be ordered via the Web site. Robert and Jean Lamothe raise a dozen or so pigs a year, which should be ordered ahead—half-size or whole hog.

Maple Bank Farm, 57 Church St. (Route 317), Roxbury; (860) 354-7038; www.maplebankfarm.com. This venerable property has been in the Hurlbut family since 1730, when John Hurlbut was granted six acres by the king of England. Cows, sheep, and pigs were the first mainstays, but over time, fruit and vegetable crops were added. Cathy Hurlbut and her husband, Howie Bronson, have been living in the "new" 1830 farmhouse since 1980, while the foundation of her ancestor, John's, original house lies visible within 100 feet of the current farm stand. Depending on the season, that stand overflows with apples, heirloom tomatoes, potatoes, carrots, garlic, fresh herbs, jams, apple cider, maple syrup, pies, pastries, and breads, as well as annuals, perennials, and garden supplies. You can pick your own blueberries in July and August. Open from

March to mid-December, Tuesday through Sunday from 10:00 a.m. to 5:30 p.m.

Maple View Farm, 276 Locust Rd., Harwinton; (860) 485-0815; mgauger@snet.net. Mark and Carole Gauger grow a variety of small organic fruits and vegetables, which they sell at farmers' markets in Torrington and Collinsville. The small farm stand is now located in their garage and operates on the honor system. Select your organic tomatoes, cucumbers, peppers, onions, potatoes, and blueberries, and put your payment in the small cash box.

March Farm, 160 Munger Ln., Bethlehem; (203) 266-7721; www .marchfarms.com. The Marchukaitis family has been farming here since 1915, with Tom March, as the surname has been shortened, the current patriarch in charge. Harvest season begins in May with salad greens, basil, and greenhouse tomatoes, then continues with blueberries in July, sweet corn and peaches in August, and sixteen apple varieties, including Ginger Gold, Honeycrisp, Mutsu, Macoun, and Paula Red, in September. All (plus pumpkins) are available as pick-your-own, or stop by the farm stand (open daily from April to just before Christmas, 9:00 a.m. to 5:00 p.m.), where you will also find honey, jams, jellies, apple products (jelly, salsa, butter, and Dutch apple jam), the cider mill's syrup, and mulled cider. And from March on, Sue March's commercial kitchen turns out pies (including peach praline and strawberry-rhubarb), cookies, and cider dough-nuts. A corn maze, after the late summer harvest, remains open until the first snowfall.

Roberts Orchard, 125 Hill St., Bristol; (860) 582-5314; e.ferrier@ att.net. An apple a day keeps the doctor away, but if you want more than that, Roberts is happy to oblige—with Macoun, McIntosh, Cortland, Honeycrisp, Jonagold, Mutsu, and Red Delicious. The Apple House farm store is ensconced in a big red barn, along with the bakery and cider-making and storage facility. There you can buy fresh cider (a wall tap enables you to draw your own into a jug), apple butter, apple cakes, mini cider doughnuts (freshly made on  Saturday and Sunday), and apple crumb pies (a specialty), along with fresh apple, cranberry apple, pecan, mince, and pumpkin pies, hot-out-of-the-oven pumpkin bread, honeywheat bread, a variety of homemade muffins, and Roberts's own homemade jams and jellies (made from peaches, raspberries, and other fruit grown on the seventy-acre farm). In addition, there are hayrides and a Pumpkin House (open weekends, with a narrated story and life-size characters). Open after Labor Day through Thanksgiving, Monday through Saturday from 9:00 a.m. to 5:30 p.m., Sunday from 10:00 a.m. to 5:30 p.m. Custom pie orders, especially for Thanksgiving, should be placed several days in advance.

Rustling Wind Creamery, 148 Canaan Mountain Rd., Falls Village; (860) 824-7084; www.rustlingwind.com. In a minuscule shop attached to the cheese-making facilities of this 204-acre farm, Joan Lamothe sells—on the honor system—all kinds of home-grown and -made products. These range from honey, jellies, jams, pickles, relishes, salsas, and maple syrup, to goat's-milk fudge and goat's-milk soap (both from the farm's thirty-some goats), to sweaters, scarves, and mittens (from the wool of the farm's fourteen sheep). The magnets are the English-style cheeses (which Joan also sells online throughout the United States): Cheshire, blue, sage, Wensleydale (including three special herbed Wensleydales), and a soft, herbed goat-cheese spread. Joan's cheeses are available during summer at farmers' markets in Norfolk and Cornwall. Open daily year-round from 8:00 a.m. to 4:30 p.m.

Starberry Farm, 81 Kielwasser Rd., Washington Depot; (860) 868-2863; starberry@snet.net. For more than thirty years Sally and Bob Futh have been leading a fruitful (ahem) existence on their twenty-five-acre farm, growing eighteen types of apples and twenty-eight types of peaches, apricots, cherries, and plums. They invite you to pick your own, from cherry time in June to the end of October or pick up some of their homemade pies, jams, and jellies. Stop by from June to Thanksgiving (even later if the weather cooperates, but call ahead), 10:00 a.m. to 5:00 p.m. daily.

Stone Wall Dairy Farm, 332 Kent Rd. South (Route 7), Cornwall Bridge; (860) 672-0261. Chris Hopkins, aided by leased land from the town of Cornwall, only began raising cows for milk in 2004.

Today twenty contented Jerseys, munching on the 120-acre farmland, supply their rich, creamy raw milk to contented customers and merchants all around the western part of the state. In a section of the big red barn, Chris also sells beef and eggs from his organically raised chickens. Vegetables are raised on the property too, by Jonathan Kirschner, and sold, also on the honor system, at a stand at the front of the farm. Open year-round; tours arranged by request.

Sullivan Farm, 140 Park Ln. (Route 202), New Milford; (860) 210-2030; www.youthagency.org. You want homegrown, you want natural? Think Sullivan's farm stand, with its seasonal vegetables, berries, honey, maple syrup, jams, jellies, chocolate and maple fudge, even pickles. Just 3 miles north of New Milford's center, Sullivan's is a 126-acre property, which now belongs to the New Milford Youth Agency. There's the Great Brook Sugar House, which has been making syrup the old-fashioned way since 1983. In February or March you might take a tour conducted by a costumed guide who walks you through three centuries of maple syrup making. (You'll find the sugar house by the steam floating skyward from its cupola.) Check the Web site for dates and hours. The farm stand is open in season Monday through Saturday, from 9:30 a.m. to 6:00 p.m., Sunday, noon to 5:30 p.m.

Tonn's Orchard, 270 Preston Rd., Terryville; (860) 675-3707 or (860) 585-1372. Herbert Tonn and family take their produce to several farmers' markets during the week, splitting time on weekends from August to October between their eight-acre peach-and-apple farm and orchard and their in-town fruit stand. You can pick-your-own on weekends from 10:00 a.m. to 5:00 p.m., starting with peaches in July, moving on to fifteen apple varieties (Paula Red and McIntosh, among others) as they ripen (beginning in August), until October. Meanwhile, Tonn's fruit stand in Burlington (418 Milford St.) sells fresh sweet corn, tomatoes, blueberries, raspberries, and cucumbers daily, from July through October, 8:00 a.m. to 6:00 p.m.

Windy Hill Farm, 18 Hillhouse Rd., Goshen; (860) 491-3021. Doug Allen has been cultivating vegetables on his 400-acre farm since 1978, while also maintaining twenty-five to thirty Herefords that he sells wholesale on the hoof and as feeder cattle. Sweet corn, tomatoes, potatoes, cucumbers, pumpkins, and other veggies are available freshly picked throughout the growing season, from mid-July to mid-October, as well as Doug's own maple syrup and fresh eggs; daily from 9:00 a.m. to dusk (call ahead for specific crops).

Food Happenings

MARCH

Maple-syrup-making Demonstrations, Flanders Nature Center, Flanders Road, Woodbury; (203) 263-3711; www.flandersnature

center.org. Demonstrations are usually the first three Saturday afternoons in March, from 1:00 to 4:00 p.m., but check the Web site to be sure.

MAY

Hotter Than Heck Festival, Waterbury area; (203) 573-0264. Things get devilishly hot around Waterbury at this festival in early May. This benefits Waterbury Youth Services, which helps 5,000 local children and families. The theme is simple: hot, hot, really hot food. Some twenty-eight restaurateurs, caterers, and specialty food vendors turn up the heat, with offerings like volcanic wings, fiery salsas, and chocolate chile-pepper cookies, fierce enough to make you cry in your beer (or beverage of choice). For the price of an admission ticket, you have access to a towering inferno of hellishly incendiary appetizers, entrees, and desserts, as well as live entertainment. Timid taste buds are welcome, too, as there are some dishes for the faint-of-palate. Check for date and locale.

JUNE

The Litchfield Summer Fest, Haight-Brown Vineyard, Chestnut Hill, Litchfield; (860) 567-4045; www.haightvineyards.com. Formerly called A Taste of Litchfield Hills, this weekend event is a magnet for hundreds of visitors, with New England and international foods and wines prepared by local restaurant chefs, food demonstrations, ice carving, upscale shopping, live music, winery tours, and vineyard hayrides. Dates are the third or fourth Saturday and Sunday in the month, held rain or shine. Check to be sure of the dates. Hours: 11:00 a.m. to 8:00 p.m. Saturday, 11:00 a.m. to 5:00 p.m. Sunday.

SEPTEMBER

Harvest Festival, Haight-Brown Vineyard, Chestnut Hill, Litchfield; (860) 567-4045. Music, grape-stomping contests, hayrides, and other festivities occur at this late September fall fête, usually held the third weekend. (Call ahead for the dates and times.)

DECEMBER

Gingerbread House Festival, St. George's Episcopal Church, Tucker Hill Road at Route 188, Middlebury; (203) 758-2165. This bazaar and fair, run by church volunteers, has been going strong since 1972. A casserole and salad luncheon is served on opening Saturday (usually the first one in December), and more than fifty gingerbread displays of miniature houses, trees, animals, and people are sold the following Saturday, at the end of the weeklong fair. For sale throughout are homemade ginger cookies (4,000 of these were gobbled up last year at $1 apiece) and such inedibles as handmade knitted scarves, hats, and gloves, and wooden decorations and tree ornaments. All proceeds go to the church. Check for hours.

Bohemian Pizza, 342 Bantam Rd., Litchfield; (860) 567-3980; $. The name seems like an oxymoron, but it is intended to suggest an offbeat pizza style (to match the funky offbeat decor). It comes down to building your own pie. The basic pie is 18 inches across, with one of three base layers (red, pesto, or white ricotta). From there you can construct your own toppings; choices include, among twenty-three options at $1 or $2 each, anchovies, spinach, basil, sun-dried tomatoes, Nodine's andouille sausage, goat cheese, and chopped clams. A complete menu features pastas, salads, spring rolls, and quesadillas, but pizzas are the indisputable stars. There's also a short wine list and some two dozen imported and microbrew beers. Open daily.

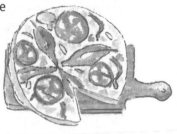

Bunker Hill Deli at Mattatuck Museum Arts & History Center, 144 West Main St., Waterbury; (203) 753-2452; www.mattatucknuseum .org; $. For a snack or break from museuming, order a sandwich, soup, salad, or dessert (or all of the above), then enjoy it (them) at the attached Gallery Café. Open Tuesday through Friday, from 11:00 a.m. to 2:30 p.m.

Chaiwalla, 1 Main St., Salisbury; (860) 435-9758; chaiwalla@ snet.net; $. Inside a little clapboard house set back from the road in the center of town, this charming tearoom has been an oasis for breakfast, tiffin, lunch, and leisurely afternoon tea five days a week (only three—Friday through Sunday—in winter) since 1989. Freshly made salads, quiches, and sandwiches are standard offerings, as are the delicious house-made tarts, pies, and cakes, like whiskey cake, carrot cake, and strawberry-rhubarb cobbler. You can count on loose brewed tea here, as owner Mary O'Reilly is a tea enthusiast. That zeal carries over to a retail and mail-order business selling fine and rare teas, which she collects from China, Japan, India, Morocco, and elsewhere in the tea-growing world. Among her selections are Sherpa, the Himalayan climbers' tea, five types of Darjeeling, Nilgiri, Terai, China Keemun, several Assams, fine green Kashmir Kawab from North India, and rare white tea. According to Mary, the name Chaiwalla means "tea bearer" in Hindi and Sanskrit. Cash or checks only, no credit cards. Regular hours: Wednesday through Sunday, from 10:00 a.m. to 6:00 p.m.

With its friendly style, tasty wholesome food, and down-to-earth prices, it didn't take long to build a loyal following for **Country Bistro,** 10 Academy St., Salisbury; (860) 435-9420; $. The mother-daughter team of Jacqueline Heriteau and Holly Hunter Stonehill assemble delicious soups, herb-roasted flank steak on a ciabatta roll, and many other choice lunch platters. The rustic one-room eatery is packed most mornings, when hearty breakfast fare is served, and the Bistro does a brisk business, too, in such popular takeout supper entrees as shepherd's pie, chicken potpie, and a layered polenta-beef casserole. Open daily for breakfast and lunch, from 8:00 a.m. to 5:30 p.m.

Movies and munchies—that's what you'll find at **Gilson Café/ Cinema,** 354 Main St., Winsted; (860) 379-5108 or (860) 379-6069; www.gilsoncafecinema.com; $. This novel cafe isn't adjacent to a theater, it is *in* the theater. Small tables are side by side so you can watch the big screen even as you eat. The five-page menu is studded with sandwiches, soups, salads, and pasta dishes. Waitresses circulate discreetly through the theater while the movie is in progress, filling orders for hot chocolate, cappuccino, carrot cake, or some other dessert. There is even a full bar.

The John Bale Book Company Café, 158 Grand St., Waterbury; (203) 591-1801; www.johnbalebooks.com; $. Mother may have admonished you not to read while you're eating. But don't tell that to folks at this two-story antiquarian bookstore. There's a small cafe on the ground floor where you'll find soups, salads, stews, and sandwiches made to order. Open from 7:30 a.m. to 4 p.m. Monday through Friday, from 10 a.m. Saturday, the bookstore also serves breakfast (muffins, fruit cups, oatmeal, egg sandwiches). There's usually background music and sometimes even a live pianist.

Panini Café, 7 Old Barn Rd., Kent; (860) 927-5083; $. Primarily a take-out place, Panini has a few tables where you can play checkers while chomping on a BLT Bad Boy (with melted provolone), Ba-Da-Bing (salami, pepperoni, artichoke hearts, provolone, ham, onion, and green peppers), or one of a dozen other toasted panini sandwiches. You might also savor a soup, salad, or one of six house-made gelatos in flavors like Cappuccino Latte, Pomegranate Blueberry, and Mango Guava Madness. Seasonal outdoor seating as well. Closed Tuesday.

Passiflora Tea Room (526 Main St., New Hartford; 860-379-8327; www.passifloratea.com; $) does double duty. One room in an historic 1850 brick house is a tearoom; the other is an herbal apothecary, with herbal and nutritional items for sale. It's the tearoom that is my magnet, with its 140 types of herbal and traditional teas, lunch menu, and yummy sweets. Many of the items are organic, with some ingredients even grown in owner Karen Tyson's garden. Hours vary; call ahead.

Rathskeller Restaurant and Bar, 88 Main St. South, Southbury; (203) 264-0186; www.rathskeller.com; $. Look for gemütlich coziness rather than high-speed bar atmosphere at this funky place, even though the bar, with its brass elbow rail, occupies a sizeable part of the room. While there are six or so draft beers available, it's the restaurant and friendly staff that attract family types. House-made soups, burgers, a dozen or more sandwich choices, buffalo wings, Carolina pulled pork on Kaiser rolls, pumpkin ravioli, and a dozen or more intriguing entrees are among the inducements that make the Rathskeller fare different

from the usual pub grub. And check out the odd salt-and-pepper shakers on each table: Locals often ask to be seated on the basis of where their favorite set is. Closed Sunday.

Learn to Cook

Carole Peck, Cooking Classes and Provence Culinary Tours, 694 Main St., Woodbury; (203) 266-4663; www.good-news-cafe.com. Carole Peck of Good News Café fame was a pioneer in cooking with natural local ingredients. She teaches classes in the spring and fall at The Silo Cooking School in New Milford (see below) and also at Delia's Culinary Forum in Wallingford. Check her and their Web sites for dates and details. Carole also leads one-week culinary tours to Provence, France, staying at her home there; there are two tours in May–June, two more in September–October, private tours by special arrangement. See her Web site for specifics.

Cooking with Adrienne, 218 Kent Rd. (Route 7), New Milford; (860) 354-6001; www.adriennerestaurant.com. Chef Adrienne Sussman, who began cooking at Commander's Palace in New Orleans, teaches cooking two Saturdays a month at Adrienne, her New Milford restaurant. Classes often follow a theme, season, or holiday (like Mother's Day or Passover) and last for three hours, from 11:00 a.m. to 2:00 p.m.

Sweet Maria's Chunkey Monkey Cake

This delicious, moist banana nut cake is filled with chocolate chunks and frosted with cream cheese icing. Maria Bruscino Sanchez calls it "perfect for dads or grads!"

¼ pound unsalted butter, softened
1 cup sugar
½ cup brown sugar
1 teaspoon vanilla extract
3 eggs
2 cups cake flour

1 teaspoon baking powder
1 teaspoon baking soda
½ teaspoon salt
2 cups mashed bananas (2–3 bananas)
¾ cup sour cream
1 cup large walnut pieces

1. Preheat oven to 350°F.
2. Grease and flour or line two 9-inch cake pans with parchment paper. Set aside.
3. In an electric mixer, cream butter and both sugars until light. Add vanilla. Add eggs, one at a time, beating well after adding each one.
4. In a medium bowl, combine flour, baking powder, baking soda, and salt. In a small bowl, combine bananas and sour cream. Pour each of these mixtures alternately into the butter mixture. Begin and end with the flour mixture. Mix just until blended. Stir in walnuts.
5. Pour batter evenly into prepared pans. Bake 20 to 25 minutes or until a tester inserted into the center of the cake comes out with a fine crumb.
6. Remove pans from the oven and place on wire cooling racks. Cool cakes in pan for 10 to 15 minutes. Carefully remove cakes from the pans and continue to cool on wire racks. Remove and discard parchment. Cool cakes completely before frosting.

Sweet Maria's

159 Manor Ave., Waterbury
(203) 755-3804 or (888) 755-4099
www.sweet-marias.com

Cream Cheese Frosting

¼ pound unsalted butter, softened

16 ounces cream cheese, softened

6 cups confectioners' sugar

1. In an electric mixer, cream butter and cream cheese on medium speed for 3 to 4 minutes, or until fluffy.
2. On low speed, gradually add confectioners' sugar until blended and smooth. Beat on high speed 3 to 4 minutes.
3. Use immediately or store refrigerated in an airtight container. Let frosting come to room temperature and briefly re-whip before using.

Assembly

Two 9-inch banana nut cake layers

One recipe Cream Cheese Frosting

2 cups chocolate chips or coarsely chopped chocolate pieces

2 cups chopped walnuts

1. Level off tops of cake layers. Place one layer, cut side up, on a cake plate or a doily-covered cake circle. Spread a layer of frosting over the cake layer. Sprinkle with chocolate chunks.
2. Place other layer, cut side down, onto bottom layer.
3. Using a metal spatula, frost the outside of the cake with remaining frosting.
4. Adhere walnuts to the sides of the cake.
5. Garnish top of cake, as desired, with chocolate chunks.
6. Refrigerate to let cake set up, about a half hour. Or store refrigerated overnight. Let cake come to room temperature before serving.

Makes one 9-inch layer cake, about 12 to 15 servings.

The Silo Cooking School at Hunt Hill Farm, 44 Upland Rd., New Milford; (860) 355-0300 or (800) 353-SILO; www.hunthill farmtrust.org. This comprehensive cooking school was begun by Ruth and Skitch Henderson in 1972 on their farm in the rolling hills outside New Milford. Classes, conducted by famous chefs, cookbook authors, restaurateurs, and noted nutritionists, cover a wide range of gastronomic interests, skills, and age groups. The Web site provides detailed descriptions of upcoming classes, as far as four months ahead, and you may register online. Courses usually consist of a single class of about three hours, mostly offered Saturday and Sunday, but occasionally on Thursday and Friday evenings. Carole Peck of the Good News Café in Woodbury and Christopher Prosperi of Metro Bis in Simsbury are two of many chefs who teach regularly at The Silo.

Sweet Maria's, 159 Manor Ave., Waterbury; (203) 755-3804; www .sweet-marias.com. In the "off-season" at Sweet Maria's Bakery, proprietor-and-baker-supreme Maria Bruscino Sanchez conducts basic cake-decorating, cookie-baking, and seasonal-dessert classes at the bakery, usually during September and October and February to March. Check the Web site for the schedule.

Kent Wine & Spirit, 24 North Main St., Kent; (860) 927-3033; www.kentwine.com. In this large, utilitarian store, proprietor Ira Smith stocks vintages from all the wine-producing areas of the globe. France, Germany, Italy, and California are especially well represented. There are also numerous specialty beers and ales (notably its fine range of Belgian ales alone) and as many as eighty-five types of single-malt scotches. Mr. Smith conducts regular wine tastings every Saturday from noon to 5:00 p.m. and is usually on hand other times to field questions about various wines, including rarities that he stocks. Check the Web site for special tastings and events.

Landmark Eateries

Adrienne, 218 Kent Rd. (Route 7), New Milford; (860) 354-6001; www.adriennerestaurant.com; $$. In 2009 chef Adrienne Sussman celebrated her thirteenth year in the eighteenth-century frame house whose looks are so compatible with the carefully prepared New American food that she serves, much of which is based on fresh, local ingredients. During summer there is outdoor seating on the expansive lawn. In winter the three small dining rooms with wood-manteled fireplaces are especially cozy and inviting. Depending on the month, Adrienne's menu, which changes seasonally, may list Maine lobster risotto with asparagus and fresh basil, grilled line-caught Rhode Island tuna, or sautéed farm-raised venison in a Massachusetts sour cherry sauce. You'll want to save room, too, for such desserts as dark chocolate mousse, puff pastry layered with rhubarb, and tangy lemon tart with a gingersnap crust. Sunday brunch—from 11:30 a.m. to 3:30 p.m.—is especially festive here. Otherwise, Adrienne is open for dinner Tuesday through Saturday.

The Boulders, East Shore Rd. (Route 45), New Preston; (860) 868-0541; www.bouldersinn.com; $$. The Boulders is worth a visit for its wide-angle lake views alone. From its tiered outdoor terrace, shaded by sheltering maple trees, the restaurant overlooks pristine Lake Waramaug. The grand view is just part of the story. The Boulders, a country inn with twenty guest rooms, has a very good kitchen and a seasonal modern American menu. Its expertise is evident in entrees like veal osso bucco, thyme-crusted beef tenderloin, and crispy lacquered duck breast with acorn squash bread pudding. Food this good comes mighty close to eclipsing that splendid view! Dinner is served Wednesday through Sunday, with brunch added on Sunday.

Carole Peck's Good News Café, 694 Main St. South (Route 6), Woodbury; (203) 266-4663; www.good-news-cafe.com; $$. There's so much to like about this sunny, informal place, which seats 170, from its roomy booths and original art on the walls to its tasteful choice of taped classical music. But what I most enjoy is the way chef-proprietor Carole Peck, a pioneer in using local, organic, seasonal farm foods, combines disparate ingredients to come up with

Carole Peck's Puree of Chestnut Soup

This is luscious, yet easy to make and good for company or on a cold winter's night.

8 ounces butter
1 pound shallots, peeled and diced
1 tablespoon ground cinnamon
2 teaspoons ground allspice
  honey
1 cup brandy

1 #202 can chestnut paste or
  5 pounds fresh chestnuts,
  roasted, shelled, and peeled
3 quarts chicken stock
Salt to taste
3 cups heavy cream
2 tablespoons sherry vinegar
1 teaspoon fresh chives, chopped

1. Melt the butter in a 1½- or 2-gallon pot. Add the shallots and sweat over medium heat till transparent.
2. Add the cinnamon, allspice, and honey. Cook about 1 minute to bloom the spices. Add the brandy and flame to burn off alcohol.
3. Next add the paste or chestnuts. Stir and cook approximately 3 minutes.
4. Pour in the chicken stock and blend well. Bring to a boil, stirring occasionally, and season with salt to taste.
5. Cook 30 minutes on a low boil; stir. Whisk in all the heavy cream but ¼ cup and bring back to a boil. Reduce heat and cook 10 minutes more.
6. Add sherry vinegar and cook 10 minutes more. Puree with an immersion blender and you are ready to serve.
7. Garnish with a dollop of whipped cream (made from the ¼ cup heavy cream left over) and snippet of fresh chives.

Makes 1 gallon or 16 cups.

Carole Peck's Good News Café
694 Main St. South (Route 6), Woodbury
(203) 266-4663
www.good-news-cafe.com

so many imaginative winners. Lobster chunks and Swiss chard in "adult" baked macaroni with provolone cheese and truffle oil is one dish that comes to mind. Wild boar schnitzel, Toulouse-style cassoulet and Nectar Hill grass-fed beef shortribs—all winter seasonal offerings—are others. Then there are the desserts, such as mile-high coconut layer cake with mango and raspberry sauce and pumpkin cheesecake with dates, toasted coconut, and spiced pumpkin seeds. Carole's round loaves of country peasant are also for sale, and a display case with Bridgewater Chocolates is an added temptation. Closed Tuesday.

Doc's Trattoria, 9 Maple St., Kent; (860) 927-3810; www.docs trattoria.com; $$. Doc's is the kind of comfortable, cozy, and laid-back place I'd like to have down the street so I could eat there often. True, this exuberant pizzeria-Italian restaurant is now more accessible than it once was, having recently been moved by new owners Roberto and Paulette Pizzo from its longtime Lake Waramaug digs to a location near the center of Kent. In three dining rooms or on an inviting terrace, you can enjoy Doc's many Italian specialties, with the prizes being the well-flavored, crunchy, thin-crusted pizzas with about a dozen different toppings. Genovese, Quattro, fromaggi, casino, margherita, and caprini are just a few. Desserts are yummy too, notably the Kahlúa-accented tiramisu and fudge-like chocolate flourless torte. Open for lunch and dinner Tuesday through Saturday, but Sunday it's dinner all day, from 1:00 p.m. to 8:00 p.m. Closed Monday.

Catherine's Speculaas Belgian Cookies

Photographer Catherine Van der Maat Brooks, aka my daughter-in-law, brought this recipe from her native Belgium. She finds it adaptable here in the Nutmeg State because of that particular heady spice. And don't use a substitute for the butter. It makes a huge difference.

2¼ cups flour
1 cup dark brown sugar
½ cup white sugar
2 teaspoons baking powder
1 teaspoon cinnamon
1 teaspoon freshly grated nutmeg

1 cup (8 ounces) salted butter, melted
1 large egg, beaten
4 ounces blanched almond slivers (optional)

1. Combine all dry ingredients in a large bowl and stir well. Pour melted butter over and mix thoroughly with wooden spoon, or knead by hand. Add egg and stir until fully incorporated. The dough should be rather stiff. Refrigerate for at least 1 hour.
2. Preheat oven to 325°F.
3. Roll half of the cold dough into a long "sausage" 2 inches in diameter. With a sharp knife, cut ¼-inch-thick slices and arrange them on a large ungreased cookie sheet, with ½ inch space between them.
4. Gently press a few almond slivers onto the surface of each slice. Bake for about 20 minutes until cookies have darkened in color. Keep a close eye on them because they burn quickly. When done, carefully remove them with a spatula and let cool on a rack.
5. Repeat steps 3 and 4 for the second half of the dough.

Tips

1. This dough can be used in flat cookie molds—large or small—as well.
2. Be creative: With a rolling pin spread the dough flat on the cookie sheet and cut out a simple shape, like a dolphin or a cat. If the contour is too complicated, the expanding dough will obliterate it. Use currants for the eyes. Makes a great personalized gift to a cookie-lover.

G.W. Tavern, 20 Bee Brook Rd., Washington Depot; (860) 868-6633; www.g.w.tavern.com; $$. This 1850 house on the Shepaug River has morphed into a restaurant for all seasons. In summer you can sit under the trees on the flagstone patio; in other seasons it's indoors before a roaring fire in the floor-to-ceiling flagstone fireplace. A portrait of G.W., aka George Washington, hangs above the fire, honoring the tavern's namesake for the time he once passed through Washington Depot. The American menu honors him even more with such old-time specialties as chicken potpie, macaroni and cheese, George Washington meat loaf, house-smoked ribs, crispy fried oysters, crocks of chili, and, oh yes, cherry pie. Open daily for lunch and dinner.

The Hopkins Inn, 22 Hopkins Rd., New Preston; (860) 868-7295; www.thehopkinsinn.com; $$. A touch of the Tyrol on a hillside overlooking Lake Waramaug—that is just the beginning of the Hopkins Inn story. Under the ownership of Beth and Franz Schober, the inn has been going strong since 1977 (with a winter break for the restaurant each year, January through March). Chef Franz brings his classical Austrian culinary training to modern versions of Wiener schnitzel, backhendl (free-range chicken and lingonberries), and kalbsrahmgulasch (veal in paprika–sour-cream sauce), among many hearty dishes. Beth runs the inn, with its eleven guest rooms and two apartments, in a comfortable, restored 1847 frame house. With the involvement of Beth's son, Toby Fossland (also a chef), a second generation now helps manage the inn's kitchen. Working with Franz and Toby is fellow Austrian Franz Reiter. There are two alpine-style

Mango Shrimp Salad

Toby Fossland of The Hopkins Inn volunteered this recipe for a delicious, different, and refreshing salad.

1 large mango, peeled, sliced thin in hemispheres

1 large ripe tomato, sliced slightly thicker in hemispheres

8 large shrimp, peeled, cooked, and butterflied

Raspberry vinaigrette

2 leaves fresh basil, cut chiffonade

12 fresh raspberries

1. Alternate mango and tomato hemispheres in a circular pattern. Stand butterflied shrimp up, tails together in center of plate.
2. Drizzle with raspberry vinaigrette (about 2 teaspoons), garnish with basil and fresh raspberries.

Serves 2 as an appetizer; adjust quantity for a light lunch entree or add mesclun greens, mâche, or Boston lettuce for more substance.

Raspberry Vinaigrette

Raspberry vinegar

Olive oil

Sugar

Salt and pepper

1. Mix vinegar and olive oil in a 1:3 or 1:4 ratio. Add sugar to taste to reduce acidity, then add salt and pepper to taste.
2. Dressing can be made in small quantities for immediate use or may be stored in larger quantities in the refrigerator indefinitely.

The Hopkins Inn
22 Hopkins Rd., New Preston
(860) 868-7295
www.thehopkinsinn.com

dining rooms, one with a fireplace, both with gemütlich Austrian touches. In summertime you may dine under a giant horse-chestnut tree on the flagstone terrace overlooking the lake. There are many extra-value touches, like the small loaf of warm, crusty bread served with appetizers—one reason The Hopkins Inn has such a loyal clientele. Desserts are traditional: peach Melba, Grand Marnier soufflé glacé, Toblerone sundae, and pear Hélène. The Schobers also bottle their popular Hopkins Inn House Salad Dressing and Hopkins Inn Caesar Salad Dressing, which they sell at the inn and at markets throughout western Connecticut. They also sell their Spinach Dressing, but just at the inn. In season, the restaurant is open for lunch and dinner each weekday (except closed all day Monday), but Sunday it's dinner only, from 12:30 p.m. to 8:00 p.m.

John's Café, 693 Main St., Woodbury; (203) 263-0188; www.johns cafe.com; $$. From a plain piperack kind of place when it opened in the mid-1990s, John's has evolved into an attractive bistro-like cafe with an open, lively manner. The modern American food (with a Mediterranean accent), always good, is better than ever under the stewardship of chef-owner Bill Okesson. There are standout dishes, like house-smoked salmon, sautéed white Gulf shrimp, house-made potato gnocchi with smoked chicken, sautéed pork Milanese, and pan-roasted duck breast. Desserts are memorable too, like the maple cheesecake with toasted pecan crust, blueberry bread pudding, profiteroles, and Key lime pie. I like the fact that the menu changes with the seasons and that there is a "wine special of the week," pegged to menu choices. Open daily for lunch and dinner, except on Sunday when it's dinner only.

The Mayflower Inn, Route 47, Washington Depot; (860) 868-9466; ww.mayflowerinn.com; $$$. Despite the Early American name, this is a highly sophisticated inn, rebuilt by Adriana and Robert Mnuchin in 1992, on the site of a former private school. It is furnished in English-country-house style, with fireplaces, a library, and comfortable lounges. The Mnuchins have since moved on, but the inn is as agreeable as ever. Although the chefs seems to move on as fast and often as a revolving door, the kitchen consistently turns out first-rate American and continental specialties regardless. On a menu that changes seasonally, there are certain "givens": house-made pastas, breads and pastries, organic herbs from the inn's gardens, house-smoked salmon, and game sausage. The extensive wine cellar has won a Wine Spectator's Award of Excellence. Dining in any of the three dining rooms is a special experience—with tables set with Limoges china, fine crystal, and silver. In warm weather you may eat on the open deck overlooking the well-kept grounds and gardens. The Mayflower is a member of the prestigious Relais & Châteaux—no surprise. Open for lunch and dinner daily.

Oliva, 18 East Shore Rd. and Route 45, New Preston; (860) 868-1787; $$. Oliva began as a minuscule cafe on the ground floor of an eccentric 1860 frame house in the town center. Success has

Baked Layered Moroccan Eggplant and Beef Ragu

According to Riad Aamar, chef-proprietor of Oliva in New Preston, this aromatic dish of his is a favorite of Oliva "regulars." And no wonder!

3 large eggplant, peeled and sliced into ½-inch pieces

½ cup extra-virgin olive oil, plus oil for brushing on eggplant

Salt and pepper

1 cup chopped onions

1 cup chopped celery

1 cup chopped carrot

1 teaspoon whole cloves

2 pounds lean ground beef (may substitute ground lamb or diced chicken breast)

3 cups tomato sauce

Dash of crushed red pepper

½ cup chopped parsley

½ cup chopped fresh mint

2 tablespoons chopped fresh cilantro

½ teaspoon ground ginger

1 teaspoon ground cumin

¼ teaspoon ground cinnamon

¼ teaspoon ground nutmeg

1 tablespoon mustard seeds

½ cup shredded mozzarella, or other cheese

¼ cup toasted pine nuts

3–6 basil leaves for garnish

caused this delightful place to expand from a mere thirty-two seats to seventy-five, and Oliva now occupies the upper floors as well and in clement weather spreads out onto the open-sided terrace. In whatever space he is allotted, chef-owner Riad Aamar accomplishes miracles. He formerly cooked at Doc's and still serves superb pizzas with a variety of toppings, as well as excellent Mediterranean and Italian dishes. That's part of the Oliva story. The Oscars, in my view,

1. Arrange sliced eggplant on a baking sheet and brush with olive oil. Roast until brown on both sides. Season with salt and pepper.
2. In sauté pan, heat olive oil and sauté onions, celery, and carrot until brown. Add cloves, cook for 1 minute, then discard cloves. Add meat and brown for at least 5 minutes. Add tomato sauce, salt and pepper to taste, and a dash of crushed red pepper. Add parsley, mint, cilantro, and the rest of the spices and cook over low heat for at least half an hour.
3. Preheat oven to 400°F.
4. In a baking dish, spread a thin layer of sauce on bottom and arrange layers of the roasted eggplant, overlapping each slice.
5. Pour half of remaining sauce over the eggplant layer, and then cover with half of cheese. Top with another layer of sliced eggplant, the remaining sauce and cheese, and bake in oven until brown.
6. Cool for at least 20 minutes; serve warm garnished with mint, basil, and pine nuts.
7. Serve with mashed vegetables, potatoes, soft polenta, couscous, or rice.

Serves 4–6.

Oliva

18 East Shore Rd. and Route 45, New Preston
(860) 868-1787

go to Riad's North African specialties, like Moroccan eggplant, a tantalizing starter with mint, mixed Moroccan spices, pecans, and lemon; baked Moroccan lamb kefta; and grilled stuffed calamari with mixed nuts, prunes, spices, and lemon. Just thinking of Chef Aamar's spice-scented entrees makes me hungry for his grilled Moroccan chicken with caramelized pear, prunes, mushrooms and almonds, and his lemon-stuffed borsellini with pecans, garlic, basil, and fresh tomato cream sauce. Seductive aromas and combinations give this restaurant real distinction. For the adventurous palate, Oliva is definitely worth a detour. Closed Monday and Tuesday; otherwise it's mainly dinner only, with lunch served seasonally. Best to call ahead.

Pastorale Bistro & Bar, 223 Main St., Lakeville; (860) 435-1011; www.pastoralebistro.com; $$. At my first dinner at this cheerful bistro, which is ensconced in a clapboard eighteenth-century house (where Noah Webster supposedly once spent a summer), I thought there was a twang of familiarity about the fine food. It turned out to be the work of Burgundy-born Frederic Faveau, who years ago put the Birches Inn on Lake Waramaug on the culinary map. Frederic and his wife, Karen Hamilton, who manages Pastorale, have made this new undertaking a charming oasis in a somewhat arid dining-out landscape. The bistro, on both floors, looks like a modern version of an old-fashioned tavern. I like the snugness of the Red Room downstairs with its oversize fireplace, but upstairs has its charms, too. The food is anything but old, with a short French/New American menu and dishes like escargot gratinee, French onion soup, chicken paillard, cassoulet, bouillabaisse, seared jumbo scallops, and boeuf bourguignonne. Good bread and superb desserts, like chocolate crème brûlée or almond-pear cake, are a few of the touches that make

Pastorale such a delightful place. Dinner only—plus a very special Sunday brunch. So eat, sip, and be merry—easy to do in such amiable surroundings.

West Street Grill, West Street, Litchfield; (860) 567-3885; www .weststreetgrill.net; $$$. Some of the area's finest cooking can be found in the stylish L-shaped dining room here that is hung with mirrors and vibrant paintings by local artists. Irish-born James O'Shea was an innovator in combining fresh ingredients in creative ways, and many of Connecticut's freshest farm-grown products— sweet corn, heirloom tomatoes, and basil—as well as eggs from free-range chickens and artisanal cheeses make their way to his tables. Several of James's chefs have graduated to restaurants of their own, but he trains each replacement well, as consistency seems to be an O'Shea passion (which may explain his success). There are many pleasing details here; note the sprightly Quimper faïence service plates and fleur de sel on each table. Part of the appeal—aside from the consistently good food—is the warm welcome provided by James and his partner, Charles Kafferman. Also fun is checking out fellow diners, often celebs like Philip Roth and Henry Kissinger, many with weekend homes nearby. Typically, such "names" can be found at table 21 and the other tables in the row down the center of the restaurant (considered prime seating to those for whom such distinctions matter). A new addition in winter is "Bistro Night" every Thursday and Sunday, when a special menu and lower prices almost have locals dancing in the aisles. Open daily for lunch and dinner.

Confit of Piquillo Peppers in Their Own Juices

This deceptively simple recipe is a favorite of James O'Shea, proprietor of West Street Grill in Litchfield, who was happy to share it.

- **1½ pounds roasted Piquillo peppers**
- **1 teaspoon sugar in the raw**
- **4 tablespoons spring water**
- **½ teaspoon Sriracha chili sauce (Thai garlic chili sauce)**
- **½ teaspoon piment doux (mostly used for a mild flavor and dark red color)**
- **4 cloves garlic, bashed (green germ removed)**
- **3 sprigs of fresh thyme (not dry)**
- **Very little fleur de sel (French sea salt)**
- **1 cup extra-virgin olive oil (Spanish being preferable)**

1. Preheat oven to 250°F.
2. Place 3 ounces (about 2 small peppers) of the Piquillo peppers in a blender with the sugar, water, chili sauce, and piment doux, and puree until well blended and totally smooth.
3. Using a deep pan or casserole, ceramic or stainless steel only, arrange half of the remaining peppers in a single layer (do not overlap). Spoon half the puree on top and smooth out. Scatter the garlic cloves and thyme on top. Sprinkle with a little fleur de sel. Make another layer with the remaining peppers. Salt again, spoon the remaining puree over the top, and smooth out. Totally cover with the extra-virgin olive oil.
4. Bake for 1½ hours until completely tender. Allow confit to cool completely. Then place in a covered container until time to serve. The shelf life is 5–7 days, refrigerated. As James says, "Hands off!"

West Street Grill

West Street, Litchfield
(860) 567-3885
www.weststreetgrill.net

The White Hart Inn, Salisbury; (860) 435-0030; www.white hartinn.com; $$. This venerable old 1806 house, later a rambling inn, has had its ups and downs gastronomically. Even in a down period, though, the setting is so cheerful in the Garden Room and so convivial in the Tap Room (both with fireplaces) that it is always a pleasant experience dining in either room. The menu is American, with a hint of the globe, and some of the dishes that might be on tap are ratatouille tamales with three sauces, cedar-roasted salmon with maple bourbon glaze and black rice, black sea bass with lobster/shrimp sauce, and Kurobuta pork two ways with guajillo chili sauce. The emphasis in the kitchen is on natural and fresh foods, and the beef, eggs, and produce mostly come from Twin Lakes Farm right in Salisbury. Open daily for all three meals.

Wood's Pit B*B*Q & Mexican Café, 123 Bantam Lake Rd. (Route 209), Bantam; (860) 567-9869; www.woodspitbbq.com; $.
Don't let the Tex-Mex specialties fool you: Like most authentic barbecue joints, Wood's looks as plain as toast, but it serves some of the best barbecue in Connecticut. Top choices are ribs, ribs, and more ribs (I am not, uh, ribbing you). Most popular are the platters of pork ribs—lean,  meaty, "dry rubbed," and full of the rich, deep-down flavor derived from slow pit cooking and green (not dry) hickory, oak, and apple woods. All platters come with jalapeño corn bread and two sides, the best being ranch-baked beans. The Rib Tickler is another winner:

lean St. Louis–style pork ribs, richly smoked. Other meat triumphs are the melt-in-your-mouth tender sliced beef brisket and pulled pork (pork shoulder smoked for eighteen hours, then shredded and seasoned with spices and sauces). Onion rings—thick pinwheels in a shroud of batter—are served in a novel way, on a wooden spindle. The house barbecue sauce—a blend of ketchup, vinegar, brown sugar, and a secret cache of spices—is lip-smackingly zesty, not overly sweet. Open for lunch and dinner, but closed Monday.

The Woodward House, 4 The Green, Bethlehem; (203) 266-6902; www.thewoodwardhouse.com; $$$. Little Bethlehem finally has the restaurant it deserves. Located in an old 1740 clapboard house on the Green, this is a delightful place for a first-rate dinner. Owners Adele and chef Jerry Reveron have turned four small dining rooms into visual gems, with their brightly painted walls hung with vibrant modern paintings. Good looks are just part of the story. The modern American food is elegant and meticulously served. While the menu changes seasonally, look for such treats as Cajun lobster bisque with lobster chunks and andouille sausage, barbecued dry-rub Colorado rack of lamb, pan-seared cod wrapped in bacon, and, for dessert, Sacher torte or apple-almond crisp tart. The well-priced two or three-course fixed-price Sunday brunch offers many delicious choices (try the stuffed French toast). The holiday season is as festive as a restaurant in a town named Bethlehem should be, with each dining room decorated in a different gala motif. Open only for dinner Wednesday through Sunday; Sunday brunch is from 11:00 a.m. to 2:30 p.m. Closed Monday and Tuesday.

Chaiwalla's Strawberry-Rhubarb Cobbler

Mary O'Reilly, whose Chaiwalla tearoom is known locally for its scrumptious desserts, says this recipe is one of Chaiwalla's most popular and also the easiest to make. Other fresh fruits can be used instead of strawberries and rhubarb.

Enough fresh strawberries and chopped rhubarb to fill a 9-inch pie tin

1 tablespoon plus 1 cup sugar
1 stick butter
1 cup flour

1. Preheat oven to 350°F.
2. Mix together berries, rhubarb, and 1 tablespoon sugar and pile evenly into a pie tin.
3. Cream butter, then combine flour and remaining sugar and add mixture to the butter. Mix well.
4. Pile butter-flour-sugar mixture evenly over the fruit.
5. Bake 45 minutes or until crunchy on top.

Serves 6.

Chaiwalla
1 Main St., Salisbury
(860) 435-9758
chaiwalla@snet.net

Adrienne's New England Clam Chowder

One of Adrienne Sussman's specialties in her restaurant, Adrienne, in New Milford, this is a favorite of mine as well.

3–4 cups canned clam juice
4–5 tablespoons vegetable oil
3 strips bacon, diced
1 small onion, diced
2 stalks of celery, diced
1 large Idaho potato, peeled and cubed

½ teaspoon dry whole-leaf thyme
¾–1 cup flour
2–3 cups canned clams, strained, reserving liquid
½ cup heavy cream (optional)
Pepper to taste

1. In a small saucepan place the canned clam juice and juice from the clams and heat to a boil over medium-high heat, then set aside.
2. In a large saucepan over medium heat, place the oil and bacon. Cook until bacon browns, then add the vegetables, potatoes, and the dry thyme. Stirring often, cook until vegetables become tender, then add the flour and mix well.
3. Now add the hot clam juice to the bacon mixture and mix very well to avoid any lumps. Heat over medium heat for about 10–15 minutes.
4. Add the cream (if used) and adjust the seasonings. Then steam or heat the clams briefly in the finished soup until well heated, stirring steadily. Serve piping hot.

Serves 14–16.

Adrienne
218 Kent Rd. (Route 7), New Milford
(860) 354-6001
www.adriennerestaurant.com

Adrienne's Lobster and Filet Mignon Wrapped in Phyllo

When I asked Adrienne Sussman of Adrienne in New Milford for a recipe to include in this book, she generously obliged with not one but two, both so compelling I couldn't choose between them—so have included both.

1 package phyllo dough, thawed
1 pound butter, melted
16 ounces lobster meat, preferably knuckle and claw

8 4-ounce filet mignon, seared (recipe follows)
2 blocks Boursin cheese, cut in quarters

1. Preheat oven to 375°F.
2. Lay out one sheet of phyllo and brush with melted butter; repeat till you have three sheets. Place one filet mignon, 2 ounces lobster meat, and one quarter of cheese in the center and fold over sides to create a package.
3. Place package on cookie tray lined with parchment paper. Repeat till you have all eight done.
4. Bake until the dough browns, about 15–20 minutes, and serve with steamed asparagus.

Seared Filets

8 4-ounce filet mignon
Salt and pepper to taste

2 tablespoons olive oil
2 tablespoons salted butter

1. Season the meat with the salt and pepper on all sides.
2. In a large sauté pan, add the oil and butter and place over medium-high heat. When the butter browns, add the filets (do not crowd the pan, because the meat won't brown) and cook till a deep brown on all sides. This should be done on as high a heat as possible so you brown the outside of the meat quickly and you don't cook them too much.
3. When the filets are seared, place on a tray and refrigerate until cooled off.

Serves 8.

Cambridge Brew House Pub, 84 Main St., Torrington; (860) 201-5666; www.cbhbrew.com; $. This is the second of two microbrewpubs in Connecticut created by partners Steve Boucino and Sacott Scanlon. In both pubs the theme is English. Ah yes, Cambridge, I get it. The bar is indeed publike, with dartboards, dominos, checkers, and of course beers and ales. Check the Web for live music schedule. The beer and ales are brewed on the premises. The beer-ale menu may change, but there are usually five or more on tap at any time. Favorites of the regulars run to Newgate Brown (light-bodied ale), an IPA (India pale ale), Old Mill Pond ESB (extra special bitter), and Copper Hill or some other Kolsch (German-style beer). Like many an English pub, Cambridge House offers a bit of substance for the body as well as the spirit, with burgers, pizzas, sandwiches, and flank steaks. The original Cambridge Brew House Pub is at 357 Salmon Brook St., Granby; (860) 653-2739; same Web site. Open daily.

Wine Trail

Connecticut Wine Trail, www.ctwine.com, provides information on state wineries and gives the latest details about places, times, tastings, and so on. The three wineries in this section are Haight-Brown Vineyard, Hopkins Vineyard, and Jerram Winery.

Haight-Brown Vineyard, 29 Chestnut Hill Rd., Litchfield; (800) 577-9463; www.haightvineyards.com. You'll know you have arrived at this oldest state winery (1978) when you see the huge wooden tun at the entrance. At the sprawling building in the center are the works, where the grapes are converted and aged. In the spacious upstairs tasting room/showroom of the main building, you may sample the end products—fourteen different wines. Self-guided tours are simple, following the Vineyard Walk. Haight-Brown hosts several annual events, beginning with the Barrel New Vintage Tasting the first two weekends of April. The tasting room is open Monday through Saturday from 10:30 a.m. to 5:00 p.m. and Sunday from noon to 5:00 p.m. in season, but only on weekends from January through March.

Hopkins Vineyard, 25 Hopkins Rd., New Preston; (860) 868-7954; www.hopkinsvineyard.com. High above Lake Waramaug and across the road from the Hopkins Inn (no connection) is the farmland settled by Elijah Hopkins after the Revolutionary War. Over the years his descendants have grown tobacco and grain crops and have raised sheep, race horses, and dairy cattle, with Bill and Judith Hopkins settling on grapes—and wines—in 1979. A huge nineteenth-century barn has been converted into a winery, with a tasting bar and showroom in the old hayloft, and Bill and Judith's daughter, Hilary, now installed as winery president. Among their thirteen wine types are chardonnay, cabernet franc, vidal blanc, and several semisweet and sweet wines (including the popular ice wine); some have won awards in national and international competitions. Enjoy a tasting and self-conducted tour. Hopkins is open for tastings and tours most of the year: daily from May 1 through December, Monday through Friday 10:00 a.m. to 5:00 p.m., Saturday until 7:00 p.m., Sunday 11:00 a.m. to 7:00 p.m.; from January 1 to daylight saving time in March, Saturday and Sunday only, same hours; from daylight saving time until May 1 Wednesday through Sunday, same hours.

Jerram Winery, 535 Town Hill Rd., Route 219, New Hartford; (860) 379-8749; www.jerramwinery.com. Jerram occupies a four-acre spread in the aptly named Town Hill district of a small town that was settled in the early 1700s. To develop the winery, owner James Jerram drew on his agriculture studies at Rutgers University, operations management at Rensselaer Polytechnic, and years in the food and beverage industries. He began his winery in 1999 with grape varieties that included chardonnay, seyval blanc, Aurora, and cabernet franc. He now offers ten wines, which include Gentle Shepherd, S'il Vous Plaît, and White Frost. Winery hours for tastings are from 11:00 a.m. to 5:00 p.m. Thursday through Sunday May through December. In January and April hours are 11:00 a.m. to 4:00 p.m. Saturday and Sunday; February and March by appointment only. The tasting room doubles as an art gallery and often as a backdrop for catered events like weddings and special parties.

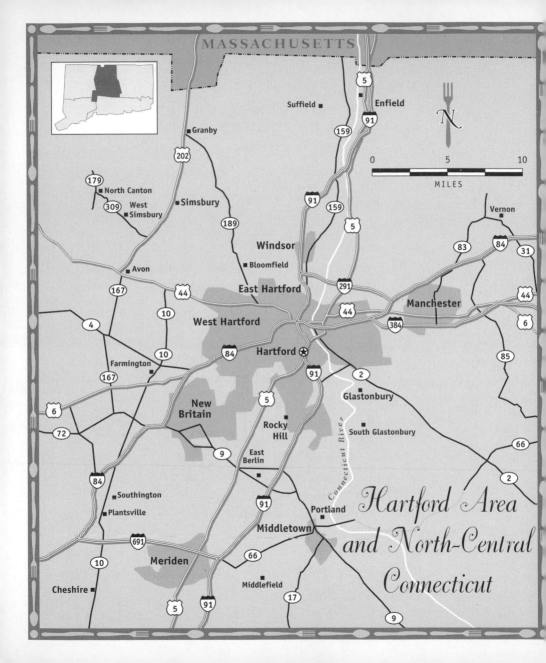

Hartford Area and North-Central Connecticut

Hartford, as the state capital, is a centripetal force that has brought to its center all kinds of artistic, cultural, political, ethnic, and culinary forces. These include a steady stream of new restaurants, ethnic grocery stores and bakeries, specialty food shops, and an influx of people from diverse ethnic backgrounds (including Vietnamese and Afghans) to enjoy them. Mark Twain, who lived in the city for twenty years, called Hartford "the best built and handsomest town I have ever seen" and would have marveled at the variety and spiciness of the city at present.

During the last century, Hartford's major culinary happenings, fiestas, and shopping took place along Franklin Avenue, the Italian neighborhood salt-and-peppered with restaurants, bakeries, Italian delis, food importers, and mom-and pop food shops, some of which are still in their original locales. One of our favorite Hartford food events is the seasonal downtown farmers' market held within the gates of the splendid Old State House, the oldest state house in the country, designed by Charles Bulfinch in the Georgian style in 1796.

Hartford spills over into leafy, suburban West Hartford, which has become an enticement for foodies, with new restaurants, cafes, coffeehouses, and all kinds of specialty food shops. Three of the state's largest international ethnic grocery markets are within its town limits.

Radiating out from Hartford in all directions are some of the state's oldest towns, like Windsor and Suffield to the north and preserved-in-amber Old Wethersfield to the south, with all its stately eighteenth-century houses locked in time. On the east side of the Connecticut River is Glastonbury, which is both sophisticated and rural at the same time, and whose well-groomed vintage houses are home to many Hartford movers and shakers. The town is tucked among orchards and farms that have been around for centuries and remain among the most productive in the state. Northeast is Manchester, with one of the best Italian restaurants in a state that has an abundance of excellent ones.

What makes this entire terrain around Hartford so appealing is that it is still agricultural, dappled with historic little towns that are surrounded by wooded hillsides, cultivated fields, and valleys. The fertile banks of the Connecticut River, which squiggles south through the middle of the region from Massachusetts, have been productive farmland for generations, and the number of small family-run farms (up to 500 acres) in this area continues to lead the state. These family enterprises produce gargantuan salad bowls of fresh vegetables and fruits, most of which they sell at their own farm stands and at farmers' markets all around the area. Many farmers invite you to pick your own berries, apples, and other crops.

An especially beautiful town is Farmington, one of Hartford's upscale suburbs, with many handsome houses, the intriguing Hill-Stead house museum, smart restaurants and food shops, and a prime location along the tumultuous Farmington River. Northeast of Hartford in neatly manicured, sedately rural Simsbury, another self-sufficient, attractive suburb, you will find several good restaurants and food outlets. South of Hartford is New Britain, an enclave so full of Polish groceries, meat markets, and restaurants, with signs written in Polish, that you may think you have landed in Warsaw. Middletown now caters to its Wesleyan University clientele, with a notable diner, vegetarian restaurant, and assorted ethnic eateries—a big change from its decades as a mill town. The surrounding countryside blossoms in spring with flowering orchards. One of the biggest, at Middlefield, has the largest indoor farm market in the state. You will read about it and others below.

Made or Grown Here

Bear Pond Farm, Old Maid's Ln., South Glastonbury; (860) 657-3830; www.bearpondfarm.com. When Craig Colvin moved from Washington Depot to South Glastonbury, he took along his most

Cilantro Couscous Salad

Kathleen Jonah Lenane, a partner at Bear Pond Farm, offered this simple-to-make recipe that really gives a welcome zap to couscous. This dish also makes a good accompaniment to a grilled meat or chicken entree and may be served warm, chilled, or at room temperature.

1 cup couscous
1½ cups fresh zucchini squash, cut into ½-inch cubes
1½ cups fresh or frozen corn kernels

3–4 tablespoons Bear Pond Farm Rich Cilantro pesto (or any pesto of your choice)
2 chopped scallions
Salt and pepper to taste

1. Cook couscous, following package directions.
2. Meanwhile, steam the zucchini and corn kernels until cooked through; drain and set aside. When couscous is cooked through, remove to a serving dish and fluff with a fork.
3. Thoroughly mix the pesto into the warm couscous. Add the vegetables and chopped scallions. Salt and pepper to taste.

Serves 2.

Bear Pond Farm
Old Maid's Ln., South Glastonbury
(860) 657-3830
www.bearpondfarm.com

valuable possessions: his recipes for pestos and tomato sauce. Thus Bear Pond Farm has started up again, and Craig's six pestos (Premium Basil, Vibrant Cilantro, Fresh Lemony, Tomato Basil, Vegan Spicy Thai, and Jalapeño Artichoke), Three-Herb Marinara sauce, three all-natural, low-fat yogurt dips, and three queso dips are being

distributed all over the state. Bear Pond is a certified organic greenhouse grower, and its nut-free products are sold at several farmers' markets, Whole Foods, and independent stores throughout Connecticut.

Giff's Original, Box 1212, Cheshire; (203) 699-8605; www.giffsoriginal.com. For the tang of New England in your cooking, there's nothing quite like the Cranberry Pepper Relish and Cranberry Ginger Chutney made by Marie "Giff" Hirschfeld. Marie began concocting relishes and salsas in her kitchen and now sells seven all-natural, no-fat, no-preservatives, low-salt products at specialty food stores all over the state, including Lyman Orchards in Middlefield and all the Highland Park Markets. In the line as well are Mango Spice Salsa, which won an award and was voted No. 1 (twice) in Connecticut in the Specialty Foods Association; and the brand-new Pomegranate Onion Relish and Tomato Lemon Chutney. Marie also sells through her Web site, shipping via parcel post or UPS.

Nip 'N Tang, P.O. Box 370416, West Hartford; (860) 231-9420; www .nipntang.com. In the late 1980s Joan Snyder combined horseradish with fruits, and the result eventually became Nip 'N Tang, sweet-hot combos that enhance meats, poultry, and many other dishes. Nip 'N Tang, subtitled "fruited horseradish delight," products are packaged in squat jars in five different compelling flavors: Apricot, Blueberry, Pineapple, Cranberry, and Pomegranate Plum. They can be found in markets and specialty shops around Connecticut and across the United States, as well as via the Web site.

Sassy Sauces, 3 Foxcroft Lane, Canton; (860) 480-9913; simmons sassy@aol.com. Former executive chef at Avon Old Farms Inn, Charles Simmons markets three of his own sharp sauces, all of which make great marinades or glazes for meat or fish: Mouthful-O-Mango Barbecue Sauce, Sweet-N-Tangy Balsamic Vinaigrette, and Spicy Citrus Sauce. Charles also imports and sells the Greek Ilianna Extra-Virgin Olive Oil. They are all available by mail order.

Thompson Brands, 80 South Vine St., Meriden; (203) 235-2541; www.thompsonbrands.com. Possibly the oldest candy maker in Connecticut, dating back to the nineteenth century, the Thompson Candy Company recently changed its name to Thompson Brands, as it now encompasses three distinct divisions: Thompson Candy, Thompson Organics, and Adora Calcium. The first makes all the molded milk and dark chocolate seasonal treats—Santas, Easter bunnies, snowmen, eggs, ducks, and other novelties—long associated with the Thompson name. Thompson Organics  is a line of chocolates, bars, and chunk chocolate for baking, made from organic cocoa beans from Central America. Adora Calcium, new and trendy, is a way to have your chocolate and eat it, too: healthful chocolate rich in calcium and vitamin D. You can buy all Thompson chocolates in the small shop attached to the factory or in stores throughout Connecticut and elsewhere. Adora Calcium chocolates are available at Shaw's, Stop & Shop, Target, and other chains.

Tulmeadow Farm Ice Cream Stand, 255 Farms Village Rd. (Route 309), West Simsbury; (860) 658-1430; tulmeadowfarm@aol .com. Two outside windows make it convenient for the crowds who line up for the rich, creamy ice cream produced at this old farm. You can go inside if you like, as the ice-cream stand is attached to Tulmeadow's farm store (see page 177 under Farm Stands). From April to mid-October, the ice-cream store is open daily from noon to 9:00 p.m., but it's best to check ahead. The ice-cream repertory consists of twenty-something flavors, available in cones, pints, and quarts, though not all flavors are available all the time. Perennial favorite is red-raspberry chocolate chip. More exotic flavors include pumpkin, Indian pudding, vanilla peanut butter cup, and ginger. There are benches and wagons outside where you can sit and savor your ice cream.

Specialty Stores & Markets

A Dong Supermarket, 160 Shield St., West Hartford; (860) 953-8903. In a space as big as an airport hangar—32,000 square feet of it—Phuong and Khiem Tran, a Vietnamese couple, have fulfilled an Asian immigrant's wildest food dream: a market with every conceivable type of comfort food from home, and then some. At first glance, A Dong looks like any big American supermarket, but then peer at the products: fresh, canned, baked, dried, pickled, and frozen foods from Vietnam, Laos, Cambodia, Thailand, China, the Philippines,

Korea, and Japan, all impeccably organized and displayed. Fresh-roasted, lacquer-colored, crispy whole ducks and suckling pigs hang from hooks. A bakery section has Banh sandwiches and bean cakes; there are fresh-produce and frozen-foods sections and even a vast department full of oriental china, pots, cooking utensils, and imported gift items. If you are an Asian-food aficionado, A Dong's is a one-stop, must-stop shopping center for sure. Open daily.

Connecticut Creative Store, 25 Stonington St., Hartford; (860) 297-0112; www.hartfordbotanicalgarden.org/ccs. In spacious quarters, as part of the Hartford Botanical Gardens in Colt Park,

this Department of Agriculture–connected store is a showcase for made-in-Connecticut merchandise—handcrafts, garden products, clothing, and food. One entire room displays food items: jams, condiments, sauces, spices, oils, mixes, and other edibles. It's a nifty way to see in one place the wide range of food enterprises (more than thirty, sometimes close to fifty) within our state—and to buy some, too. The store is open Wednesday through Saturday 10:00 a.m. to 4:00 p.m.

Crown Super Market, 2471 Albany Ave., West Hartford; (860) 236-1965. Picture a New York–style Jewish delicatessen enlarged to supermarket size and you'll have an idea of what Crown Super Market is like, stocked with every imaginable type of kosher food, including a wide assortment of baked goods, poultry, and meats.

There are many nonkosher foods as well, mainly natural and organic. Closed Saturday.

Daybreak Coffee Roasters, 2377 Main St., Glastonbury; (800) 882-5282; www.daybreakcoffee.com. Tom Clarke's shop is more than just a place to have a terrific cuppa. He sells forty different types of fresh, high-quality green coffee beans from around the world (regular, decaf, Organic Fair Trade, flavored), which he roasts before your eyes. While sipping a latte, espresso, cappuccino, or one of Tom's special roasts, either in the shop or outdoors in warm weather, you may chew on a fresh Daybreak-baked scone, muffin, turnover, or cookie. This is a good source for gifts, too, with about thirty gift or custom-packed baskets from which to choose and all kinds of food items, many made by other Connecticut gourmet food producers. Tom also sells his coffees wholesale. You will find them at Java Palooza! in Middletown, Cavey's in Manchester, Common Ground in Litchfield, and Village Café in Canton, among many other outlets. Open daily.

DiBacco's Market, 553 Franklin Ave., Hartford; (860) 296-7365; www.dibaccofoodimports.com. Like so many of the Italian stores along Franklin Avenue, DiBacco's, after thirty-nine years in business, has extremely loyal customers, who come for the wide array of imported Italian foods—an incredible variety of dried pastas, olive oils, cheeses, coffees, and packaged, canned, and dried goods. Then there are Mario and Angela DiBacco's fresh-baked Italian breads and pizzas, store-made Italian sausages (which are also sold to other retailers), soups, and grinders made daily for lunch take-outs or to eat at one of the four tables on the premises. Open daily.

Everybody's Market, 1021 South Main St., Cheshire; (203) 272-2266; www.everybodysmarket.com. While this efficient market's slogan, "Where You're Somebody," is somewhat silly (aren't we all somebody everywhere?), nothing else is dubious about this superlarge (about 35,000 square feet) supermarket, whose variety of good foods, organic and otherwise, is awesome. The origins go back to the 1930s, but the market is now twenty-first-century up-to-date, with every edible an eager foodie might desire. According to manager Chris McKenna, the market's forte is its diverse perishables: fresh produce, meats, pastries, deli items—even gourmet box lunches. There's a great variety of cheeses, a fresh-flower-and-plant area, even a coffee bar with three tables where you can sip and nibble pastries or sandwiches while you shop. The European-style bakery offers cookies, tarts, tortes, cakes, pies, and artisanal breads. The market also does catering. Open daily.

Gulf Shrimp Seafood Company, 240 Atwater St., Plantsville; (860) 628-8399; www.gulfshrimp.info. Forget the idea of Gulf shrimp. Chad Simoneaux, proprietor, was honoring his home state of Louisiana when he set up his wholesale seafood business in 1991, but the reams of seafood he buys fresh five days a week in Boston have nothing to do with the Gulf. In his enormous 18,000-square-foot plant, Chad has fish and shellfish so fresh that the many restaurants and retailers he sells to (like Metro Bis in Simsbury and

The Hopkins Inn in New Preston) swear by his wares. No wonder, as wholesale delivery six days a week is made within twelve hours of the catch. In late April and May, he gets Connecticut River shad and shad roe, and from mid-May to September, he stocks fresh soft-shell crabs. Retail orders, via FedEx, get overnight delivery. Chad also has retail space in his plant, where he sells his fresh seafood directly to the public, Monday through Saturday, from 9:00 a.m. to 5:00 p.m. Among the more popular critters are blue prawns, farmed Hawaiian Kampachi, and fully prepared fresh-frozen items, including stuffed shrimp, clams casino, seafood chowders, soups, fried whole-belly clams, and seafood egg rolls.

Modern Pastry Shop, 422 Franklin Ave., Hartford; (860) 296-7628; www.modernpastryshop.com. This old-fashioned, otherworldy Italian pastry shop specializes in over thirty different Italian and French pastries, cakes, and cookies. Among those are some devilishly rich cakes, like Italian rum cake, lemon mousse, creampuff cake, and tiramisu. As you linger over your choices by the well-worn counter, you might make like a regular and order a cuppa coffee. Closed Monday; other days the shop opens at 6:00 a.m.

Mozzicato De Pasquale Bakery & Pastry Shop, 329 Franklin Ave., Hartford; (860) 296-0426; www.mozzicatobakery.com. De

Pasquale's bread shop, a Hartford fixture since 1908, was bought by Gino Mozzicato in 1975, when he combined it with his pastry shop. The spacious, immaculate quarters became the best of two worlds: marvelous breads (Italian, Tuscan, rye), rolls and heaven-sent cakes (rum cake, tiramisu, torta al cappuccino, lemon and raspberry mousse, hazelnut, Napoleon, almond tortes, Italian cherry nut, Easter, Christmas, special-occasion), and more than twenty types of delectable cookies (pignoli, amaretti, canali, rococo, taralli, crescents). Elaborate wedding cakes are a bakery staple, too, as are pastries like cannoli, profiteroles, cheesecakes, and marzipan. Mozzicato also makes thick-crusted pizzas daily, as well as Italian-style gelatos in twelve luscious flavors. In warm weather, lemon granita is added to the lineup, as tartly refreshing as any you'd find on the streets of Napoli. Next door, through a separate entrance, is **The Mozzicato Caffè,** a large room seating forty, where you can enjoy an espresso, cappuccino, or latte with a Mozzicato pastry or pizza and perhaps a cordial. Historic Franklin Avenue has undergone many changes in recent times, but Mozzicato De Pasquale continues to thrive, a favorite of Italians and new arrivals alike. Open daily, from 7:00 a.m. to 9:00 p.m.

Omar Coffee Company, 41 Commerce Court, Newington; (860) 667-8889 or (800) 394-OMAR; www.omarcoffeecompany.com. Since 1937 the Costas family has been importing eighty-plus kinds of green coffee beans from all over the world and slow-roasting them to sell retail and wholesale to outlets across New England and elsewhere. This spacious store, attached to the factory, is like a club lounge with comfy chairs and bar stools. It makes a great rest stop for a cup of one of the daily specials, along with biscotti for dipping. There are also coffee gift baskets and bulk coffee for sale. Omar funds a scholarship program at the University of Connecticut, so buying any of four Husky Blends aids the program. Open Monday through Friday from 7:30 a.m. to 4:00 p.m.

Rein's Delicatessen, 435 Hartford Turnpike (Route 30), Vernon; (860) 875-1344; www.reinsdeli.com; $$. Just off I-84, at exit 65, Rein's Deli, in an unexceptional low-slung building, seems rather unassuming to be a pilgrimage site. But for generations of expatriated New Yorkers and others who crave New York Jewish deli food, Rein's has been satisfying their culinary lusts since 1972. Nova, lox, borscht, matzoh balls, kreplach, chopped herring, pastrami, roast and corned beef, bagels, cheese blintzes, potato pancakes, name it, you'll find it at Rein's. You'll also find tasty soups, some forty

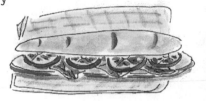

sandwiches, and house-made desserts like marble halvah and orange poppy seed pound cake. Open daily, except holidays, from 7:00 a.m. to midnight, Rein's is also a full-fledged restaurant (called "the way-off Broadway lounge"), serving breakfast, lunch, and dinner.

Say Cheese!, Simsburytown Shops, 928 Hopmeadow St. (Route 10), Simsbury; (860) 651-9000; www.saycheeseofsimsbury.com. Yes, emphatically, say cheese—more than one hundred varieties of

An International Bazaar
on Farmington Avenue

On two blocks of Farmington Avenue in West Hartford, near the Hartford line, a trio of ethnic food markets cater to an international clientele and are chock-full of imported foods that appeal to adventurous home cooks.

Cosmos International, 770 Farmington Ave., West Hartford; (860) 232-6600; www.cosmosinternational.com. A veritable supermarket of mostly Indian and Pakistani foodstuffs, Cosmos sells huge sacks of rice, dried fruits, nuts, spices, jars of hot sauces, pickles, chutneys, pappadum mixes, chappati flour, a variety of teas, curry pastes, butter ghees, cooking oils, and spicy mixes. There is a fresh produce section with Indian eggplant, okra, and fiery chiles, and even a deli case with Indian specialties prepared by a Cosmos chef—lamb vindaloo, chicken tika masala, masala dosas, pakoras—ready for take-out. There are foods from Egypt, Greece, Israel, and elsewhere in the Middle East as well. Open daily.

Delicacy Market, 774 Farmington Ave., West Hartford; (860) 236-7100; www.delicacymarket.com. Two doors down from Cosmos, Delicacy Market is crammed with Russian, Ukrainian, and other eastern European favorites. They include Estonian, German, Russian, and Polish sausages; cold cuts and twenty-nine salamis from all over; forty-six types of smoked fish; Lithuanian and Latvian breads; seventeen imported cheeses, including Swedish; grains, lentils, and beans; Ukrainian and Russian hard candies; Russian teas; dried fruits, nuts, and seeds; salted and pickled vegetables; store-made pierogies, blintzes, and raviolis; and yogurts and butters from Israel, Latvia, and Poland. There are also fresh fruits and vegetables, hot soups, and meals for take-out, like potato pancakes and stuffed cabbage. Open daily, Monday through Saturday from 9:00 a.m. to 7:00 p.m., Sunday from 10:00 a.m. to 6:00 p.m.

Tangiers International, 668 Farmington Ave., West Hartford; (860) 233-8168; www.tangierswh.com. Though this huge store, on the corner of Prospect, might more aptly be named Athens for all the Greek products it contains, there is something for every Middle Eastern–food fancier here, whether North African, Jewish, Turkish, Armenian, Syrian, Egyptian, even Bulgarian. Some foods are premises-made, like hummus, baba ghanoush, stuffed grape leaves, kibbe, tabbouleh, and spanakopita. Others are imported: jars of Bulgarian eggplant and spiced whole tomatoes, tubes of harissa (the spicy North African seasoning), Greek olives in brine, Lebanese berry syrups, all kinds of grains, dried lentils and beans, sumac and other herbs, Greek and Bulgarian cheeses, Turkish delights, even a well-stocked frozen-food section. There is a vast refrigerated case full of baklava and other honey-accented Middle Eastern pastries. A lunch counter in the rear is a gathering place for coffee and daily specials like a lamb gyro or falafel sandwich, to eat here or take home. Pause a minute to enjoy the Babel of languages. Open daily, Monday through Saturday from 10:00 a.m. to 8:00 p.m., on Sunday to 6:00 p.m.

Metro Bis's Beef, Corn, and Pepper Salad

As the harvest season begins to wind down, chef Chris Prosperi occasionally cooks at local farmers' markets. He sets up a small tabletop gas grill, then wanders through the market with a basket gathering the freshest produce he can find. Back at his table, he prepares dishes on the spot that highlight the bounty of the farms. Not long ago he combined kebab meat from a local cattle farmer with maple syrup he found at another stand. Paired with fresh Connecticut corn, peppers, and tomatoes, he created an improvised beef salad that was a hit with market shoppers, who begged him for the recipe. No need for you to beg: Here it is.

1 pound beef kebab meat
2 teaspoons kosher salt
2 teaspoons maple syrup
4 teaspoons curry powder
2 teaspoons oil
2 large red peppers
3 ears fresh corn, husked

2 large tomatoes, each cut into
    3 thick slices
2 tablespoons balsamic vinegar
1 tablespoon olive oil
2 tablespoons maple syrup
¼ cup chopped fresh basil

1. Preheat the grill.
2. Place the beef cubes in a medium mixing bowl and toss with 1 teaspoon kosher salt, 1 teaspoon maple syrup, 2 teaspoon curry powder, and 1 teaspoon oil, then mix well.

imported cheeses are for sale in this gourmet shop, as well as more than twenty varieties of coffee beans, imported crackers, biscuits, jams, vinegars, oils, sauces, syrups, mustards, teas, cookies, candies, and chocolates. Now owned by Rich Wagner, the shop also

3. Chop off the tops and bottoms of the peppers, removing the stems. Clear the seeds and pith from the pepper, cutting the body into 4 rectangular pieces.

4. Add the pepper pieces to another medium mixing bowl and toss with 1 teaspoon kosher salt, 1 teaspoon maple syrup, 2 teaspoons curry powder, and 1 teaspoon oil.

5. Place the beef cubes on a preheated grill and sear on each side until the meat is cooked to medium rare—about 3–5 minutes. Remove from the grill and let rest.

6. Place the peppers and husked corn on the grill and cook until slightly charred on each side. The corn may take 1 minute or more. Now grill the tomato slices for about 1 minute on each side.

7. Slice the beef cubes as thin as possible against the grain, then place in a clean mixing bowl. Dice the peppers and tomatoes into ½-inch cubes. Remove the corn from the cob with a sharp knife right into the mixing bowl.

8. Combine the sliced beef and vegetables with the balsamic vinegar, olive oil, maple syrup, and fresh basil, mixing well. Adjust the seasoning with salt.

9. Serve over freshly shredded lettuce or with good crusty bread.

Makes about 6 cups.

carries fancy gift baskets packed with goodies, as well as high-end cooking utensils, wineglasses, cheeseboards, Polish pottery, and other accessories. Open Monday through Friday from 10:00 a.m. to 6:00 p.m., Saturday until 5:00 p.m.; closed Sunday.

For up-to-the-minute information about dates and times, call the Connecticut Department of Agriculture at (860) 713-2503, visit the Web site at www.state.ct.us/doag/, or e-mail ctdeptag@po.state .ct.us.

Bethany Farmers' Market, airport property (Route 63), Bethany. First and Third Saturday of every month, from July through October.

Bloomfield Farmers' Market, Bloomfield Town Hall, 800 Bloomfield Ave., Bloomfield. Saturday from 9:00 a.m. to 1:00 p.m., early July through October.

Collinsville Farmers' Market, Town Hall parking lot, Main Street, Collinsville. Sunday from 10:00 a.m. to 1:00 p.m., late June to October.

East Hartford Farmers' Market, Raymond Memorial Library, 840 Main St., East Hartford. Friday from 9:00 a.m. to 1:00 p.m., early July through October.

East Windsor Farmers' Market, Revays Gardens, 840 Main St., East Windsor. Friday from 9:00 a.m. to 1:00 p.m., early July through October.

Ellington Farmers' Market, Arbor Park, Town Center, 35 Main St. (Route 286), Ellington. Saturday from 9:00 a.m. to 12:30 p.m., early May to end of October.

Enfield Farmers' Market, Town Green (Route 5), Town Hall, Enfield. Wednesday from 3:00 to 6:00 p.m., early July to October.

Farmington Hill-Stead Museum Farmers' Market, 35 Mountain Rd., Exit 39 off I-84, Farmington. Sunday from 11:00 a.m. to 2:00 p.m., mid-July to October.

Hartford Asylum Hill Farmers' Market, Asylum Hill Congregational Church, 814 Asylum Ave., Hartford. Wednesday from 11:00 a.m. to 2:00 p.m., early July through October.

Hartford–Billings Forge Farmers' Market, grassy courtyard on Billings Forge campus, north of Firebox restaurant, 519 Broad St., Hartford. Monday and Thursday from 11:00 a.m. to 2:00 p.m., late May through October.

Hartford Capitol Avenue Farmers' Market, First Presbyterian Church of Hartford, 156 Capitol Ave., next to Bushnell, Hartford. Monday from 10:00 a.m. to 1:00 p.m., early July through October.

Hartford Old State House Farmers' Market, Old State House, 800 Main St. entrance, Hartford. Monday, Wednesday, and Friday from 9:00 a.m. to 2:00 p.m., May through December.

Hartford Park Street Farmers' Market, Walgreen's parking lot (corner of Park and Washington Streets), Hartford. Monday from 9:30 a.m. to 1:00 p.m., first week of July through October.

Hartford Regional Market, exit 27 off I-91, 101 Reserve Rd., Hartford. Open daily year-round from 5:00 a.m. to 9:00 p.m.; the largest food-distribution terminal between New York and Boston.

Hartford West End Farmers' Market, United Methodist Church parking lot, 571 Farmington Ave., Hartford. Tuesday and Friday from 4:00 to 7:00 p.m., early July through September.

Marlborough Farmers' Market, 45 North Main St., Marlborough. Sunday from 11:00 a.m. to 3:00 p.m., mid-June to November.

Manchester Farmers' Market, town parking lot, corner of Main and Forest Streets, Manchester. Saturday from 8:00 a.m. to 12:30 p.m., early July through October.

Manchester C.C. Farmers' Market, MCC Band Shell parking lot, Great Path Rd., Manchester. Wednesday from 2:00 to 5:00 p.m., first week of June through October.

Meriden Farmers' Market, Butler St. parking lot (corner of West Main and Grove Streets), Meriden. Saturday from 8:00 a.m. to noon, mid-July through October.

Middlebury Farmers' Market, Middlebury Senior Center, 1172 Whittemore Rd., Middlebury. Tuesday from 10:30 a.m. to noon, from end of June through October.

Middletown Farmers' Market, South Green on Old Church St., Middletown. Tuesday and Thursday from 8:00 a.m. to 1:00 p.m., mid-July through October.

Middletown II Farmers' Market, parking lot of It's Only Natural Market, Middletown. Friday from 10:00 a.m. to 1:00 p.m., mid-July through October.

New Britain Farmers' Market, St. Ann's Church, 109 North St., New Britain. Thursday from 10:00 a.m. to 1:00 p.m., mid-July through October.

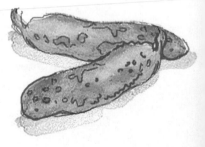

New Britain/Urban Oaks Farmers' Market, 225 Oak St., New Britain. Friday from 3:00 to 6:00 p.m. and Saturday from 10:00 a.m. to 1:00 p.m., August through October.

Rocky Hill Farmers' Market, Town Hall, Center St., Rocky Hill. Thursday from 4:00 to 6:00 p.m., July through October.

Simsbury Farmers' Market, Simsmore Square, 540 Hopmeadow St. (Routes 10 and 202), Simsbury. Thursday from 2:00 to 6:00 p.m., June to mid-October.

Southington-Plantsville Farmers' Market, 997-1003 South Main St., Plantsville. Friday from 3 to 6:00 p.m., early July through October.

Suffield Farmers' Market, Town Green, North Main and High Streets, Suffield. Saturday from 9:00 a.m. to noon, mid-June through mid-October.

West Hartford Farmers' Market, LaSalle Rd. public parking lot, across from post office, West Hartford. Tuesday and Saturday from 9:00 a.m. to 1:00 p.m., Thursday from 11:00 a.m. to 3:00 p.m., May through December.

West Hartford Whole Foods Farmers' Market, Whole Foods parking lot, across from Blueback Sq., 50 Raymond Rd., West Hartford. Monday from 3:00 to 6:00 p.m., early June to end of October.

Wethersfield Farmers' Market, Keeney Memorial Center, 200 Main St., Wethersfield. Thursday from 4:00 to 7:00 p..m., end of May through October.

Wilson/Windsor Farmers' Market, Connecticut Service for the Blind, 184 Windsor Ave., Windsor. Tuesday from 3:00 to 6:00 p.m., mid-July through October.

Windsor Farmers' Market, corner of Maple Ave. and Broad St., Windsor. Thursday from 4:00 to 7:00 p.m., mid-July through October.

Farm Stands

Arisco Farms, 1583 Marion Rd., Cheshire; (203) 271-0549. At Alex and Beverly Arisco's fifty-acre farm, you are welcome to pick your own tomatoes and peppers. Also for sale at their farm stand are sweet corn, eggplants, squash, and other veggies. The Ariscos have farmed here since the late 1950s. You will find them at their stand between 9:00 a.m. and 6:00 p.m. every day from mid-July to Thanksgiving, but it's best to call ahead to be sure of hours.

Arlow's Sugar Shack, 101 Bushy Hill Rd., Granby; (860) 653-3270. Arlow Case, here for more than forty years, calls his self-service farm stand the Sugar Shack, where he sells a wide range of seasonal vegetables, including cucumbers, peppers, pumpkins, summer and winter squash, zucchini, and tomatoes, produce from other farms, and his own homemade maple syrup (available year-round). Stand hours: July through September, Monday through Saturday from 9:00 a.m. to 5:00 p.m. The honor system applies.

Belltown Hill Orchards, Farm Market & Bakery, 483 Matson Hill Rd., South Glastonbury; (860) 633-2789; www.belltownhillorchards .com. Donald and Mike are the third generation of the Perelli family who have farmed in Glastonbury's rolling hills since 1910. They follow the CORE Values approach—ecologically balanced growing practices and Connecticut State Pest Management techniques for ecologically based agriculture. You are welcome to pick your own berries, pears, peaches, sweet and tart cherries, apples (twenty-four varieties), pumpkins, and tomatoes. There are also twelve varieties of red, green, and blue grapes (ready in mid-August). In the bakery: fruit pies, whoopee and cream pies, sugar-free pies, fruit squares and crisps, apple cider doughnuts, and caramel and fudge apples vie for attention with jams, jellies, and other canned products in Grandma's Pantry. Open from June through October, Monday through Friday 9:00 a.m. to 6:00 p.m., Saturday and Sunday 8:00 a.m. to 6:00 p.m. From November 1 to December 31, hours are Monday through Sunday, 9:00 a.m. to 5:00 p.m.; in January, weekends only, 10:00 a.m. to 4:00 p.m.

Botticello Farms, 209 Hillstown Rd., Manchester; (860) 649-2462; www.botticellofarms.net. With more than 50,000 square feet of greenhouse space, planting on this 350-acre farm begins in December. At the farm stand, veggies make the world go round, the likes of squash (zucchini, summer, acorn, butternut, buttercup, and Hubbard), nine peppers (among them cubanelles, habañeros, jalapeños, Thai hots, Hungarian hots, and Italian sweets), onions, cucumbers, seven tomato types, eggplants, corn, pickles, sugar pumpkins, jack-o'-lanterns, gourds, potatoes (Green Mountain, Yukon Gold, Chefs, and red), and Indian corn. Also for sale are seasonal fruits from other local farms and orchards: strawberries, raspberries, blueberries, peaches, nectarines, many kinds of apples and plums, and several pear varieties. The pick-your-own vegetable season runs from April to December, daily from 8:00 a.m. to 7:30 p.m.

Bushy Hill Orchard & Cider Mill, 29 Bushy Hill Rd., Granby; (860) 653-4022; www.bushyhill .com. Nora and Harold Law bought Bushy Hill in 1976 and now have 15,000 trees on seventy-five acres. The apple trees are all limited to 6-foot heights, and the peaches are on trellises up to 7 feet high, making it easy for pick-your-own efforts, which also extend to two acres of raspberries and an acre of blueberries. To pollinate apple blooms, Nora and Hal have thirty-two beehives, but bears persist in snatching their honey! Their bakery turns out doughnuts, cookies, Amaretto muffins, apple, blueberry, and pumpkin pies, even puff pastry Bavarian strudel—and their famous cider doughnuts. Also on the grounds: a cider mill and ice-cream parlor with farm-made ice cream. And there are tractor wagon tours of the orchards in spring when the apple trees (seventeen varieties) are in bloom. Call for hours and days.

Deercrest Farm, 3499 Hebron Ave., Glastonbury; (860) 633-4407. The Bronzi brothers, Huchinson and Jonathan, and their wives are turning out a cornucopia of fresh fruit and vegetables at their 100-acre Deercrest Farm each year. Their farm stand reflects that abundance in all manner of produce, from twenty kinds of apples, eight types of pears, apricots (which Jonathan calls "fussy and delicate"), nectarines, and berries, to beans, peas, three types of peppers, eggplants, broccoli, cauliflower, eight types of squash, including turban, oh yes, and peaches. Farmers on this land have been known since 1900 as "the peach growers." The Bronzis' father bought the property in 1965 and continued the tradition. The stand is open from May to the end of December, 9:00 a.m. to 6:00 p.m. daily.

Dondero Orchard Farm Stand & Bakery, 529 Woodland St., South Glastonbury; (860) 659-0294; www.donderoorchards.com. The Dondero family began farming in 1911. Succeeding generations are still going strong, growing twelve types of apples and three types of pears, plus such miscellaneous fruits and vegetables as strawberries, rhubarb, lettuce, peas, asparagus, and, appearing later in the growing season, nectarines, corn, blackberries, raspberries, cabbage, turnips, onions, winter squash, and pumpkins. The bakery part of the business is responsible for homemade fruit pies,

tea breads, strawberry shortcakes, apple dumplings, cookies, caramel apples, jams, pickles, jumbo eggs, and, for "man's best friend," Fat Paw Homemade Dog Biscuits. The Donderos close just before Christmas Eve and reopen when their first crops ripen. Open June to December, daily from 8:00 a.m. to 6:00 p.m.

Drazen Orchards, 215 Wallingford Rd., Cheshire; (203) 272-7985; gordraz@sbcglobal.net. The Drazens have been farming their thirty-acre spread for fifty-five years. The current crops, all grown by Gordon Drazen, with the weekend help of his son and local workers, consist of eighteen varieties of apples (including McIntosh, Empire, Liberty, Jonagold, Gingergold, Gala, Mutsu, and Cortland), eight types of peaches, both yellow and white, nectarines, and two types of pears, all of which are available for picking from mid-August until the end of October. Note that the apples are dwarf varieties for easy picking. Not in the mood to pick your own? No problem, the Drazen farm stand carries all those fruits, along with sweet corn, tomatoes, flowers, cider, and more. Open from the second week in August until Thanksgiving from 10:00 a.m. to 5:30 p.m. daily.

Easy Pickin's Orchard, 46 Bailey Rd., Enfield; (860) 763-3276; www.easypickinsorchard.com. Brian Kelliher's family has been farming their fifty acres since 1951. This family affair includes help from Brian's brother and two sisters and their families, who live nearby. The pick-your-own harvest runs from such vegetables as tomatoes, peppers, eggplants, Spanish onions, leeks, beans, cabbage, cauliflower, and beets to herbs (basil, cilantro, dill, parsley, and others) and apples (225 apple trees, nineteen varieties, including Macoun, Gala, Jonagold, Kinsei, Rubinette, and Sayaka), Japanese and prune plums, Asian pears, yellow and white peaches, raspberries, blueberries, and pumpkins—in their seasons. The Kellihers offer Sunday wagon rides after Labor Day at 2:00, 3:00, and 4:00 p.m.; on the third Sunday in October, there is an annual gourd hunt. Open July to November, Friday through Sunday from 9:00 a.m. to 5:00 p.m. and Monday through Thursday from 9:00 a.m. to noon.

Flamig Farm, 7 Shingle Mill Rd., West Simsbury; (860) 658-5070; www.flamigfarm.com. Flamig is an educational resource farm, but you can buy farm-fresh eggs there. And children love the petting zoo, summer camp, and haunted hayrides. In season open daily from 9:00 a.m. to 5:00 p.m.; closed from mid-November to early April.

Gigi's Native Produce, 48 Shaker Rd., Enfield; (860) 881-8297; www.gigisnativeproduce.com. Gina (Gigi), Ron, and daughter Olivia Veser sell a whole alphabet of fresh produce at their awning-shaded roadside cart, all grown on their twenty-five-acre farm: strawberries, sweet corn, tomatoes, peppers, squash, pole beans, cucumbers, native potatoes (Red Bliss and Yukon Gold), and melons in season. There are also herbs, homemade pies, and fresh flowers. Open July to September, daily from 9:00 a.m. to 7:00 p.m.

Gotta's Farm, 661 Glastonbury Turnpike (Route 17 south), Portland; (860) 342-1844. It is pick-your-own time when the apples ripen at Richard Gotta's from September onward. There is fresh cider, too. But be sure to visit the farm stand earlier for the sweet corn, tomatoes, peppers, squash, and melons, which ripen at various times. There is also a bakery with pies, breads, and desserts. Check it out from June to October, daily from 9:00 a.m. to 6:00 p.m.

Hippest Hartford-Area Bistro

Metro Bis—7B Simsburytown Shops, 928 Hopmeadow St., Simsbury; (860) 651-1908; www.metrobis.com; $$—boasts the charm and insouciance of a French bistro, with banquettes, antique hutch, a wall of mirrors, and front doors from a Paris Metro. This personable cafe serves contemporary American food with some Asian spins at surprisingly affordable prices. Chef Christopher Prosperi, who owns the bistro with his wife, Courtney, is an enthusiastic booster of Connecticut products, which enhance his creative cuisine, and even occasionally cooks at local farmers' markets. The first time I visited I knew I was in good hands when delicious sesame-seed-crusted Italian bread arrived along with a spread of red-pepper hummus. There are Thai, Korean, and Middle Eastern touches, mostly in the appetizers, that add to the pizzazz of the intriguing menu. House-smoked salmon, crispy Thai spring rolls, crispy marinated calamari, grilled tandoori marinated leg of lamb, and chili-seared, farm-raised catfish are a few of our memorable choices from a menu that changes often. And how could I forget desserts like Key lime tart and maple white chocolate bread pudding? Be sure to pick up some of Chris's own bottled salad dressings as you leave. There are three: Caesar, Tomato Ginger, and Balsamic Vinaigrette, all deliciously tangy. Metro Bis also hosts cookbook authors and wine dinners once a month. Open six days a week for lunch and dinner; closed Sunday.

Hickory Hill Orchards, 351 South Meriden Rd., Cheshire; (203) 272-3824; www.hickoryhillorchards.com. Lynn and Fred Kudish have been busy at their farm for more than twenty years, keeping up with the sales of their own and other local produce. Their pick-your-own fruits, available after mid-August, include fourteen types of apples (among them McIntosh, Macoun, Red and Golden Delicious, Ida Red, Rome, Fuji, Mutsu, Winesap, and Cortland). They sell flowers from local nurseries through December. There are also hayrides, picnics, and weekend events. Open mid-August through December from 10:00 a.m. to 5:30 p.m. daily.

High Hill Orchard, 170 Fleming Rd., Meriden; (203) 294-0276. Wayne Young, the manager of High Hill Orchard, runs a busy farm selling his tomatoes, onions, peppers, beans, eggplants, pumpkins, peaches, apples, pears, blueberries, flowers and fresh-pressed apple cider in season. Peaches, Bosc pears, and four of twelve apple varieties are available for picking, too. Open mid-July to Christmas, Saturday and Sunday from 10:00 a.m. to 5:00 p.m. After Labor Day to Thanksgiving, it's weekdays as well—Tuesday through Friday, noon to 6:00 p.m. Closed Monday.

Karabin Farms, 894 Andrews St., Southington; (860) 620-0194; www.karabinfarms.com. If you seek variety in pick-your-owns, visit Diane and Michael Karabin's fifty-acre farm, which they have run since 1984. They have 2,000 fruit trees and sell fourteen types of apples, six types of peaches, pumpkins, and, in December, Christmas trees. Their new farm store also offers cheeses, their own eggs and maple syrup, honey, and flowers (raised in four attached greenhouses). The store is open daily from April 1 to Christmas Eve, 9:00 a.m. to 5:00 p.m. For picking your own, there are hayrides (weekends only) to the pumpkin fields and apple orchards from Labor Day to just before Halloween. Call or check the Web site for hours and availability.

Lyman Orchards, junction of Routes 147 and 157, Middlefield; (800) 349-6015 or (860) 349-1798 (store); www.lymanorchards.com. The Lyman family, now in its eighth generation, has been farming here as far back as 1741; its spread now covers 1,100 acres, with 300 acres of berries, apples, peaches, pears, and pumpkins. Lyman Orchards includes an 18-hole golf course and club and the state's largest indoor farm store, the **Apple Barrel Farm Market,** which is to farm stands what a Humvee is to a Geo—humongous. There, year-round, you will find the orchard's fruit, cider, cider doughnuts (and holes), other bakery goods, preserves, vinegars, salsas, applesauce, and condiments, as well as many other Connecticut-made food products. Deli items include soups, salads, specialty sandwiches, and hearty country breakfasts. The orchards are open for farm tours; pick-your-own apples, peaches, pears, blueberries, strawberries, and raspberries are available from June to October. Lyman's calendar is packed with events: an Easter apple hunt, summer music festival, blueberry bake-off, apple-pie baking contest, and Winterfest celebration; check for dates. The orchards and market are open daily year-round from 9:00 a.m. to 6:00 p.m., but from 9:00 a.m. to 7:00 p.m. during September and October.

Ogre Farm, 180 Old Farms Rd., Simsbury; (860) 658-9297; www .georgehallfarm.com. George Hall, who comes from a long farming line, works, with his son George Jr., a fifty-acre spread that has been largely organic since 1967 and certified organic for more than twenty years. Their roadside stand is stocked with all their home-grown produce, which they also sell at the farmers' markets in West Hartford, Naugatuck, Simsbury, and New Haven. Ogre's seasonal produce—everything picked fresh daily—includes lettuce, carrots, beets, parsley, potatoes, various tomatoes, sugar pumpkins, lots of sweet corn, spinach, eggplant, sweet potatoes, herbs, cabbage, and cauliflower. They also sell honey from eight hives, free-range eggs (from some 250 chickens, fed on nonmedicated grain), and large jack-o'-lantern-size pumpkins (not organic). Open from the first week of July to Halloween. In season open daily from 9:00 a.m. to 5:00 p.m.

The Pickin' Patch, 276 Nod Rd., Avon; (860) 677-9552; www .thepickinpatch.com. The name sounds whimsical, but farming is serious business to Janet and Donald Carville. Janet's grandfather was the seventeenth generation of Woodfords who settled this property, which once totaled 500 acres and is one of the state's ten oldest farms (and Avon's oldest business). The Carvilles specialize in small fruits—blueberries, strawberries, raspberries, and melons—along with peas, beans, spinach, various lettuces, squash, beets, ten tomato varieties, peppers, sweet corn, and, in October, pumpkins. From their thirteen greenhouses, they sell cut flowers, perennials, and potted vegetable plants. Their farm stand is open daily May through October from 8:00 a.m. to 6:00 p.m.

Rogers Orchards—Home Farm, 336 Long Bottom Rd., South-ington; (860) 229-4240, and **Rogers Orchards—Sunnymount Farm,** Meriden-Waterbury Turnpike (Route 322), Southington; (203) 879-1206; www.rogersorchards.com. Eight generations of Rogerses have farmed here since 1809; currently John and his son Peter till 250 acres. They include twenty apple varieties, the most popular being McIntosh, Macoun, Cortland, and Empire. You may pick your own on weekends in September and October. Available at both Rogers farm stands are peaches, pears, nectarines, apricots, plums, vegetables, apple cider, doughnuts, honey, and apple and other fruit pies. Both stands are open daily from late July to mid-May the following year. Hours at the Home Farm stand are 8:00 a.m. to 6:00 p.m. and at Sunnymount Farm stand 9:00 a.m. to 5:00 p.m.

Rose's Berry Farm, 295 Matson Hill Rd., South Glastonbury; and **Rose's Berry Farm at Wickham Hill,** 1200 Hebron Ave., Glastonbury; (860) 633-7467; www.rosesberryfarm.com. The Rose family operation has existed since 1908; its apple trees and berry patches now cover one hundred acres of rolling hills. At the South Glastonbury farm, you may pick your own apples, strawber-ries, blueberries, raspberries, and pumpkins

and also enjoy Sunday breakfast (early June through October, 8:30 a.m. to 1:00 p.m.) on the deck overlooking apple orchards, ponds, and scenic vistas. The farm store stocks farm-fresh pasteurized apple cider, six types of homemade pies, muffins, jams, and fruit vinegars. At the greenhouse you may buy blueberry plants and, in season, Christmas trees. Summer hours are Monday to Thursday from 8:00 a.m. to 8:00 p.m., Friday and Saturday from 8:00 a.m. to 6:00 p.m., and Sunday from 9:00 a.m. to 5:00 p.m. Rose's farm stand is situated a few miles north in Glastonbury on Wickham Hill, where most of the farm produce is retailed from May to October, Monday to Friday from 10:00 a.m. to 6:00 p.m. and Saturday and Sunday from 9:00 a.m. to 5:00 p.m. There are fall school tours by appointment only.

Scott's Orchard & Nursery, 1838 New London Turnpike, Glastonbury; (860) 633-8681; www.scottsorchardandnursery.com. Woody and JoAnn Scott welcome you to Apple Hill from mid-March through December 24. Their pick-your-own fruits include eight varieties of peaches (ripening August through September), three of plums (into October), pears (September through October), and nine types of apple, including Cortland, Macoun, Empire, McIntosh, and Winesap (August through October). Additionally, there are horse-drawn hayrides weekends from mid-September to late October. Check the Web site for the pick-your-own schedule.

Hartford—Home of the First American Cookbook

A signature year for American cooking was 1796, when Amelia Simmons (about whom little is known), published a forty-seven-page paperback, entitled *American Cookery*. Until then, English cookery books were the standard, but the different climate, crops, and facilities begged for a book indigenous to America. Amelia included foods unheard of in Europe: cranberry sauce, pumpkin and mince pies, Rye 'n' Injun (a dark bread made with molasses, yeast, and white corn), spruce beer, watermelon-rind pickles, and five recipes using cornmeal. For the next thirty-five years, her recipes were reprinted, often without credit. No copyright or royalties for poor Amelia!

Tulmeadow Farm Store, 255 Farms Village Rd. (Route 309), West Simsbury; (860) 658-1430; tulmeadowfarm@aol.com. Don Tuller and his relatives work the 265-acre Tulmeadow Farm, as their ancestors have since 1768. They grow greenhouse tomatoes, assorted greens, and other vegetables, but sweet corn and pumpkins are their biggest crops. All are available in season in their farm store, along with fresh fruit (grown by neighbors), Lamothe's maple syrup, honey from Jones Apiaries, Griffin Farmstead goat cheese, goat milk and cow milk yogurt, farm-raised beef, fruit pies, chicken potpies, herbs, cut flowers, and perennials. The store is open daily year-round, but hours change with the seasons, so it is best to call or e-mail ahead. In one of the store's two rooms, farm-made ice cream is sold from April to mid-October (see page 149, under Made or Grown Here). While the farm doesn't raise turkeys itself, it does take orders for them for Thanksgiving.

Urban Oaks Organic Farm, 225 Oak St., New Britain; (860) 223-6200; www.urbanoaks.org. If you expect a conventional farm, Urban Oaks will surprise you. It consists of four large greenhouses on four acres on a city street. There, certified organic farming is done under strictly supervised climatic and atmospheric control, with strict supervision of the process. Urban Oaks is a nonprofit farm project that sells year-round, primarily to restaurants, specialty markets, and retail stores. Public access is limited to August through October, Friday from 3:00 to 6:00 p.m. and Saturday from 10:00 a.m. to 1:00 p.m., when you may buy fresh specialty salad and other greens (lettuce, kale, and chard), carrots, herbs, peppers, zucchini, apples, pears, and produce from Urban Oaks and eight other certified organic farms in Connecticut and neighboring states.

Woodland Farm, 575 Woodland St., South Glastonbury; (860) 633-2742; woodlandfarm@cox.net. Arden and Harold Teveris have been farming here since 1963. Now, with their third son, Peter, his wife, Nancy, and a bevy of visiting grandchildren, they tend their thirty-acre farm and produce fruit jams, prize freestone peaches, summer and late-harvest apples, red and yellow plums, pears, nectarines, and sweet and sour cherries. They are known for their blueberries, raspberries, and strawberries and in the fall for fresh-pressed apple cider. Open daily from August through December, 9:00 a.m. to 6:00 p.m.

Food Happenings

FEBRUARY

Wine on Ice, Hartford; (800) 287-2788; www.wineonice.com. Connecticut Public Television's annual wine auction has become a tradition, with 200 lots of fine and rare wines up for bid. Starting off the gala event is a champagne reception, followed by dinner with fine wines and then the auction. Proceeds go to the educational programming on CPTV and WNPR. The site and date change from year to year, so call for current dates and locale.

MAY

Dionysos Greek Festival, St. George Greek Orthodox Church, 301 West Main St., New Britain; (860) 229-0055. This annual three-day event always begins on the Friday of Memorial Day weekend and ends Sunday at 8:00 p.m. In between you can feast on homemade Greek foods—the likes of spanakopita, gyros, shish kebab, and baklava, fresh from the church kitchen. In addition, you will find Greek jewelry and handcrafts, Greek music, dancing, and entertainment. A Dionysian happening for sure. Opa!

FOOD LOVERS' TIP

If it's an authentic Italian meal you crave, you'll find one on Franklin Avenue, Hartford's old-time Italian neighborhood. In four long blocks, from 318 Franklin to 624 Franklin, there are numerous Italian restaurants, including these well-known ones: **Francesco's** at 318; **Casa Mia** at 381; **Chef Eugene** at 428; **Franklin Giant Grinder** at 464; **Ficara's Ristorante** at 577; **Carbone's** at 588; and **Capriccio** at 624. Buon appetito!

JUNE

The Connecticut Chefs Showcase, Hartford; (800) 287-2788. Usually held in mid-June at a floating location, this stellar annual event benefiting Connecticut Public Broadcasting has been going strong for more than ten years. Featuring a silent auction of fine, collectible wines, wine dinners prepared by five distinguished statewide chefs, and a "Mystery Box" to be bid on, this does indeed showcase superior foods and wines. Call them for information about the next event, the chefs participating, date, price, and location.

North Canton Strawberry Festival, North Canton Community United Methodist Church, 3 Case St. (corner of Route 179), North Canton; (860) 693-4589; www.gbgm-umc.org/northcantonumc. Going strong the third Saturday of June since 1951, this strawberry celebration includes bake and tag sales, plant and burger booths, an auction, and activities for children. The festival is most famous for its towering super-duper strawberry shortcake, made with home-made biscuits, butter, strawberries, and yards of fresh whipped cream. Hours are 11:00 a.m. to 5:00 p.m.

Ye Olde-Fashioned Strawberry Festival, Plantsville Congregational United Church of Christ, 109 Church St., Plantsville; (860) 628-5595. Since 1993 this daylong festival (from 5:00 to 8:00 p.m., always on a Friday in mid-June) has been a celebration of the strawberry. Centerpieces are luscious strawberry shortcakes, but visitors—usually about 500 of them—also enjoy hot dogs and nostalgic music.

SEPTEMBER

Celebration of Connecticut Farms, (860) 247-0202; www .ctfarmland.org. Usually held on the Sunday after Labor Day, this moveable feast changes venue every year. (For details contact Henry Talmage, executive director, Connecticut Farmland Trust, 77 Buckingham St., Hartford.) This annual outdoor fund-raising event—usually a sellout weeks ahead—benefits the Connecticut Farmland Trust, which protects the state's dwindling farmlands. The celebration is co-chaired by a big name like Meryl Streep or the late Paul Newman and leading chef Jacques Pepin and features twenty-five to thirty of the state's best chefs, who prepare dishes from Connecticut-made foods. There are cheese artisans, local vintners, ice-cream makers, and other food

Best for Barbecue and Blues

At **Black-eyed Sally's BBQ & Blues** in Hartford (350 Asylum St., Hartford; 860-278—RIBS(7427); www.blackeyedsallys.com; $–$$), the midnight-blue, tin-tiled walls and ceiling provide a funky backdrop for some of the best barbecue in the Nutmeg State, with Cajun and Creole specialties as well. Add colorful paintings of Muddy Waters and other blues greats and live entertainment Monday (jazz) through Saturday evenings, and what more does a body need? James and Dara Varano opened Sally's in 1995 and made it the jumpingest blues joint around. Headline acts have included Johnny Rawls and Sonny Rhodes Blues Band. As for the slow-smoked ribs, Sally's forte, I recommend the falling-off-the-bone-tender Memphis-style pork rib platter—a quarter rack with Bayou slaw, corn bread, and rice and beans. If you like your ribs more incendiary, rub on some of Sally's red-hot Cajun beer barbecue sauce. Dynamite! You might begin your meal with Louisiana gumbo, Uncle Jaimo's spicy barbecue wings, or Cajun popcorn (nubbins of deep-fried Louisiana crawfish tails in a zesty Tennessee tartar sauce). For a finale, there's bourbon pecan pie or Mississippi mud pie. Closed Monday.

producers, as well as music, art, and tours. For food lovers, this event is often a must.

Cheshire Fall Festival and Marketplace, Bartlem Park (Route 10), Cheshire; (203) 272-2345; www.cheshirechamber.com. An annual one-day event since 1991, sponsored by the Chamber of Commerce and coordinated with the town of Cheshire, this becomes more popular with every passing year. There is live entertainment, a craft fair, and booths galore, with some eighty displays by the town's civic and business organizations. Between six and ten booths are sponsored by local restaurants, dispensing—among other tasty treats—chowder, fried dough, sandwiches, and the famous Blackie's hot dogs. Parking is free, as are the fireworks and the festival. The festival usually takes place the second weekend of September.

OCTOBER

Apple Harvest, Welles St., Glastonbury; (860) 659-3587. Right after Columbus Day in mid-October, you can depend on this free, annual two-day harvest event at the Community Center to be apple-polished, as it has been for more than thirty years. Expect to find apple pies, puddings, cakes, and other apple-centered delicacies provided by about 200 vendors, with an emphasis on local farmers and products, along with farm trucks piled high with shiny fresh apples. The Chamber of Commerce sponsors an Apple Pie Booth. Other foods include old standbys: soups, stuffed potatoes, and ice-cream sandwiches. A noon parade from town hall is followed by carnival rides, singing groups, and, of course, apples galore. In all, the event attracts some 200 volunteers in what is an ebullient community effort. The time is from 10:00 a.m. to 5:00 p.m. both days. Call for specific dates.

Apple Harvest Festival, Town Green, Main St., Southington; (860) 628-8036; www.appleharvestfestival.com. This two-weekend festival gives locals a double whammy. It begins the last Friday, Saturday, and Sunday of September, then leapfrogs to the next weekend (first weekend of October) for more fun and games. It's been going strong for more than thirty-eight years! The festival kicks off with a road race, a parade, crowning of the queen, a street fair, and live music until 8:00 p.m., with dozens of apple products and other goodies for sale. Hours vary on different days; call the above-listed phone number or check the Web site for details.

Nibbles

Top dogs can be found at **Capitol Lunch,** 510 Main St., New Britain; (860) 229-8237; www.capitollunch.com; $. But what makes patrons stand in line to order isn't the frankfurters (aka Cappie dogs), it's the Famous Sauce, a thick, brown, clove-scented meat sauce lathered over the crisp-skinned dog. You can also order burgers, onion rings, and fries, but it's the sauce that's been the magnet at this tidy, modest place since 1929. To-go pints of Cappie's Famous Sauce are available. Open daily, but hours vary; it's wise to call ahead.

At **Harpo's Bakery and Café,** 908 Main St., South Glastonbury; (860) 657-4111; $, you might expect to see a bewigged live replica of Harpo Marx. But *this* Harpo is Dave Slade, who gained the nickname as a kid when he had curly blond hair. That curly mane is gone now, but the bakery recipes, many of which were a legacy of his grandparents, who owned an Italian bakery for more than fifty years, live on. Among Harpo's gems are crusty Italian bread, pizza, many cookies (biscotti, almond paste, butter balls, and then some), cupcakes, turnovers, and seven types of muffins. The bakery has two large tables, where you can sit and chomp on sweets or Harpo's breakfast sandwiches, burgers, chili dogs, omelets, or other comestibles. Open from 5 a.m.; closing hours differ daily, but Harpo's is always open until at least 4 p.m.

Main Street Creamery, 271 Main St., Old Wethersfield; (860) 529-0509; www.mainstreetcreamery.com, $, is a great little lunch stop if you are touring the historic houses of the old town. Hefty sandwiches, like the favorite corned beef or pastrami on rye, soups, and twenty-eight flavors of Praline's ice cream are staples in this down-home place. Open daily, mid-March through October. Cash only.

Since 1941 **O'Rourke's Diner** (728 Main St., Middletown; 860-346-6101; $) has been a much loved, if slightly grungy, Main Street mainstay and tourist attraction. But in 2006 O'Rourke's burned down, to the dismay of its many fans.

Aided by the fund-raising of alumni of neighboring Wesleyan University, owner Brian O'Rourke rebuilt in record time. Famous for its comfort food, especially breakfast items, the diner features thirty-three different omelets (including the aptly named six-egg

Belly Buster), ten types of eggs Benedict, banana bread French toast, and Irish Galway (poached eggs over grilled brown bread with smoked salmon, bacon, hollandaise, and home fries). Open daily from 6 a.m. to 3 p.m., but Friday and Saturday open also for dinner, from 5 p.m. to 9 p.m. BYO.

One of Hartford's little secrets is **Pond House Café,** 1555 Asylum St., Hartford; (860) 231-8823; www.pondhousecafe. A delightful cafe on a pond in rose-filled Elizabeth Park, it is especially tranquil when the roses are in bloom, sitting outside on the patio or covered porch. Inside is pleasant any season because of the great window views. Nibble on a few starters or pizza or enjoy a full meal, new American style. BYO. Sunday brunch is a great time to be here, but reservations are almost a "must."

Shady Glen, 840 East Middle Turnpike, Manchester; (860) 649-4245; $. A mural of elves and pixies picnicking on ice cream in a shady glen is a reminder of Shady Glen's main product: some of the best ice cream in the state. The ice cream is made one level below the diner in as many as thirty flavors, most with natural flavorings. Chocolate Almond Joy and chocolate peanut butter are among the favorites. Another reason folks flock to this hamburger "joint"/ diner: unusual cheeseburgers, with cheese that oozes over onto the grill, ending up both soft and crunchy. A second Shady Glen is at 360 West Middle Turnpike, Manchester; (860) 643-0511. Open daily for lunch and dinner at both Shady Glens.

Scott's Jamaican Bakery, 1344 Albany Ave., Hartford; (860) 247-3855; www.scottsjamaicanbakery.com; $. Small and bustling, Scott's, located at the corner of Kent, is a mecca of West Indian baked goods, with fresh-baked corn bread, cinnamon bread and rolls, plantain and coconut tarts, and a host of other Caribbean pastries. A small freezer contains Scott's popular Jamaican beef patties, shaped like empanadas, ready to take home for a quick meal. Two other locations are at 3381 Main St.; (860) 246-6599 and 630 Blue Hills Ave.; (860) 243-2609.

Sweet Harmony Café and Bakery, 158 Broad St., Middletown; (860) 344-9646; www.sweetharmonycafebakery.com; $, has the old-fashioned charm of a village tearoom. Even so, it turns out some delicious modern dishes, like a variety of quiches and—its signature—unusual housemade cakes. Trang Tran, the chef, is responsible for such delights as a coconut-frosted mango cake filled with pineapple mousse; pistachio cake with strawberry mousse; and kumquat cake with passion fruit mousse. Hours are irregular; it's best to call ahead.

Learn to Cook

Ann Howard Apricots, 1593 Farmington Ave., Farmington; (860) 673-5405; annhoward_FEM@SBCglobal.net. Ann Howard, noted restaurateur and baker, gives occasional "hands-on" cooking classes in her home. Call or e-mail for the current schedule, details, and prices.

Spiritus Wines, 220 Asylum St., Hartford; (800) 499-WINE; www .spiritus.com. This celebrated wine shop, which opened in 1982, has educated the wine palates of thousands. The current owner, Gary Dunn, became a wine lover while living in France. After moving to the Hartford area, he found and bought Spiritus from Barrie and Martin Robbins-Pianka, who were known for their fine wine selections from America and abroad. In addition to the monthly **Spirit Writings** newsletter, a Web site that is continuously updated with wine news, and wine tastings (call for dates and times), the wine selection is as select as ever. Ask about Spiritus's legendary food/wine dinners at specific restaurants in the area. Spiritus now offers free delivery on orders over $100 within the Hartford area.

Landmark Eateries

Ann Howard Apricots, 1593 Farmington Ave. (Route 4), Farmington; (860) 673-5405; www.apricotsrestaurant.com; pub $, restaurant $$. Facing the surging Farmington River, Ann Howard

THE STATE'S UNIQUE GUSTATORY TWOFER

Cavey's Restaurant, 45 East Center St., Manchester; (860) 643-2751; www.caveysrestaurant.com; $$ (Italian), $$$ (French), is really two separate and distinct restaurants (northern Italian and modern French with some Asian accents) both in the same freestanding building, under the same ownership, though with separate kitchens and different but equally well-trained waitstaffs. Open for dinner only and closed Sunday and Monday, both restaurants are superb. No wonder then that they have been Hartford-area favorites since the Cavagnaro family first opened them in 1933. The Italian Cavey's two ground-floor dining rooms are as airy as a Mediterranean villa. I like the warm, friendly ambience and modern interpretation of northern Italian cooking. House-made pastas are really special, as in farfalle with chicken and peppers or grandmother's ravioli in brown butter or Bolognese sauce. I also savor Cavey's carpaccio, mussel, and polenta soup and fresh figs wrapped in prosciutto with Gorgonzola dolce. But really, almost everything the kitchen produces is a winner.

Elegance remains the operative word (along with priciness and jackets for men) in the French Cavey's formal belle époque decor, making this the place for a special-occasion evening. Still, in the spirit of this more casual era, the classic French menu has been modernized, with recent gems including starters of seared foie gras with braised Swiss chard and cranberry cassis sauce; duck confit with braised red cabbage and cauliflower; and grilled calamari with Asian stir-fry in a sweet chili sauce. Excellent also are grilled loin of lamb, pan-roasted Broken Arrow Ranch antelope, and herbed monkfish medallions in a buttercup squash sauce. The wine list is a wonder as well. Dinner only, from 5:30 p.m. to 9:30 p.m. in the Italian, from 6:00 p.m. in the French. Both closed Sunday and Monday.

Apricots is a delightful place for lunch or dinner. A onetime trolley barn, the two-story building boasts three separate dining rooms on the second floor, a pub on the ground floor with its own full menu and more casual fare, and a patio by the river where lunch is also served. From the upstairs windows, you have a wonderful river view. Warm, inviting, yet unpretentious are words that fit both the decor—with delicate apricots painted on the walls along with some exposed brick—and the contemporary American cooking. Ann Howard, a prize-winning baker of note, was one of the first to emphasize the freshest of ingredients. Lunch dishes like baked sole Oscar, Apricots' signature chicken potpie, and colossal spinach Florentine ravioli are memorable. So are such dinner entrees as sautéed fillet of North Atlantic cod with hot crab soufflé and honey-roasted organic "frenched" chicken breast with apple-walnut stuffing. And the praise keeps piling up. Open daily for lunch and dinner.

Arugula, 953 Farmington Ave., West Hartford; (860) 561-4888; cgehami@aol.com. Christiane Gehami opened Arugula, a Mediterranean bistro, in 1996 and it has been going strong ever since. Not only is the food well prepared, but the informal setting adds to a pleasurable dining experience.

Brix, 1721 Highland Ave. (Route 10), Cheshire; (203) 272-3584; www.brixct.com; $. There's nothing fancy about Brix, but I like

Barcelona Beckons

Barcelona Restaurant & Wine Bar, 971 Farmington Ave., West Hartford; (860) 218-2100; www.barcelonawinebar.com; $$. With six outposts in its mini-empire, Barcelona is a name to reckon with, suggesting tapas and other intriguing tidbits. Like its siblings, this Barcelona offers a convivial atmosphere, offbeat art, and decor, where a youngish crowd likes to hang, nibbling lighthearted snacks and meals suited to sophisticated urban tastes. The menu highlights thirty or more tapas (little plates) so intriguing they invite lots of mixing and matching. Irresistible choices include spinach/chickpea casserole, sautéed shrimp with garlic, sherry-braised short ribs, ham and chicken croquettes, cornmeal-crusted skate wings, and lots of mussels and other seafood combos. The Spanish-accented and Mediterranean entrees are terrific, too—dishes like paella, pan-roasted wild striped bass, Rioja-braised lamb shank—as are desserts and assorted Spanish cheeses. There's also a late-night menu. The wine list—with some marvelous Spanish choices, along with South American, U.S., and other nations—is a oenophile's dream. The other Barcelonas are **Barcelona SoNo,** 63–65 North Main St., South Norwalk, (203) 899-0088, the first; **Barcelona Greenwich,** 18 West Putnam Ave., Greenwich, (203) 983-6400; **Barcelona Fairfield,** 4180 Black Rock Turnpike, Fairfield, (203) 255-0800; **Barcelona Stamford,** 222 Summer St., Stamford, (203) 348-4800; and **Barcelona New Haven,** Omni Hotel, 155 Temple St., New Haven, (203) 848-3000. West Hartford is open daily for dinner, lunch Monday through Friday. Other Barcelonas vary; in South Norwalk and New Haven, no lunch is served at all. Check with individual Barcelonas for their schedule and hours.

its trim, cheerful simplicity. It isn't often you find a roadside restaurant with this much instant appeal, which is intensified by the Mediterranean-Italian menu. Most dishes are well-made, and dining here is a thoroughly pleasant experience. I'd heartily recommend the housemade gnocchi al telefono, osso bucco Milanese, penne Bolognese, and various pizzas. Closed Mondays.

Cracovia, 60 Broad St., New Britain; (860) 223-4443; $. In a small city where Polish seems like the second language, this café, owned by Gregory Adamski, is one of four Polish restaurants and is considered the best. At first sight, what sets Cracovia (named for Crakow, or Krakow, Poland's second city) apart from an ordinary luncheonette is the beautifully executed mural on the wall behind the long lunch counter: a Polish knight in armor on horseback wielding a lance. Another knight graces the rear wall. Nothing else here is fancy, but it is a neat and tidy local hangout in what is predominantly a Polish neighborhood. If you want a crash course in Polish cooking, try the roast pork stuffed with plums, goulash with dumplings, cheese blintzes, pirogi, golabki (cabbage stuffed with ground meat and rice in a tomato sauce) or potato pancakes. You might sample one of six Polish beers to go with your meal. Cracovia also does a hearty breakfast with French toast, omelets, and egg sandwiches with ham, bacon, or Polish kielbasa sausage. Fair warning: Portions are enormous. Open 8:00 a.m. to 8:00 p.m. daily.

Feng Asian Bistro, 93 Asylum St., Hartford; (860) 549-3364; www.fengrestaurant.com; $$. This may be Hartford's most stunning restaurant, with luminous lighting, gleaming wood floors, and rough-hewn tan stone walls. And the food matches. In three rooms—main dining room, sushi bar, and lounge—you'll eat well on Asian food presented in a novel way. As an example, lobster bisque is not served in a bowl but as "lemongrass lobster latte" in a mug—dramatic and still delicious. That sets the tone. You may cook your own Kobe beef or let others do the work and simply sit awestruck and enjoy the results. Whether you go pan-Asian or stay with various sushi combinations, you'll have an enjoyable evening. I know I did. Open daily, but on Saturday and Sunday it's dinner only.

Firebox, 539 Broad St., Hartford; (860) 246-1222; www.fireboxres taurant.com; $$. The name, Firebox, sounds down-to-earth, but the handsome decor and elegant food at this modern American restaurant are upscale and memorable, without being wildly expensive. There are two dining rooms, the front one with exposed brick arched windows and 30-foot-high vaulted ceilings, the rear one with whitewashed brick walls, Amish farm tables, and a gas fireplace set in the wall at eye level like a work of art. A hallmark of the food is that much of it, especially the produce, is locally grown. Firebox was originally a wing of a late-nineteenth-century brick factory (called Billings Forge), near the Capitol in Frog Hollow, a run-down neighborhood. The building was bought and restored by the Melville Charitable Trust, a national philanthropic organization based in Hartford.

Metro Bis's Brussels Sprouts, Bacon, and Honey

Chris Prosperi, chef-owner of Metro Bis in Simsbury, loves brussels sprouts—the little "heads" growing on stalks that hold dozens of them—which is one reason he always looks forward to the autumn harvest. "If picked in early fall, before the frost," Chris says, "these members of the cabbage family have a bitter, nutty taste. Harvested after a couple of chilly nights, the sprouts actually sweeten with the freeze."

Chris developed this recipe at the Litchfield Farmers' Market using early-harvest brussels sprouts, which he sweetens with local honey. "As the season progresses, simply adjust the amount of honey depending on the bitterness of the vegetable."

1 tablespoon oil
1 cup diced onion
¾ cup minced carrot
1 teaspoon kosher salt
5 strips bacon, chopped
1 pound brussels sprouts, sliced

½ cup water
1 tablespoon rubbed sage
2 teaspoons curry powder
3 tablespoons honey
1 tablespoon red wine vinegar

Much of Firebox's staff is drawn from the immediate neighborhood, and it further supports the local economy by relying on local products as much as possible and underwriting a farmers' market in the adjacent parking lot. Firebox is living proof that you can have your cake and support a worthy cause at the same time. Through its success, the Trust aims to encourage other vendors and merchants

1. Heat the oil over medium high heat in a heavy-bottomed pan, then add the diced onion.
2. Cook for 1 minute or until lightly caramelized, then stir in the carrots and kosher salt. Add the bacon and cook for 2–3 minutes.
3. Mix in the sliced brussels sprouts. Cook for an additional minute and then pour in the water.
4. Lower the heat to medium and cook for 8–10 minutes or until brussels sprouts are soft. Be careful not to cook with the pan dry. Add water 2 tablespoons at a time if necessary, until sprouts are done.
5. Stir in the sage and curry powder, then cook for 30 seconds.
6. Remove from the heat, then add the honey and vinegar. Taste and adjust the seasoning with salt and more honey if necessary.

Makes about 1 quart.

Metro Bis

7B Simsburytown Shops
928 Hopmeadow St., Simsbury
(860) 651-1908
www.metrobis.com

to join it in helping to rehab the area. So enjoy your honey-pepper-roasted chicken, corn and shrimp risotto, Stonington flounder, and other Firebox treats, knowing that in doing so, you're making a worthwhile contribution, too. Open daily, but Saturday and Sunday it's dinner only.

It's Only Natural, 386 Main St., Middletown; (860) 346-9210; www.ionrestaurant.com; $$. After winning awards as best vegetarian restaurant in the state, chef Mark Shadle and his fellow co-owner Renara Magee turned their place totally vegan. But the dishes are so creative at this unconventional place, you don't have to be a vegetarian or vegan to enjoy them. On a menu that changes four times a year and often borrows from many cultures, you may find hummus platters, spicy Cajun tempeh cutlets, sweet potato enchiladas, and the ever-popular sweet potato fries. It's Only Natural has two dining areas and an outdoor patio. Portions are gargantuan; organic wine and beer are now available. Open for lunch and dinner, but closed Sunday.

Peppercorn's Grill, 357 Main St., Hartford; (860) 547-1714; www.peppercornsgrill.com; $$–$$$. This stylish restaurant with a dramatic glass façade is near the Wadsworth Atheneum. It exists on two levels, having recently expanded into space formerly occupied by Spiritus, the wine shop (now on Asylum Street). Peppercorn's attracts a youngish, thirty-something crowd and also Italian-food mavens, who consider it among the best Italian restaurants in

a city full of good ones. I like especially the carpaccio, calamari fritti, the wonderfully crisp salads, various risottos, the gnocchi-of-the-day, and the luscious pastas (ravioli all'arancia is particularly winning). Even the desserts, not usually an Italian-restaurant strong suit, are

Mini-Empire, Maxi-Fun

Max Downtown, City Place, 185 Asylum St., Hartford; (860) 522-2530; www.maxdowntown.com; $$$. There are now seven Maxes in the Hartford area, each different. My favorite is still Max Downtown, the flagship. The Maxes are not a chain (no clones here) but a mini-empire created by entrepreneur Richard Rosenthal, who has a flair for matching very good food with a contemporary "with-it" environment and friendly service. At Max Downtown I like the bold good looks, the vibrant mural on the upper wall, the buzz and

bustle of business diners, and the robust menu. It features items like crispy tempura lobster, basil-crusted rack of lamb, and grilled veal chop stuffed with caramelized onions, mascarpone, and pancetta, plus Max's signature Kansas City strip steak, steak au poivre, and hickory-smoked "cowboy cut" beef rib chop with chili onion rings. For lunch, nothing tops Max's super cobb salad, an all-time favorite. An excellent, globally diverse wine list offers two dozen wines by the glass. Other Maxes are **Max Amore** and **Max Fish,** both in Glastonbury, **Max a Mia** in Avon, **Max's Oyster Bar** and **Max Burger,** both in West Hartford, and **Max's Tavern,** over the line in Springfield, Massachusetts. All have different looks, decor, and menu emphasis. All are maximum fun. Open daily, but on weekends it's for dinner only. Other Maxs have their own schedules, so check individually.

superb, especially the warm chocolate Valrhona cake and chocolate bread pudding. Open for lunch and dinner during the week, for dinner only on weekends.

Shish Kebab of Afghanistan, 36 Lasalle Rd., West Hartford; (860) 231-8400 www.afghancuisine.net; $. As what may be the only Afghan restaurant in the entire state, Shish Kebab offers a fine way to become acquainted with Afghan culture, at least its culinary aspects, at really reasonable prices. The restaurant has two stories and a patio, with the dining area upstairs (there's an elevator); the rooms are pleasingly decorated with Afghan artifacts. If you find Indian cuisine too spicy, Afghan food might fit you to an A (for Afghan). It uses many of the same ingredients and is well seasoned and tangy enough for most palates without being incendiary. Among a host of delectable dishes, I'm partial to several kebabs (lamb is particularly tasty), ashak (stuffed with chopped spinach, beef, yellow split peas, garlic, and coriander), mantoo (steamed dumplings with onions, ground beef, and house-made yogurt), kabeli palow, and desserts like baklava and fernee (rice pudding with rose water and cardamom). There is a small wine list and several Indian beers, which go well with the food. You might finish with Afghan tea, a sweet-spicy blend of black tea with cardamom and milk. There is live Afghan music Friday night. Open daily for lunch and dinner.

Trumbull Kitchen, 150 Trumbull St., Hartford; (860) 493-7417; www.maxrestaurantgroup.com; $$. I love the "buzz" at this non-Max Max, a high-energy brasserie that is the only Richard Rosenthal-owned "Max" with a different name. Richard co-owns it with chef Chris Torla. Together they have made it the place to be for the under-forty crowd. The cool look and modern decor are backdrops for dishes like braised lamb osso bucco, Hilda's meat loaf, and light fare like tapas, stone pies (pizzas), creative salads, dim sum, and sushi. The Rosenthal touch is also evident in the well-chosen wine list that navigates the planet. Open daily, but on Sunday for dinner only.

Brewpubs & Microbreweries

Cambridge Brew House, 357 Salmon Brook St., Granby; (860) 653-2739; www.cambridgebrewhouse.com; $. The inspiration of partners Steve Boucino and Scott Scanlon was to create this brewpub in the likeness of an English pub, complete with dartboards, checkers, and dominos. To beer drinkers, the pizzas, burgers, sandwiches, and flank steaks are secondary. What counts are the beers and ales brewed on the premises, often five or so available at a given time. While the beer menu changes, some of the favorites are Abijah Rowe, an award-winning IPA (India pale ale), ESB (extra special bitter), Newgate Brown (light-bodied ale with cocoa under-currents), and Kolsch (German-style beer). A second Cambridge Brew House is at 84 Main St., Torrington; (860) 201-5666; www.cbhbrew.com. Open daily, except closed Monday.

City Steam Brewery Café, 942 Main St., Hartford; (860) 525-1600; www.citysteambrewerycafe.com; $$. An awesome Romanesque three-story brownstone structure, designed by architect H.H. Richardson in the 1870s, was completely renovated in 1979 and now houses a Marriott Residence Inn and the City Steam Brewery Café. The cavernous premises also include a comedy club, billiard hall, and restaurant with seating on seven levels. Brewmaster Ron Page is in charge of the handcrafted beers. Some of his popular quaffs are Colt Light Lager (named for gun maker Samuel Colt, a Hartford native), Naughty Nurse Pale Ale (a sunset-hued best-seller), and Original City Steam (an English-type brown ale). Hours are Monday through Thursday from 11:30 a.m. to 10:30 a.m., Friday and Saturday from 11:30 a.m. to midnight, and Sunday from 4:00 to 10:00 p.m.

Eli Cannon's Tap Room, 695 Main St., Middletown; (860) 347-3547; www.elicannons.com; $, is neither a brewpub nor a micro-brewery. So why, you may ask, is it included here? As the purveyor of the most diverse, exciting, and captivating list of worldwide brews, it belongs on any dedicated beer drinker's "must visit" list. With thirty-six beers that rotate on tap (among twenty-two to thirty-six spigots), domestic and imported, this is probably beer nirvana—a favorite watering hole (since 1994) for Wesleyan students and suds lovers all over Connecticut. Emphasis is on microbrews and typically might include Lagunitas, Smuttynose, Dogfish Head, and Avery. Proof of its seriousness, the pub displays portable blackboards listing each beer available and the date the keg was tapped. Along with cold beer, Eli Cannon's serves up a warm atmosphere and hot food, describing its offbeat menu as "Irish/English Pub/American Trailer Park Fusion." You'll find competently made sandwiches, spicy wings, burgers, fish-and-chips, plus real meals, salads, and desserts. Claim a seat on the attractive, umbrella-shaded, flower-decked patio out back (dubbed the "beer garden of Eden") when the weather warrants being outdoors. Open six days a week for dinner, Tuesday through Friday for lunch as well. Closed Mondays.

Hops Grillhouse & Brewery, 3260 Berlin Turnpike, Newington; (860) 594-8808; www.hops restaurants.com; $$. Hops has been hopping across the country since its modest beginnings in Clearwater, Florida, in the 1980s. This is Connecticut's only outpost, though as a mini-chain, one never knows when another might hop along. Known for its jumbo Gulf shrimp, steaks, Key lime pie, and lively atmosphere, Hops also has a handful of microbrews. They include Alligator ale, Clearwater Light, and Thoroughbred Red ale. Hours are Monday through Thursday from 11:30 a.m. to 10:30 p.m., Friday and Saturday from 11 a.m. to 11:30 p.m., Sunday from 11 a.m. to 10 p.m.

John Harvard's Brew House, 1487 Pleasant Valley Rd., Manchester; (860) 644-2739; www.johnharvards.com; $$. From platters of burgers and fries to juicy New York strip steaks, the food at this brewpub, part of a small Boston-based group, is solid, if unspectacular, like the rather sterile atmosphere. The beers are something else; some have been recognized nationally for their excellence. One medal winner is the fruity John Harvard's Pale Ale. Others to savor are Old Willy IPA and seasonal brews like Queen Bee Honey (in April/May), Oktoberfest, and Holiday Red. Hours Monday through Saturday are 11:30 a.m. to 1:00 a.m., Sunday to 10 p.m.

Olde Burnside, 780 Toland St., East Hartford; (860) 528-2200; www.oldeburnsidebrewing.com; $$. In what was his family's old ice-making factory, Bob McClellan established his new microbrewery, dubbed Olde Burnside, in the early days of this century. In short order Olde Burnside's smooth, mellow Ten Penny Ale was voted in a reader's poll in the *Hartford Advocate* "Hartford's best microbrew" in 2005, 2006, and 2007. Keeping it company now are two other ales, the hearty black'n'tan-style Dirty Penny Ale and Penny Weiz (hey, I get it, penny wise), a version of a Belgian witbier or wheat beer (50 percent wheat, 50 percent barley). According to head brewer Joe Lushing and assistant Chris Parrott, all are available on draft or in distinctive half-gallon Growler bottles.

Thomas Hooker Brewing Company, 16 Tobey Rd., Bloomfield; (860) 242-3111; www.hookerbeer.com. Named after one of Hartford's founding fathers, this newish brewery dubs its fresh-tasting products "Connecticut's beer." A beer fancier might take a Saturday tour (the small fee includes a tasting glass), between noon and 5:00 p.m., to learn how the beer is made and even have a sampling of four draft beers in the tasting room. Every first and third Friday between 5:00 p.m. and 8:00 p.m., there's also an open house with tasting. Hooker makes and packages nine beers in all. These include a dry, aromatic American Pale Ale, the bitter citric Hop Meadow IPA, Irish Pale Ale, and a smooth Hooker Lager.

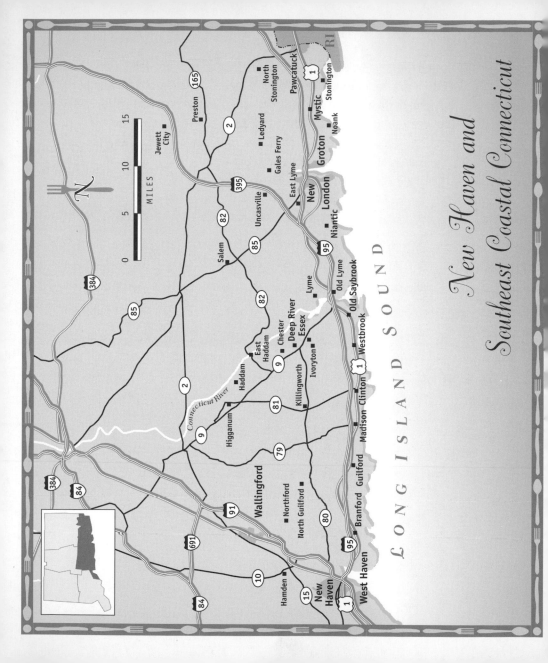

New Haven and
Southeast Coastal Connecticut

New Haven and Southeast Coastal Connecticut

As a college town—home to Yale University and the University of New Haven—the Elm City is a "happening" in and of itself. New Haven is the cultural magnet of this Long Island Sound coastline—with Yale University, two art museums, three theaters, symphonies, lectures, and arts events. The city's sixteen-acre Green is the site of music concerts and many arts festivals and events. And in the past few years, New Haven has also become one of the state's best, most wide-ranging restaurant cities, with a gastronomic variety—reflected in its Japanese, Chinese, Malaysian, Thai, Vietnamese, Korean, Turkish, Ethiopian, Lebanese, French, and Italian restaurants—as amazing as its cultural diversity. Wooster Street, the old Italian neighborhood, has its own ambience—with tiny stores, gelato parlors, pastry shops, restaurants, and pizzerias. There are so many pizzerias—and really good ones—in Greater New Haven that it is no surprise the city calls itself the pizza capital of America.

The entire southeast area of Connecticut has much to offer visitors who love good food and the good life. Just following the shore can keep you in seafaring and seafood nirvana, with stops at the picturesque seaside towns of Branford, Guilford, Madison, Clinton, and Westbrook along the way. Favorite summer habitats of vacationing New Yorkers, these towns have as their heritage beaches (including the expansive Hammonasset Beach State Park), inlets, points, and coves for fishing, swimming, and boating, as well as grassy New England greens and colonial houses. The 1639 Whitfield House in Guilford is believed to be the oldest stone building in New England. Guilford alone has several hundred seventeenth-, eighteenth-, and nineteenth-century houses and five distinguished historic house museums. It also has a village green that is considered one of the prettiest in the entire Northeast. Of equal appeal to visitors are the

various food options all along the shore: clam and lobster shacks, ice-cream parlors, delis, coffeehouses, cafes, and restaurants with water views.

The entire southeast coast is scalloped with scenic shore villages that are popular fishing and boating centers: Niantic, Waterford, Groton, and Noank. Of special nautical interest are this threesome: New London, at one time a whaling center, home to one of the United States' greatest playwrights (Eugene O'Neill) and now to the U.S. Coast Guard Academy; Mystic, with Mystic Seaport, the reconstructed nineteenth-century New England whaling village (where parts of the movie *Moby Dick* were filmed); and Stonington, almost too postcard-pretty to be real, with its old lighthouse and long, narrow Water Street.

Inland a few miles at Ledyard and Uncasville are Connecticut's two Indian casinos, Foxwoods and Mohegan Sun. Their prime interest to food lovers is not the gaming but the fifty-eight eateries they boast between them, at least two of which are upscale establishments run by famous Boston chefs Todd English and Jasper White. No more than a few miles in from this easternmost shore are orchards, fields of vegetables, and dairy and cattle farms.

Add to the litany of the area's prime attractions a clutch of delightful Connecticut River towns with four distinguished village inns among them, all noted for fine food. At East Haddam is Goodspeed Opera House, a landmark musical theater overlooking the river. Gillette Castle State Park, the former fantasy house-fortress of William Gillette (who popularized Sherlock Holmes on stage in the early twentieth century), roosts high above the river; its ample grounds are a state park, which welcomes picnicking and hiking. Essex, with its photogenic marina, Connecticut River Museum, and vintage steam train that runs on 12 miles of tracks along the river, is celebrated for its strict zoning code (no neon signs) and even more so for the fabulous Sunday brunch at its village inn. The river itself is the habitat of Connecticut's official state fish, the native shad; along the riverbanks you will see an occasional shad shack, where you can purchase this seasonal fish and its delicious roe.

Linking all the towns in the southeastern part of the state is an awakened commitment to fine food. Superb fresh seafood is a longtime "given," but in recent years there has been a flowering of new restaurants: Indian, Mexican, Thai, Vietnamese, and the like. They have been accompanied by excellent gourmet markets, delis, cheese shops, and bakeries that did not exist here twenty-odd years ago. The discoveries awaiting you are many.

Made or Grown Here

Chabaso, 360 James St., New Haven; (203) 562-7205; www
.chabaso.com. When Charles Negaro opened the cafe in his Atticus Bookstore in New Haven in 1981, he produced yummy pastries, bars, and cookies but tried in vain to find top-quality sandwich bread. Thus daunted, in 1995 he started his own bakery: Chabaso (named after his three children). Chabaso turns out a variety of breads—seven kinds of ciabatta, pugliese, seven-grain, country sourdough, cranberry-pecan multigrain, raisin, three kinds of baguettes (wheat, seeded, and Parisian)—and scores of delicious rolls, sweet rolls, and desserts. In addition to supplying Atticus, Chabaso wholesales to more than fifty stores in Connecticut, including Costco, Trader Joe's, Nica's in New Haven, Cilantro in Guilford, and Stony Creek Market in Branford. The late Julia Child once said, "How can a nation be great if its bread tastes like Kleenex?" With Chabaso around, Julia might have stopped worrying.

The Great Pizza War . . .
and the Winner Is—

In New Haven, the self-styled pizza capital of the world, the contest between **Frank Pepe Pizzeria Napoletano** (157 Wooster St.; 203-865-5762; www.pepespizzeria.com; $) and **Sally's Apizza** (237 Wooster St.; 203-624-5271; www.sallysapizza.com; $) has extended far beyond the confines of the old Italian neighborhood of Wooster Street. Fans (as in fanatics) of each are ready to fight (or eat) to the last savory bite. Pepe's is older, dating back to 1925, Sally's to 1938. Both serve thin-crusted, crispy-edged, smoky-flavored pies, whose dough is fed into authentic coal-fired brick pizza ovens at the ends of long-handled wooden peels. Both pizzerias feature a New Haven creation: white clam pie, made with fresh-shucked clams, garlic, oregano, olive oil, and grated pecorino cheese. The owner of Sally's once worked at Pepe's. I give the edge to Pepe's, smitten with its paper-thin, slightly salty, chewy crusts, fine-flavored ingredients, and the option of a dozen or more different toppings. It's fun to watch the Rhode Island littleneck clams being shucked for the white clam pizzas. Fans enjoy the pared-down basics of the pizza parlor itself, with its modest booths, plain metal trays lined with white butcher paper on which the oval pies are served, and pitchers of beer. Check out Sally's, too, as well as **The Spot,** owned by Pepe's, also located on Wooster Street, which in our book is Pizza Plaza, USA. Flash! Pepe's now has outposts in Fairfield (238 Commerce Dr.; 203-333-7333) and in Manchester (221 Buckland Hills Dr.; 860-644-7333), both in the same top form as the New Haven original.

The Cupcake Truck, various locations, New Haven; (203) 675-3965; www.followthatcupcake.com. Baking eight basic cupcakes fresh each day, then packing them into a refurbished bread truck, driving throughout the New Haven area to sell them one-on-one, like Good Humors: That's the concept Marsha and Todd Rowe developed. What's made it a successful recipe, aside from the freshness of the cupcakes, is the rich variety of the Rowe-made frostings, which allow customers to customize their confections. There are a few exotic favorites, like Chocolate Ruin, Red Velvet Jones, Sweet Potato Pecan, Lemon Meringue, and Loco Coconut, with special occasions and holidays meriting new creations. The truck parks at noon with the Cedar Street Food Carts but can be seen all over the downtown. Best advice is to "follow that cupcake."

Dryden & Palmer Co., 16 Business Park Dr., Branford; (203) 481-3725; www.rockcandy.com. This family-owned company has been making and wholesaling rock candy since 1880—crystals, swizzle sticks, rock candy on a string—selling to such stores as Chocolatier in Guilford and Munson's many stores, among other outlets.

Fabled Foods, 500 South Main St., Deep River; (860) 526-2666. Not only are the foods (i.e., breads) fabled but so is the story. This thriving artisan bakery began in 2000 in Deep River (having moved from New Milford, where Ina Bomze and her late husband, Austin Laber, ran a restaurant and bakery) and now wholesales its fabulous breads to upscale restaurants, markets (like Whole Foods), and shops all over the state (Gold's Deli in Westport for one). Austin

Fabled Eggplant, Pepper, and Onion Spread

Ina Bomze, proprietor of Fabled Foods in Deep River, is a dedicated cook and devout foodie. She shares this quick-to-assemble spread, which is easy to make and always a hit with guests. Try it with ciabatta crisps or sourdough crostini.

½ cup extra-virgin olive oil
3 tablespoons minced garlic
Pepperocini (according to your taste)
2 eggplants, cut into ¾-inch cubes

2 large red onions, cut into ¾-inch cubes
4 medium red bell peppers, cut into ½-inch pieces
¼ cup chopped parsley
Freshly ground black pepper to taste

1. Preheat oven to 450°F.
2. In a large bowl, mix olive oil, garlic, and pepperocini. Add eggplants, onions, and peppers and toss to coat.
3. Divide mixture between two large sheet pans. Roast, turning occasionally, until lightly browned. Cool for about 15 minutes.
4. Transfer half to food processor. Process until coarsely pureed (pulse). Transfer to a bowl and repeat with the rest of mixture. Season with pepper and mix in parsley. Serve at room temperature.

Makes 4 cups.

Fabled Foods
500 South Main St., Deep River
(860) 526-2666

Ina's Cannelini Beans and Escarole

This recipe of Fabled Foods' Ina Bomze's can be served as part of a vegetarian meal or as accompaniment to veal, beef, or another meat entree. As Ina says, "Mangia!"

1¼ cups dried Cannelini beans	6 garlic cloves, minced
2 tablespoons olive oil	1 large can plum tomatoes (San
¼ teaspoon red pepper flakes	Marzano preferred)
2 heads escarole, washed and	Rind of Parmigiano Reggiano
torn into pieces like a salad	2 tablespoons balsamic vinegar

1. Soak beans for 8 hours (or overnight). Drain.
2. Cook beans in a large pot with a generous amount of water covering them. Bring to a boil. Lower to a simmer for about an hour or hour and a half, depending on beans. Check beans for consistency after about an hour.
3. When beans are done, drain, reserving some of the liquid.
4. In a very large pot, heat oil, then add red pepper flakes. Add escarole with water clinging to the leaves. Then add garlic. Toss with tongs to coat everything. Add beans and toss to mix (gently).
5. With clean hands, tear the plum tomatoes over the pot into bite-size chunks. With a cleaver or chef's knife, cut rind of Parmigiano Reggiano into small pieces. As the cheese cooks over low heat, add a little bit of the reserved liquid from the beans to the mixture and sprinkle in the balsamic vinegar.
6. Continue simmering over a low flame for about 10–15 minutes. Then transfer to serving dish and serve.

Serves 4.

Fabled Foods
500 South Main St., Deep River
(860) 526-2666

was a self-taught baker, but with his untimely death in 2002, Ina is now the spark plug of this enterprise. Supported by a talented bake staff, she produces a best-selling sourdough bread, sourdough olive and rosemary, sourdough pecan raisin, several Italian rustic breads (pugliese and ciabatta), rye, pumpernickel, semolina batards, asiago boule, multigrain (with twelve grains), twelve-grain cranberry walnut, challah (Friday only), six-grain spelt (Saturday), and focaccia and caramelized onion rolls.

4 & Twenty Blackbirds Bakeshop, 610 Village Walk, Guilford; (203) 458-6900. At wicker chairs and tables outside, patrons sit next to flower-filled window boxes, reading *The New York Times* while sipping a cup of coffee and nibbling a fresh-baked muffin or almond scone. That is the modus operandi at this nifty bakeshop. If you sit inside, the pleasures also involve inhaling all the delicious baking aromas as batches of cookies, ruggelach, cakes, tortes, tarts, pastries, or pies (no, no blackbirds) emerge from the oven, which is visible behind the counter. Fruit tarts follow the local growing season. Saturday is specialty-bread day (like focaccia), but the scrumptious cakes and cheesecakes are daily delights. Mainly known for its exquisite desserts, the shop also sells a select array of chocolates, olive oils, imported pastas, and other high-end comestibles. Closed Monday.

Gelato Giuliana, 168 North Plains Industrial Rd., Wallingford; (203) 269-2200; www.gelatogiuliana.com. The fruit flavors in Giuliana Maravalle's gelatos have no dairy or fat; they are purely, intensely fruity, which is what makes them so delicious. In all, Giuliana's gelatos come in some thirty-seven flavors, plus five yogurt-based gelatos. There are also seasonal flavors, like pumpkin and panetone. Choosing is difficult. Will it be apple cobbler or honey pecan? Panna cotta or s'mores? Maybe peanut butter and chocolate. The gelatos are available at upscale shops, groceries, and restaurants in Connecticut and elsewhere in New England.

> "I doubt whether the world holds for any one a more soul-stirring surprise than the first adventure with ice cream."
>
> —Heywood Broun

Hallmark Drive-In, 113 Shore Rd., Old Lyme; (860) 434-1998; $. What is better on a sweltering day than an old-fashioned ice-cream stand along the shore? That's what Hallmark is, an unpretentious drive-in, in business for one hundred years in 2009. Gary and Peg Legein have owned it since 2000 and now make—in five-gallon batches at a time—twenty-five flavors, like strawberry and fresh peach in season, ginger (with imported ginger), grape nut, mint chip, Black Hall Mud (coffee, chocolate chips, Oreo cookies, and walnuts), banana nut, raspberry, and peanut-butter-cup crunch, all with 16 percent butterfat content. Still, in spite of the great flavor range, the most popular are vanilla, chocolate, and black raspberry. There is now a restaurant indoors, where you can get breakfast, as well as grinders and clam rolls. But on a warm day, nothing beats sitting outside in the picnic area, licking your ice cream and watching the Saybrook Point lighthouse in the distance. Open mid-March to mid-November.

Judies European Bakery, 63 Grove St., New Haven; (203) 777-6300; www.judies.net; $. Judies is a twofer: a bakery making appealing breads (sold retail and wholesale all along the shore) and a cafe specializing in lunches made from those breads. The breads include peasant and Italian baguettes, sesame breads, and panini. In addition to those regulars, every day a different specialty bread is baked, such as English oatmeal, Russian black, English cheddar, challah, herb bread, orange ricotta, brioches, and blueberry teacakes. The cafe, open weekdays, does a lively trade in soups and grilled sandwiches of all kinds, and it is a great place to stop by for coffee, cappuccino, or espresso.

Madison Chocolates, 908 Boston Post Rd., Madison; (203) 245-4335; www.madisonchocolates.com; $. Chocolatier Paul A. Staley, a CIA graduate and longtime chef, is living his dream, making limited batches of chocolates, using Felchlin Swiss chocolate. He creates twenty-seven types of truffles (Grand Marnier, hazelnut frangelico, and passion fruit among them), pavés (espresso, black currant, caramel crunch, et al.), solid chocolate bars (in milk chocolate, special-edition dark, dark, and bittersweet), and novelty pops in fun shapes. Boxed truffles are available in two- to-fifteen-piece assortments. This delightful shop also sells eight types of sandwiches, specialty cakes, and eleven flavors of handmade gelato daily. On weekends, Paul does a rousing breakfast business, too, with his own fresh-baked croissants and breads, eight different breakfast pastries, and three breakfast sandwiches. Call for hours.

Old Lyme Ice Cream Shoppe, 34 Lyme St., Old Lyme; (860) 434-6942; www.oldlymeicecream.com; $. Local folks swear by the creamy 16 percent butterfat content ice cream made here—with reason. Owners Lou Mae Albert and her son Steve Albert make thirty-five flavors in all (sixteen available daily), plus house-made Italian ices (try the lemon or strawberry kiwi). There are a few tables inside and out front where you may also enjoy take-out soups, sandwiches, muffins, and Danish pastries. But the ice cream and ices are the big draw, along with coffee from the self-serve bar just inside the door. Closed January to mid-March, depending on the weather.

Palmieri Food Products, Inc., 145 Hamilton St., New Haven; (800) 845-5447; www.palmierifoods.com. Since 1920 the Palmieri family has been making all-natural, additives-free pasta sauces. At

present they have twelve tomato-based sauces, along with horseradish and cocktail sauces, a salsa, a barbecue sauce, and a buffalo-chicken-wing dip, all distributed and sold around the state at Stop & Shop stores, Shaw's, XPECT Stores, and Geissler Markets and, in this area, at Robert's Food Center, Madison. The spaghetti sauce remains Palmieri's most popular item. Palmieri's is also a bottling facility for many small producers, such as farmers who want to transform excess crops into bottled sauces and spreads, to sell at their farm stands.

Pasta Cosi, 3 Linden Ave., Branford; (203) 483-9397; www.billys pastacosi.com/store. Pasta Cosi, a line of five robust, flavorful Italian sauces, was developed in Billy DiLegge's funky little Italian restaurant, **Billy's Pasta Cosi,** at this Branford location. There are fourteen sauces in the line. They include roasted garlic, vodka, arrabbiata, puttanesca, and marinara and are sold at Andy's Food Mart in East Haven and stores throughout the state. They are also available at the restaurant and via mail order.

Sankow's Beaver Brook Farm, 139 Beaverbrook Rd., Lyme; (860) 434-2843; www.beaverbrookfarm.com. Suzanne and Stanley Sankow are multitaskers. Using the wool from their Romney sheep—part of a flock of 700 that roams their 175-acre farm—they make blankets, sweaters, caps, hats, scarves, and mittens, which are sold in the wool shop on the grounds. From the East Frisian sheep and Jersey cows (all raised free of growth hormones and antibiotics), Suzanne produces some great farmstead cheeses (Summer Savory, feta, Pleasant Valley, Nehantic Abbey, and Farmstead among them), ricotta, and thick yogurt, available in the farm market shop on the grounds, along with USDA-inspected lamb roasts, chops, patties, and sausages (salami, pastrami, Land Jäger, and garlic-fennel). Pleasant Cow, Sankow's most popular cow's-milk cheese, was chosen by *Saveur* magazine as one of the fifty best cheeses made in the United States. This is one of the few dairies in the state licensed to sell raw milk.

Products made in Sankow's farm kitchen by Stuart London, former chef at the Old Lyme Inn, are sold in the farm market shop as well: shepherd's pie, lamb-and-feta turnovers, lamb curry stew, cheese spreads like horseradish ricotta and Greek tzatziki, and ten delicious ice-cream flavors. The two shops are open from 9:00 a.m. to 4:00 p.m. daily.

Sankow products, including Stanley's heirloom and greenhouse tomatoes, are available at farmers' markets in Greenwich, Westport, West Hartford, and Wooster Square in New Haven, as well as at Whole Foods, Highland Park, and Bishop's Orchards markets. On the Saturday and Sunday after Thanksgiving, Sankow's holds its Annual Farm Days, when visitors may watch the sheep shearing, sample meats and cheeses, enjoy a horse-drawn hayride over the grounds, and watch spinning demonstrations. It's a fun time down at the farm.

Stonington Seafood Harvesters, 4 High St., Stonington; (860) 535-8342. This small, one-family company is famous among discerning Connecticut chefs for its sea scallops, which Captain Billy Bomster Jr. and his brothers Joe and Mike dredge from the Atlantic Ocean depths on their western-rigged scallop trawler, the *F/V Patty Jo.* What makes the Bomster scallops different is that they are shucked by the crew and flash-frozen in heavy, one-pound plastic pouches within minutes of coming onboard, instead of sitting on ice in the hold for two weeks before the boat lands.

This quick process protects the flavor, color, and firmness, leading family patriarch Bill Bomster to believe they are the "world's finest all-natural, unadulterated, scrumptious sea scallops." Judge for yourself. You can order with UPS next-day delivery to your door. The scallops come in five one-pound pouches shipped in a foam box that preserves their cryogenic condition. At the Bomster self-service freezer (address above), the scallops, along with fresh-frozen local seafood (cod, flounder, tuna steaks, handcut salmon fillets), are for sale on the honor system. You can also buy them from McQuade's Marketplace in Mystic, among many area outlets. Seasonally, from July to November, the Bomsters sell Key West pink shrimp, too. Open year-round every day, dawn to dusk.

Walking Wood, 104 Seymour Rd. (Route 67), Woodbridge; (203) 393-1029; wooziewikfors@snet.net. Woozie Wikfors began raising poultry in 1998 when a friend gave her two adolescent emus. They're still laying and may for another forty years—emus live long productive lives. She sold their huge deep forest green eggs at a premium and soon found herself raising chickens as well. She now has thirty different heritage breeds, which include Cochin and Polish crested hens, and now raises ducks too. All the livestock are free-range and organic, scampering over her five-and-one-half acres (which back on to 300 acres). Woozie calls them "my girls" and praises to the sky the merits of free-range and organic. During the season, Woozie sells her eggs at several farmers' markets. She also sells chickens and rabbits.

"One cannot think well, love well, sleep well, if one has not dined well."

—VIRGINIA WOOLF, *A Room of One's Own*

Wentworth Homemade Ice Cream, 3697 Whitney Ave., Hamden; (203) 281-7429. Since 1988 Regina Banos's homey ice-cream parlor, in an old house with a gazebo and yard, has been going strong. Her forty flavors of natural house-made ice creams are delicious, with 16 percent butterfat content and all-natural flavorings. The coffee ice cream begins with brewed coffee, and the peach, banana, and other fruit ice creams are all made with real fresh fruits. Flavors include butter pecan, rum raisin, Heath bar crunch, Snickers cheesecake, mint Oreo, mocha lace, and chocolate fudge brownie, plus, in the fall, coconut-pineapple and pumpkin. There's even ice cream for dogs: K-9 crunch (cay-nine, get it?). A second Wentworth branch is at 44 Center St., Wallingford; (203) 265-2814. Both stores are open Monday through Thursday from 11 a.m. to 9:30 p.m., Friday and Saturday until 10:00 p.m. year-round. Cash only.

> Thornton Wilder, who lived twenty-nine years in Hamden, once wrote, "My advice to you is not to inquire why or whither, but just enjoy your ice cream while it is on your plate."

Specialty Stores & Markets

Andy's Food Mart, 670 Main St., East Haven; (203) 467-2639; www.andysfoodmart.com. Calling itself "your window to Arthur Avenue and Italy," this multipurpose market carries Pasta Cosi sauces and many of the fresh pastas that Billy DiLegge makes for his Branford Pasta Cosi restaurant (penne, fusilli, lasagna, linguine, rigatoni, and bucatini among them). In addition, Andy's sells all kinds of cheeses (Italian, Irish, and Quebec cheddars, and Beltane Farm's goat cheese, to name a few), prepared dinners (chicken marsala, meat loaf, venison, and others), and various imported Italian food treats.

Ashlawn Farm, 78 Bill Hill Rd., Lyme; (860) 434-3636; www.farm coffee.com. Chip and Daphne Dahlke have turned their century-old, one-hundred-acre family farm into a coffee roastery. Some twenty types of coffee beans, from all over the coffee-growing world, eight decafs, and more than seven flavored coffees are roasted in the old milking barn. Chip sells to upscale shops and restaurants in this area and claims coffee doesn't get any fresher than Ashlawn's. Closed Sunday and Monday.

Atlantic Seafood, 1400–1410 Boston Post Rd., Old Saybrook; (860) 388-4527. New and larger space is a backdrop for the freshest of fish and shellfish presented on immaculate trays in refrigerated display cases in this compelling market. The freezer packed with seafood dishes—stuffed clams, clam chowder, lobster bisque, marinated mussels, fish entrees, seafood pies, eight to ten different salads, house-made crab cakes, and other dishes (all made in-house)—is especially attention-grabbing. "Only the Freshest" is the Atlantic Seafood motto, and you are urged to call ahead to find out what piscine wonders have just arrived from Point Judith, Rhode Island, or New Bedford, Massachusetts, the seagoing sources of all these nautical treasures of the deep. If you're planning an

old-fashioned clambake, Atlantic Seafood can be the source for everything you need, except the logs and sandpit. Wild Alaskan salmon, sushi-fresh yellowfin tuna, littleneck and steamer clams, Mystic River oysters, sea scallops, mako shark, whole live lobsters, and all kinds of tasty fresh fish are available.

Bon Appetit, 2979 Whitney Ave., Hamden; (203) 248-0648; www .bonappetitct.com. In 1971 Roland and Andrea Blakeslee opened their gourmet food shop and have stayed ahead of the curve ever since. Today this attractive, well-organized shop is like a wish list of every delicacy you can imagine: condiments, dips and spreads, dessert sauces, deli meats and salads, jams, mustards, oils, olives, rices, teas, vinegars. A large assortment of local, regional, and international cheeses is flanked by glass-covered displays of fresh croissants, bagels, Danish, pastries, cookies, and luscious cakes. Tables, cupboards, display cases, even wine barrel tops are covered with good things to eat from all over the world, including Connecticut.

Caseus Fromagerie & Bistro, 93 Whitney Ave., New Haven; (203) 624-3373; www.caseusnewhaven.com. Caseus is two-faced: a remarkable cheese shop and a bistro serving lunch and dinner ($$). As a cheese shop (whose name means milk curds separated from the whey into molds), Caseus on its two levels unfolds a wide world of wonderful artisanal cheeses (more than one hundred), both domestic and imported. Keeping the cheeses company are olives, honeys, unusual pickles, Vosges and Poco Dolce chocolates, Raphael jams from France, Valderrama extra-virgin olive oil from Spain,

Jim's organic Wonderbrew coffee, and other select food items. As a bistro, in limited space, Caseus functions no less well, serving both French-inspired lunch and dinner. The shop is open Monday and Tuesday from 10:30 a.m. to 5:00 p.m., Wednesday through Saturday until 6:00 p.m. For bistro hours check the Web site.

The Cooking Company, Swing Bridge Market Place, 1610 Saybrook Rd., Haddam; (860) 345-8008. Subtitled "A Prepared Food Market," this is no small-potatoes operation. Chef-owner Susan Bauer and two assistants prepare a vast panoply of delicious foods for customers to take away, reheat, and consume at home. (It is also possible to nosh on the premises at one of eight seats or, in warm weather, just outside.) Fresh salads (like grilled chicken Caesar pasta, Greek, or Cobb), soups, prepared entrees (walnut-crusted pork loin, Greek chicken, chicken enchiladas, among a rotating list), frittatas, sandwiches (twelve different ones, including grilled panini), and multilayered wraps are a few of the freshly made possibilities. There are deli items (Genoa salami, maple-smoked turkey, spicy capocollo ham) and a small frozen-foods section, where soups, appetizers, and desserts are showcased. To tempt the sweet tooth, there are fruit pies, cookies, brownies, and cakes. A coffee bar with Daybreak and Ashlawn Farm coffees is just inside the entrance, and a rear room is stocked with fancy gourmet items: olive oils, vinegars, pickled vegetables, preserves, and other comestibles. A second, larger Cooking Company shop is at 187 Route 81, Killingworth; (860) 663-3111. It has a patio and make-your-own salad bar, plus double the seating.

Cook's Kitchen, 620 Boston Post Rd., Guilford; (203) 533-4325; www.cooks-kitchen .com. Debbie and Stan Harris have moved from their Madison location with their cooking shop concepts intact—lock, stock, and cutting knives. Their sparkling new facility carries high-end cookware, cutlery,  and culinary tools. They also offer gourmet foods, from aged balsamic vinegars and various oils from around the world, to truffles, Madagascar vanilla products, and Stonewall Kitchen's jams, chutneys, and mustards. There is ample space for cooking classes. (See below under Learn to Cook.) The Harrises also conduct culinary tours to Tuscany, Umbria, and Chile. Open Monday through Saturday 10:00 a.m. to 5:00 p.m. Closed Sunday.

Dr. Lankin's Specialty Foods, 220 Route 12, Suite 5 #391 Rd., Groton; (888) 256-6635; www.awesomealmond.com. For a primary-care physician to develop a side business selling almonds may sound slightly, um, nutty, but these almonds are for real. So is Dr. Ken Lankin. Studying almonds for a college thesis on nutrition gave him a desire to experiment with roasting and flavoring these tasty nuts. Eventually he created Awesome Almonds in three flavors: orange-vanilla, cinnamon-vanilla, and cocoa-java. According to the good doctor, the California-grown almonds are good for cholesterol, heart disease, obesity, and other health problems. You can buy the Awesomes directly from the firm's Web site or at Mystic Sweets & Ice Cream Shoppe in Mystic and Lee's Oriental Market in New London, among many shops in this area. The nuts have no preservatives, salt, cholesterol, or added oils and are a vegan and kosher-certified product.

Fromage Fine Foods and Coffees, 873 Boston Post Rd., Old Saybrook; (860) 388-5750; www.fromagefinefoods.com. In moving from square footage of 300 to 1,800, this delightful gourmet shop has prospered and now has more tasties than ever. Owner Christine Chesanek sells some 150 different international cheeses, intriguing house-made cheese spreads, and customized gift baskets and cheese platters. On display are containers with eighteen types of olives, a charcuterie sec- 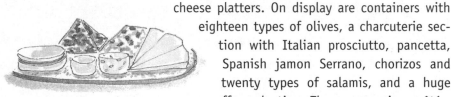 tion with Italian prosciutto, pancetta, Spanish jamon Serrano, chorizos and twenty types of salamis, and a huge coffee selection. There are venison pâtés, interesting breads, fresh pastries, teas, spices, condiments, olive oils, and a frozen-food section with ready-to-heat duck breasts, phyllo hors d'oeuvres (sold by the dozen), and other items. In short, it's one-stop shopping if you're planning a party. With all the extra space, Christine has added a fine display of high-end glass- and tableware, teapots, and other table accessories.

Given Fine Chocolates & Indulgences, 696 Boston Post Rd., Madison; (203) 245-4646; www.givenchocolates.com. It's a "given" that this is the place to shop for all kinds of candies, so you might as well give in. The selection ranges from Garrison and Moonstruck chocolate truffles to Knipschildt (whom some consider the Tiffany of handmade chocolates). Given's distinctive robin's-egg blue boxes make great gifts. Create your own truffle collection, chocolate platter, or holiday gift baskets. Indulge the kiddies in your care at the "candy wall"—lined with huge glass jars of jelly beans, other penny candies, and retro candy bars.

Hong Kong Grocery, 71 Whitney Ave., New Haven; (203) 777-8881. Cluttered aisles and crammed-together cans, bags, and jars of all kinds of Chinese foods do not deter the crowds from this diminutive, if sometimes confusing, market. A prime source of fresh Chinese produce, twenty-five-pound sacks of rice, and scores of hard-to-find Chinese and other Asian items, it is no wonder the place is jammed most of the time.

Lee's Oriental Market, 432 Williams St., New London; (860) 443-9665. What this small market lacks in size it makes up for in variety and orderliness. A fresh-food case has, among other veggies, napa cabbage, daikon, Korean radishes, bitter melons, lemongrass, and soybean sprouts. In the freezer are soybean kernels, egg-roll wrappers, gyoza skins, fish and fish cakes, grated cassava, and shumai dim sum. There are shelves full of various teas, a wide range of rice (including twenty-five-pound sacks of Thai jasmine rice and sticky rice), dried mushrooms, roasted sesame seeds in quantity, gallon tins of soy sauce, packaged soups, and assorted candies and sweets. Chinese foods dominate, but there are Japanese, Filipino, Korean, and Thai goods as well, all neatly presented in well-kept surroundings.

The Life of Riley Irish Imports, 881 Boston Post Rd., Old Saybrook; (860) 388-6002 or (800) 404-7956; www.lifeof rileyirishimports.com. Begorrah, all kinds of Irish goods, perfumes, Celtic jewelry, Galway Irish crystal, figurines, walking sticks, books, and cards are displayed in Tracey Riley's compact shop devoted solely to the Emerald Isle. Food products include Bewley's and other Irish teas, biscuits, cookies, scone mixes, Hogan's brown bread, jams, mustards, candy, and frozen foods like Galtee bacon, bangers, and black pudding (blood sausage). The shop opened in 1986 and is still going strong.

Liuzzi Cheese, 322 State St., North Haven; (203) 248-4356; www .liuzzicheese.com. As Italian delis go, Liuzzi Cheese is a standout. It not only sells numerous cheeses (including Spanish Garrotxa and Natural Valley's raw goat cheese from Wisconsin), as its name suggests, but also stocks all kinds of cold cuts, twenty types of olives, marinated mushrooms and anchovies, and scores of dried goods like olive oils and pastas. In addition, there are take-home entrees (ham pie, house-made meatballs, spinach lasagna) and fresh-frozen pastas. All this and a butcher counter with fresh cuts of meat. Open Monday through Saturday, 8:30 a.m. to 6:00 p.m.

Mystic Market East, 63 Williams Ave., Mystic; (860) 572-7992; www.mysticmarket.com. This intriguing market specializes—in its words—in "catering * cuisine * confection." The confections are awesome: elegant cakes, cannoli, tarts, éclairs, pies, and dessert trays of miniature pastries. There are cheeses from all over the world, humongous varieties of fresh-baked breads, condiments, and other comestibles to satisfy most gourmet needs. If you want someone else to do the work for your party, wedding, or other special "do," the market, in its catering wing, called **Coastal Gourmet,** offers numerous specialty menus. Open Monday through Saturday 7:00 a.m. to 7:00 p.m, Sunday 8:00 a.m. to 5:00 p.m. **Mystic Market West,** a second Mystic Market, is at 375 Noank Rd. (Route 215); (860) 536-1500.

Saeed's International Market, 464 Ocean Ave., New London; (860) 440—3822; $. This popular Middle Eastern–Mediterranean grocery has space galore—3,500 square feet of space. Owner Potti Said carries cheeses from France, Italy, Spain, Albania, Bulgaria, Syria, and Israel. A deli case features meats, spinach and cheese pies, baklava, and other honeyed pastries. An olive bar displays twelve different bins of briny olives. Grains include couscous, mograyeh (Israeli toasted couscous), and lentils, plus all kinds of nuts, spices, and seeds. Also available: kosher and Italian organic lines; olive oils from all over the Mediterranean and other oils (walnut, almond, grape seed, basil, sesame, hazelnut, and pepper); hummus, Greek yogurt, and taramasalata; and a variety of breads and baked goods. At any of ten tables, you can sit and munch gyros and other hot sandwiches or, for breakfast, fresh-baked croissants, bagels, and assorted pastries, along with a cup of coffee from an expanded coffee list.

Open Monday through Saturday from 9:00 a.m. to 7:00 p.m. Closed Sunday.

Simon's Marketplace, 17 Main St., Chester; (860) 526-8984; $. Tiny as Chester is, it has blossomed into a real "foodie" town. Credit this large, wonderfully inclusive market, now owned by Jim and Jody Reilly, for some of the local excitement. The spacious store has twenty-four seats for breakfast, lunch, and snacking. Other attractions include a gourmet delicatessen case with salads, meats, and sausages by the pound; an appealing imported cheese selection; Jim's organic Free Trade coffees in bulk; ten flavors of Salem Valley Farms ice cream; and such staples as milk, yogurt, cream cheese, and butter. Takeout dishes, like shepherd's pie and stuffed eggplant, are made on the premises. Another big draw: fresh-made scones (different each day); four types of buckwheat crepes and six sweet ones; and a slew of sandwiches. Open Monday through Saturday 8:00 a.m. to 6:00 p.m., Sunday to 5:00 p.m.

Star Fish Market, 650 Village Walk, Guilford; (203) 458-3474; www.starfishmkt.com. I am not out to sea when I call this the prettiest seafood store I have ever seen, with displays so artistic you might think you are in an art gallery. The fish are displayed on plates in the refrigerated glass case, one fillet or fish per plate, sometimes with a single sprig of herb adorning it—sea-fresh, pristine, immaculate. The entire shop is just as beautiful, with shelves and tables full of deluxe products: olive oils, dried pastas, sauces, seafood accoutrements. A section with frozen and smoked fish, sausage, Niman

MYSTIC PIZZA . . .
MAYBE ONLY JULIA KNOWS FOR SURE

Not to stoke fires of rivalry, but **Mystic Pizza,** a pizzeria in Mystic, claims it is the site and inspiration for the movie *Mystic Pizza,* which catapulted Julia Roberts to fame. But don't tell that to folks in Stonington, who claim the movie was filmed at a pizzeria, now defunct, on Water Street in their town, not Mystic.

Ranch meats, chicken, and game is also inviting, as are the large and choice imported cheese selections and bread display. Star Fish, a sterling little store in an upscale shopping complex, is a work of art, a still life of perfection. Open Tuesday through Friday 9:00 a.m. to 6:00 p.m., Saturday to 5:30 p.m. Closed Sunday and Monday.

Sweet Cioccolata, 28 North Colony St. (Route 5), Wallingford; (203) 294-1280; www.sweetcioccolata.com. Since 1998 Rachel Ceste has been selling her unusual chocolates, wholesale and retail. "Create your own gift" is her motto, and the shop is full of baskets and individually wrapped chocolates (like almond bark, chocolate peanut clusters, and chocolate-covered pretzels), to be individually selected by you and popped into the basket (there are preassembled baskets too if you don't want to choose your own). House-made treats include chocolate-dipped strawberries, dried apricots and pears, chocolate-covered Oreos and shortbreads, and chocolate turtles. Very popular are caramel-dipped, chocolate-covered apples and pears. Open Monday through Friday 9:00 a.m. to 5:00 p.m., Saturday to 3:00 p.m. Closed Sunday.

Farmers' Markets

For up-to-the-minute information about dates and hours, which can change from year to year, call the Connecticut Department of Agriculture at (860) 713-2503, visit the Web site at www.state .ct.us/doag, or e-mail ctdeptag@po.state.ct.us.

Branford Farmers' Market, parking lot behind Town Green, Branford. Sunday from 10:00 a.m. to 1:00 p.m., mid-June through October.

Chester Village Farmers' Market, town center, Chester. Sunday from 9:00 a.m. to 1:00 p.m., mid-June through October.

Clinton Farmers' Market, 48 Main St., Clinton. Friday from 3:00 to 6:00 p.m., end of May through October.

Clinton-Chamard Vineyards Farmers' Market, 115 Cow Hill Rd., Clinton. Sunday from noon to 3:00 p.m., late May to October.

Deep River Farmers' Market, Deep River Library, Main St., Deep River. Thursday from 3:30 to 7:00 p.m., June through mid-October.

Deep River Lace Factory Farmers' Market, 161 River St., Deep River. Wednesday 3:00 to 6:30 p.m. and Saturday 9:00 a.m. to 1:00 p.m., early June to November.

Durham Farmers' Market, Town Green (Route 17), Durham. Thursday from 3:00 to 6:00 p.m., early May to early September.

East Haven Farmers' Market, East Haven Town Hall, East Haven. Sunday from 9:00 a.m. to noon, from mid-July to first week of October.

East Lyme Farmers' Market, East Lyme High School parking lot, East Lyme. Sunday from 10:00 a.m. to 1:00 p.m., mid-July to October.

Essex Farmers' Market, Main St., behind the Griswold Inn, Essex. Friday from 3:00 to 6:00 p.m., from mid-June through October.

Griswold/Jewett City Farmers' Market, Griswold Town Hall, 28 Main St., Jewett City. Monday from 3:00 to 6:30 p.m., mid-June to early November.

Groton Farmers' Market, Groton Shopping Plaza, next to the post office (Route 1), Groton. Wednesday from 2:00 to 6:00 p.m., mid-July through October.

Hamden—Downtown Farmers' Market, Town Center Park, next to Miller Library, 2663 Dixwell Ave., Hamden. Friday from 11:00 a.m. to 3:00 p.m., end of June to first week of October.

Hamden–Spring Glen Farmers' Market, Spring Glen Church, 1825 Whitney Ave., Hamden. Tuesday from 3:00 to 6:00 p.m., from late June through October.

Higganum Village Market Farmers' Market, Town Green, Higganum. Friday from 3:30 to 7:00 p.m., late May through October.

Ledyard Farmers' Market, Route 117, Tri-Town Center parking lot, Ledyard. Friday from 3:00 to 6:00 p.m., early June to early October.

Madison Farmers' Market, 261 Meeting House Rd., Madison Historic Town Green, Madison. Friday from 3:00 to 6:00 p.m., early June through September.

Mystic/Denison Farmers' Market, across from Denison/ Pequotsepus Nature Center, 120 Pequotsepus Rd., Mystic. Sunday from noon to 3:00 p.m., early June through September.

Mystic Farmers' Market, Quiambaug Fire House, 50 Old Stonington Rd., Mystic. Tuesday from 2:00 to 6:00 p.m., May through October.

New Haven Edgewood Park Farmers' Market, Edgewood Park, corner of West Rock and Whalley Ave., New Haven. Sunday from 10:00 a.m. to 2:00 p.m., late June to late November.

New Haven Downtown Farmers' Market, Church St. at the Green, New Haven. Wednesday from 11:00 a.m. to 3:00 p.m., mid-June to late November. Like all the New Haven farmers' markets listed here, this is a project of CitySeed, a local nonprofit dedicated to promoting local development and sustainable farming (203-773-3736; www.cityseed.org). All the market items are from Connecticut farms, and most are organic or pesticide-free.

New Haven Fair Haven Farmers' Market, Quinnipiac River Park, corner of Grand Ave. and Front St., New Haven. Thursday from 3:00 to 7:00 p.m., ealy July through October.

New Haven State Street Farmers' Market, grassy lot next to 1013 State St., in front of State and Mechanic, New Haven. Saturday from 9:00 a.m. to 1:00 p.m., August 1st to late November.

New Haven Wooster Square Farmers' Market, Russo Park, DePalma Ct. between Chapel and Wooster Streets, New Haven. Saturday from 9:00 a.m. to 1:00 p.m., mid-May through mid-December; then every other Saturday from 10:00 a.m. to 1:00 p.m., from the second week of January to May. This is the only New Haven farmers' market to be open throughout the year.

New London Farmers' Market, Municipal Parking Lot, corner of Eugene O'Neill Dr. and Pearl St., New London. Tuesday and Friday from 10:00 a.m. to 2:00 p.m., early July through October.

New London-Fiddleheads Food Coop Farmers' Market, 13 Broad St., New London. Saturday from 9:00 a.m. to 4:00 p.m., year-round.

North Guilford–Dudley Farmers' Market, 2351 Durham Rd., North Guilford. Saturday from 9:00 a.m. to 12:30 p.m., first week of June through October.

Old Saybrook Farmers' Market, Cinema Plaza, 210 Main St., Old Saybrook. Saturday from 9:00 a.m. to 1:00 p.m. and Wednesday from 10:00 a.m. to 1:00 p.m., late June through October.

Orange Farmers' Market, Orange city fair grounds, 525 Orange Center Rd., Orange. Wednesday from 3:30 to 6:30 p.m., late June to October.

Stonington Farmers' Market, Town Fishing Fleet Pier, Stonington. Saturday from 9:00 a.m. to noon, early May to November.

Wallingford Gardeners' Market, Railroad Station Green, Quinnipiac, Hall Ave. and Colony Rd. (Route 5), Wallingford. Saturday from 9:00 a.m. to noon, early July through mid-September. Cooking demonstrations feature local produce and gardeners' products.

West Haven Farmers' Market, West Haven Green, corner of Campbell and Main, West Haven. Thursday from 11:00 a.m. to 6:00 p.m. and Saturday from 10:00 a.m. to 2:00 p.m., early July through October.

Farm Stands

Bishop's Orchards, 1355 Boston Post Rd., Guilford; (203) 458-7425; www.bishopsorchards.com. This is one big operation with a market, bakery, and winery—like a mini supermarket. Five generations of Bishops have farmed here since 1871. Of the farm's 320 acres, 140 are devoted to apples alone, 22 to peaches, 27 to pears, plus miscellaneous parcels for strawberries, blueberries, raspberries, and pumpkins. You may pick your own from June through October. Seasonal fruits are offered as they ripen: strawberries first, in mid-June; blueberries next, July to September; raspberries and peaches, in mid-August; pears and apples at the end of August; and apples and raspberries continuing into mid-October. Oh yes, pumpkins ripen in late September and are around for Halloween. Bishop's sells their produce, their own pies and breads, apple cider, apple butter and other preserves with their label, cut flowers, fruit baskets, and gift packs (which they will ship). The market also sells some grocery items made elsewhere. Open daily year-round, Sunday 9:00 a.m. to 6:00 p.m., Monday through Saturday 8:00 a.m. to 7:00 p.m.

A second, seasonal Bishop's location at 1920 Middletown Ave. in Northford (203-458-PICK) specializes in pick-your-own apples only. It is open September through October, weekends only, from 9:00 a.m. to 5:00 p.m.

Four Mile River Farm & Greenhouse, 124 Four Mile River Rd., Old Lyme; (860) 434-2378; www.fourmileriverfarm.com. Teaching history for years in Hamden wasn't enough for Nunzio Corsino II, so in 1985 he began to farm his eighteen acres, raising, without chemicals, antibiotics, or growth hormones, Yorkshire pigs (twelve at a time), Angus, Hereford, and Charloisis cattle (a herd of thirty to thirty-five), and free-range laying hens (one hundred). The certified meats are cut, processed, vacuum-packed, and flash-frozen. Nunzio markets directly from his farm, at five farmers' markets, and to area restaurants (River Tavern in Chester and Flood Tide in Mystic, for instance). The Corsino farm stand (with a freezer inside one of the outbuildings) has fresh eggs, steaks of various sizes, beef patties, beef kielbasa, mulch hay, and handcrafts made by Irene, Nunzio's wife—all sold on the honor system. Pigs are by special orders with customers requesting in advance the desired division: chops, roast, ham steaks, bacon, and the like.

Hindinger Farm, 835 Dunbar Hill Rd., Hamden; (203) 288-0700; www.hindingerfarm.com. From the hills here you can see across Long Island Sound, a view Ann Hindinger, her late husband, Bill, and their children George and Liz have enjoyed for years, as did Bill's grandfather when he bought the farm in 1893. The produce is raised using modern techniques and sold at the Hindingers' farm stand. Depending on the season, you'll find apples, peaches, pears, strawberries, and such vegetables as asparagus, rhubarb, peas, cucumbers, beans, eggplant, and especially sweet corn and tomatoes. All these are at the stand, as they ripen, beginning the first of May right up to Christmas, from 9:00 a.m. to 6:00 p.m. Tuesday to Friday, to 5:00 p.m. weekends. In addition to this fresh bounty, the Hindingers have added jellies, jams, salsas, maple syrup, fresh flowers, and gifts. Each year the family holds a strawberry festival in June, with shortcake, ice cream, and pies, plus hayrides using their two tractors—and those wonderful views; call for date and time.

Holmberg Orchards, 12 Orchard Dr., Route 12, Gales Ferry; (860) 464-7107; www.holmbergorchards.com. Here's another big farm and orchard beckoning you to pick fruit as it ripens: fifteen varieties of apples, peaches, pears, nectarines, blueberries, raspberries, and pumpkins in season. You can finish up at the big farm market building for its freshly baked pies, turnovers, muffins, applesauce and apple crisp, newly harvested vegetables, and fresh-pressed apple cider. Stop by in the fall for their bales of hay, gourds, corn-stalks, winter squash, and dried flowers. Open year-round, daily from 9:00 a.m. to 6:00 p.m., with pick-your-own fruits available from July through October. Postscript: Russell Holmberg, fourth generation of Holmbergs to work the farm, partners with Margaret Chatey of Westford Hill Distillers in producing pears in her eau-de-vie bottles. To some 429 Bartlett pear blossoms he attaches her fancy Italian bottles with, sometimes, as many as twenty-five bottles "sprouting" on a single tree. Then—voilà!—in time the pear grows within each bottle. The end result is Westford Hill's Poire Prisonnière eau-de-vie.

J. DeFrancesco & Sons, Forest Rd., Northford; (203) 484-2028; defrancescofarm@att.net.com. Anthony DeFrancesco began truck farming here in the 1900s, gradually expanding the farm—and his family, eventually siring four sons—with his wife, Philomena. At present, their grandson Joe, his wife, Linda, and *their* four sons run the one hundred acres that now include seven acres of greenhouses for flowers. Outdoor plantings of fruit and vegetables include peas, beans, strawberries, tomatoes, eggplants, cantaloupes, watermelons, a dozen varieties of sweet corn, and pumpkins. These are sold to stores, restaurants, and at the farm stand, over which Linda reigns. The stand is in a venerable old horse-and-carriage barn and is open daily from Palm Sunday through Halloween, from 7:00 a.m. to 6:00 p.m. in summer. Call for specific days and hours in other seasons. The proceeds of the admission fee to the corn maze go to treat autism.

Digesting Hamburger History

Louis' Lunch, 261–263 Crown St., New Haven; (203) 562-5507; www.louislunch.com; $; is a local celebrity and here's why. New Havenites insist that the hamburger was born in their city, the creation of Louis Lassen in 1900. According to Louis's grandson Ken, it was midday when a man dashed in to Louis's luncheonette and breathlessly ordered a quick meal he could eat on the run. Louis slapped a freshly broiled beef patty between two slices of bread, and the customer rushed away, unaware he was part of history. Louis' (pronounced "Louie") Lunch is a pocket-size landmark on the National Register of Historic Places. Moved from its original spot in 1967, the tiny redbrick building with its red-shuttered windows was reconstructed, with bricks contributed by hundreds of nostalgic devotees. Ken Lassen still uses Louis's original recipe, broiling each fresh-ground beef patty—reportedly more than 90 percent lean, ground fresh each morning—on the antique vertical cast-iron grill, serving it between toasted bread slices. Cheddar cheese spread, fresh tomato, and caramelized  onion are the garnishes of choice. And whatever you do, don't ask for mustard or ketchup, which are taboo to Louis purists. Closed Sunday, Monday, the second week of January, Good Friday through Easter Sunday, and all of August for "the annual spoon inventory."

Simple Chicken Piccata

This dish is a favorite of Debbie Harris of Cook's Kitchen in Guilford. It is both a cinch to make and a sure hit with guests.

4 boneless chicken breasts

2 eggs (mixed together with water to make an egg wash)

Panko bread crumbs (seasoned or unseasoned)

3 lemons

Extra-virgin olive oil to coat bottom of pan

White wine

2 tablespoons butter

½ cup chicken broth

Salt and pepper to taste

Four sprigs of fresh parsley

1. Preheat oven to 325°F.
2. Dredge chicken breasts in egg wash and then panko.
3. Slice 1½ lemons in thin rings, carefully popping out seeds. Ream other 1½ lemons and reserve juice.
4. Using a nonstick pan to maintain coating, heat pan, and sauté chicken breasts in the butter and extra-virgin olive oil until golden brown on both sides. Remove chicken breasts and place on ovenproof serving platter and keep warm in oven for no more than ten minutes. Meanwhile, place slices of lemon in pan and sauté a few minutes on each side until slightly translucent. Remove and reserve.
5. Deglaze pan with white wine, and add chicken broth, salt, and pepper to taste. Remove serving dish from the oven.
6. Place slices of lemon on chicken pieces, pour sauce over chicken, garnish with parsley, and serve.

Serves 4.

Cook's Kitchen
620 Boston Post Rd., Guilford
(203) 533-4325
www.cooks-kitchen.com

Maple Lane Farm, 57 Northwest Corner Rd., Preston; (860) 889-3766, twenty-four-hour picking hot line (860) 887-8855; www .maplelane.com. This onetime cow pasture has evolved into Allyn Brown III's pristine 120-acre farm where you can pick your own strawberries, raspberries, and blueberries all summer long, plus twelve apple varieties and peaches into fall, and you can cut your own Christmas trees in December. There is no farm stand *per se* here now, but picking one's own is definitely "in." And with the dwarf trees, picking is much easier and safer. During the fall pumpkin season, there are weekend hayrides. Open April through Christmas, daily from 8:00 a.m. to 6:00 p.m.

Medlyn's Farm Market, 710 Leetes Island Rd., Branford; (203) 488-3578. With a range of vegetables that includes eggplants, beans, peas, sweet corn, tomatoes, squash, potatoes, peppers, and pumpkins, you're not likely to go home disappointed. The market also has melons, rhubarb, and strawberries in their growing seasons plus free-range eggs, flowers, jams, and jellies. Open June to October daily from 10:00 a.m. to 6:00 p.m.

Pond Hill Farm, 900 Clintonville Rd., Wallingford; (203) 981-0900. On his eleven acres, containing the oldest brick house in Connecticut (1756), Bill Wallace taps 200 sugar maple trees to make maple syrup. Visitors are welcome to watch the process anytime in February and March, the tapping season—if they call ahead. They might also buy the delicious maple syrup in the old post-and-beam sugarhouse by appointment throughout the year.

Scott's Yankee Farmer, 436 Boston Post Rd. (Route 1), East Lyme; (860) 739-5209; www.scottsyankeefarmer.net. Wainwright and Audrey Scott planted orchards and opened a farm stand in the

Moveable Feasts

The **Cedar Street Food Carts,** at the corner of Cedar and York Streets, New Haven, are a phenomenon and one of the Elm City's best-kept food secrets. As many as twenty-two food carts, each equipped with its own shade umbrella, arranged on both sides of Cedar in a pocket-park setting, sell a smorgasbord of ethnic foods between noon and 2:00 p.m. every weekday (not quite so many on weekends). The reason for this culinary constellation? To provide a quick, easy, and inexpensive lunch to hospital personnel and visitors at the nearby Yale New Haven Hospital. So stroll along and take your pick: Japanese, Chinese, Malaysian, Thai, Mexican, Caribbean, Indian, Pakistan, soul food, Ethiopian, Middle Eastern, hot dogs, Italian ices, and a newcomer, The Cupcake Truck. It is a short "flight" to some intriguing gastronomic adventures. Some carts are outposts of local restaurants—like Bangkok Thai, for instance—giving a sample of what you might find at the source and a chance to participate in a spontaneous New Haven happening.

1960s. Now son Tom and his wife, Karen, have taken over the 125 acres, cultivating apples, strawberries, raspberries, and blueberries for picking fresh during the growing season, June through October. Also for sale are vegetables, cider, jams, honey, pies, homemade doughnuts, and more. There are weekend wagon rides in autumn and a corn maze operating until Halloween weekend. The farm stand is open 9:00 a.m. to 5:30 p.m. year-round.

Smith's Acres, 4 West Main St., Niantic; (860) 691-0528; www .smithsacres.com. The busiest stand in several farmers' markets belongs to Joe and Teri Smith, where buyers line up patiently to buy the Smiths' big juicy ripe tomatoes, apples, and, in the fall, various types of squashes, parsnips, and other root veggies. Open daily 9:00 a.m. to 5:00 p.m., from two weeks before Easter until Christmas Eve.

Food Happenings

APRIL–MAY

Taste of the Nation—New Haven; (203) 430-6453; www.strength .org. This is New Haven's largest, most successful annual fund-raising event, going strong since 1987, and benefiting the Connecticut Food Bank and Christian Community Action. Many of the area's finest restaurant chefs participate each year, with more than fifty different wines available for the sampling, as well as cooking demonstrations, a champagne seminar, and an auction. The locale changes, so it's imperative to check ahead.

JUNE

Annual Shad Bake, Essex Elementary School, Centerbrook; www .essexrotary.com. The year 2009 was the fiftieth of this genial family event, which customarily begins at 4:30 p.m. and continues until early evening. Fresh shad, cooked on oak planks, is the big draw (though hot dogs and chicken are on hand for non-shad eaters). There's live music, children's rides, and family activities, with funds from the event going toward Rotary good works. The bake is usually held on the first Saturday in June, but check the Web site to be sure.

Branford Festival, Town Green, South Main St., Branford; (203) 488-5500 or (203) 488-8304; www.Branfordfestival.com. For more than twenty years, this has been a tasty (and tasting) perennial three-day event over Father's Day weekend in June. It begins Friday evening with food, music, and entertainment. Saturday's highlight is a craft and community expo, with 180 displays. The festival ends on Sunday with a road race. Call for schedule and details.

JULY

Clinton Bluefish Festival, Clinton Andrew Memorial Town Hall, Clinton; www.clintonbluefishfest.com. This town has gone all out for bluefish for thirty-four years and is proud of its sobriquet

"Bluefish Capital of the World." The two-day festival each year (usually in mid-July) begins on Friday from 6:00 to 10:00 p.m. and picks up again Saturday noon until 11:00 p.m. There are numerous food booths, sponsored by restaurants and local organizations, that serve seafood, pulled pork, fish chowder, fried dough, and more. The popular seafood chowder cook-off is a singular event in which patrons can taste-test the winning entries. There's live music both days, games, entertainment, and a fishing tournament, in which dedicated anglers compete to land the biggest bluefish ever.

Lobster Festival & Arts & Crafts Show, Pennsylvania Ave., Niantic; (860) 739-2805; www.nianticlions.org. If it is the first weekend of July, it's time for Niantic's annual Lobster Festival, combined with a juried arts and crafts exhibition. For almost thirty years, this has made the weekend a summer highlight. The major star is always the lobster, but there will also be plenty of fresh clam chowder, fresh strawberries and shortcake, fried dough, curly fries, and other delicious consumables. Expect to find craftspeople, painters, and sculptors displaying their newest wonders both for sale and pleasure. A major fund-raiser of the Lions Club, the event's proceeds help support the club's many worthy activities. Hours are noon to 7:00 p.m. Saturday, noon to 6:00 p.m. Sunday.

Market **"En Plein Air,"** at Florence Griswold Museum, 96 Lyme St., Old Lyme; (860) 434-5542; www.florencegriswoldmuseum.org or www.flogris.org. This is an event within an event. Historic Old Lyme celebrates the annual town-wide Midsummer Festival, usually the last Saturday/Sunday in July, which about 6,000 people attend (see www.oldlymemidsummerfestival.com for details). There is usually a Friday-evening live concert at 7:00 p.m. on the riverbank, and on Saturday from 9:00 a.m. to 3:00 p.m., the beautiful grounds and gardens of the Florence Griswold Museum become "En Plein Air," a French-style, open-air market. It bursts with top-quality Connecticut products—fresh produce, breads, fine cheeses, meats, specialty foods, and flowers—as well as imaginative fun projects and activities and a chance to visit the museum at a reduced admission charge. Call for dates and hours.

OCTOBER

Annual Apple Festival, Town Green, Route 85, Salem; (860) 859-1211; www.congregationalchurchsalem.org. Having hosted these celebrations since 1969, Salem's Congregational Church really knows the drill. Traditionally held the last Saturday in October, this exuberant festival opens at 9:00 a.m., after weeks of preparation by church volunteers busy making apple pies, turnovers, crisps, Bettys, crumbs, Swedish apple puddings, applesauce cakes, and other apple goodies for the big event. Various apple treats are available in the Old Center School building, as well as outside at such sundry stands as the Apple Fritter booth, the Apple Sundae & Hot Dog booth (in which apple sauerkraut is served with the weiners), and the Piece of the Pie booth (apple pie with or without cheddar cheese). At the crafts booths stuffed teddy-bear dolls wear an apple theme: a slick Jonathan or a Delicious femme fatale with feather boa. The Tea Room features hot apple pancakes served with tea or coffee. There is continuous music in the Gazebo. The party's over when all the apple goodies have been sold, usually by around 1:00 p.m.

Apple Festival & Craft Fair, Old Saybrook Middle School, Sheffield St., Old Saybrook; (860) 388-0121. Traditionally held Columbus Day weekend (or as near to it as possible), this annual one-day Saturday festival features apples in many tempting forms, other edibles (including homemade sauerkraut, hot dogs, and chili), and an abundance of handcrafts. The festive event is sponsored by the Old Saybrook Women's Club and benefits a scholarship and autism/Asperger's research. Hours are usually from 9:00 a.m. to 4:00 p.m., but it is always prudent to call ahead to confirm the date and times.

Celebrate Wallingford, Fishbein Park at railroad station, Wallingford; (203) 284-1807; www.wallingfordcenterinc.com. For close to twenty years, Celebrate Wallingford has been a popular annual event, highlighted by "Taste of Wallingford," in which local restaurants offer their specialties at street-side booths. The celebration, held the first weekend of October, lasts two days, with the fun including live entertainment, arts, crafts, and activities for children and by civic groups. Hours are usually Saturday from 11:00 a.m. to 7:00 p.m., Sunday from noon to 6:00 p.m. Call or e-mail for the current year's date.

NOVEMBER

Elm City Legends, Omni Hotel, 155 Temple St., New Haven; www .marchofdimes.com/connecticut. Held on a Monday night in mid-November, this laid-back food event is a major annual fund-raiser for the Connecticut March of Dimes. Chefs from more than a dozen area restaurants (along with other vendors) set up gourmet tastings

FOOD LOVERS' TIP

More clams come from Connecticut waters than anywhere else on the East Coast. The state clam is officially a *Mercenaria mercenaria*, known throughout New England as a quahog. A sure sign of summer's advent is when all the clam shacks along US 1 from West Haven to the Rhode Island line open their windows and begin their ritual deep-frying of bucketsful of ocean-fresh clams. The fried-clam season typically runs through October, depending on the weather, giving you plenty of time to work your way up the shore, searching out the best. Which are best is your call.

of some of their favorite dishes. They also participate in silent and live auctions by donating such appetizing packages as cooking lessons with a master chef, a cocktail party for guests in a local restaurant, a wine dinner with experts, lunch with a local television personality, or a catered dinner for eight in your home. For details call (860) 812-0080.

> "There's nothing in Christianity or Buddhism that quite matches the sympathetic unselfishness of an oyster." —SAKI

Nibbles

Atticus Bookstore Café, 1082 Chapel St., New Haven; (203) 776-4040; www.atticusbookstorecafe; $. What began in 1981 with a couple of tables, a counter, and display cases at the edge of the bookstore has insinuated its way into one-third of the store. Now there are eighteen tables for two and two large group tables, proof that readers and shoppers like a handy place for a wholesome sandwich or quick pick-me-up. Fresh-tasting soups, sandwiches, and delicious muffins, cookies, and tarts are the standards here, with the combo of a cup of soup and a huge half-sandwich one of the better deals. Breads and baked goods come from Chabaso Bakery, which just happens to have the same ownership. Café opens at 7:00

a.m., bookstore at 8:00 a.m.; both close at 9:00 p.m., except Friday and Saturday when it's 10:00 p.m.

The Blue Oar (16 Snyder Rd. [off Route 154], Haddam; 860-345-2994; $$) is a real sleeper. In fact, it sleeps most of the year, only open April to early October. That's because the cafe is outdoors at the edge of a marina hugging the Connecticut River. Whether lounging under a shade tree or at a sprightly painted picnic table on an open-sided deck, I can't imagine a better way to while away a summer day or evening, savoring the Blue Oar's lobster rolls, steamers, or even a grilled seafood dinner. This is no-frills eating at its most pastoral, which explains why locals like CBS's Morley Safer and chef Jacques Pepin enjoy it, too. Open 11:30 a.m. to 8:00 p.m.; closed Monday and Tuesday.

Brie & Bleu, 84 Bank St., New London; (860) 437-2474; www .thamesriver.com; $$. There's more to this cheese shop, facing the Thames River, than meets the eye, tempting as the cheeses are. The shop doubles as a bistro, and at thirteen tables patrons sample from a short bistro menu that is mated with wines. Choices might include short ribs, seared duck breast, organic free-range chicken, cheese combos, and various bruschettas. As if cheese and bistro weren't enough to keep them busy, proprietors Charlotte Hennegan and Fred Argilagos also own **Thames River Wine & Spirits** next door (connected to the shop/bistro).

The brick cellar of the wineshop is a trip in itself, like entering a spooky vault. (*Cask of Amontillado,* anyone?)

Celtica, 260 College St., New Haven; (203) 785-8034; www.gotirish .com; $. Begorrah, for afternoon or anytime tea, this is the place in downtown New Haven for a "drop by." The shop is a veritable bazaar of Irish goods, from nubbly sweaters to delicate glass and porcelain. In the rear is a modest tearoom with four tables, where shoppers can pause to enjoy a cup of Bewley's Irish tea and a scone with clotted cream and jam, anytime from noon to 4:00 p.m. daily. Celtica sells a few other food products as well—but not for shop consumption— the likes of assorted teas, Kate Reilly's Irish Soda Bread mix, Tommy Moloney's sausages, and various biscuits and cookies. The shop is open Monday through Saturday from 10:00 a.m. to 6:00 p.m., Sunday from noon to 5:00 p.m.

Du' Glace Bistro and Patisserie, 156–158 Main St., Deep River; (860) 526-2200; $$. Even better than the pairing of bacon and eggs is a bistro married to a pastry shop. Especially a very good pastry shop. That's what makes this bistro/patisserie so special. It's like a kid let loose in FAO Schwarz. What do I eat first? The aromas are intoxicating—and so are the flavors of croissants, raspberry crois- sants, almond (or coconut) macaroons, Napoleons, cream puffs, and tarts of all types (head for the Key lime or pear and frangipane). The non-dessert tarts are equally wonderful, like the bacon-leek tart appetizer. The bistro also offers lively French classics like coq au vin, cassoulet with duck, and frogs' legs Provençale. The patisserie is open Tuesday through Sunday, from 7:00 a.m. to 6:00 p.m., the bistro Tuesday through Thursday plus Sunday from 5:00 p.m. to 9:00 p.m., Friday and Saturday to 10:00 p.m. Closed Monday.

Nibbling at **Feast Gourmet Market** (159 Main St., Deep River; 860-526-4056; www.feastgourmetmarket.com; $) can mean robust sandwiches on good bread, with natural and/or organic ingredients from neighboring farms and vendors. It might also mean hot pasta lunches made daily or anytime-snacks of sandwiches and fresh pastries. Keep in mind there's also gourmet takeout and catering available.

In New Haven the name **Libby's Italian Pastry Shop,** 139–141 Wooster St.; (203) 772-0380; $, is synonymous with Italian ices. Liberato Dell Amura began making gelatos and granitas in 1922, and his family continues the tradition. In this unassuming little Wooster Street shop (near Frank Pepe's Pizzeria), you will find twenty-five flavors of intensely delicious Italian ices. Besides the usual flavors, there are piña colada, blue raspberry, sambuca, amaretto, mango, and cranberry. Libby's also sells Italian pastries. Signatures are the twenty varieties of Sicilian cannoli and ten types of biscotti. Inside the shop is a semi-enclosed area called **Caffè Villa Gina,** where patrons enjoy various coffees and desserts in the evening. Hours: Sunday and Monday 11:30 a.m. to 9:00 p.m., Wednesday and Thursday to 10:00 p.m., Friday and Saturday to 11:00 p.m. Closed Tuesday.

Lobster Landing, 152 Commerce St., Clinton; (860) 669-2005; $$, is wedged between a tackle shop and a marina. What could be more appropriate for a lobster shack? This one, resting on pilings directly over the waters of Long Island Sound, dates back one hundred years and has been knocked down twice by hurricanes and rebuilt. For fans, it's worth it. The lobster is caught daily and served in rolls dressed with butter and lemon. Seating—for sixty—is outdoors, shaded by awnings. Open daily from 10:00 a.m. to 6:00 p.m. from last week in April through December.

Pasta Cosi, 3 Linden Ave., Branford; (203) 483-9397; www.pasta cosi.com; $. Plain and simple decor, delicious pasta. That pretty well sums up this small luncheonette-like place. Go with the pastas, all made in-house, all with natural house-made sauces, all served in steroid-muscular portions. Owner Billy DiLegge's sauces are marketed elsewhere, though you can buy them (and the pastas) here as well (see listing under Made or Grown Here, page 217). I'm partial to the fusilli Gorgonzola di marino (with chicken breast, toasted pine nuts, spinach, herbs, and cheese). The house cappuccino is great too. Closed Monday.

The Place Restaurant, 901 Boston Post Rd. (US 1), Guilford; (203) 453-9276; $$. What makes this modest spot (holding sway since 1971) different from your usual clam shack, where the standard m.o. is fried everything, is that The Place grills with hardwood, giving all the briny items a pleasing smoky quality. Fire-roasted clams, bluefish, catfish, shrimp, salmon, and lobster are among many goodies, as well as landlubber dishes like grilled chicken and rib eye steak. Corn on the cob is the only side on the menu, but feel free to bring your own salads, chips, and wine or beer. All the cooking is done outdoors, back in an oak tree-shaded parking area. The adjacent seating consists of cut tree stumps, so if it rains you are out of luck. Cash only. Open from summer to mid- or late October, depending on the weather.

R.J. Café, 768 Boston Post Rd., Madison; (203) 318-8008; $. Bookstore cafes are often utilitarian places for a quick bite while shopping. That is not the case at R.J. Café, where tasty meals are the norm. Tucked in the rear of the state's most famous independent bookstore, R.J. Julia, the cafe offers daily specials in soups, sandwiches, quiches, salads, and entrees. There are also BLT and grilled panini sandwiches, as well as some nifty desserts (like house-made carrot cupcakes, brownies, cookies, and scones). Open Monday through Saturday from 10:00 a.m. to 8:00 p.m., on Sunday from 10:00 a.m. to 6:00 p.m.

Tea and Company: **Sundial Gardens,** 59 Hidden Lake Rd., Higganum; (860) 345-4290; www.sundialgardens.com. On a back road in Higganum, Sundial Gardens, a teatime treasure, is worth the hunt. Proprietor Ragna Tischler Goddard is both a tea and garden expert, and a visit here allows you to enjoy both. "Tea Events" are held once a month. For a small registration fee, Ragna offers a tasting of three teas, a dessert made by Ragna's husband, Tom (a skilled pastry chef), a brief lecture on tea, and a demonstration of tea implements. The teas are for sale at the tea shop and via her online catalog, along with Ragna's herbal tisanes, teapots from China, and tea accessories. There's a tiny fee to visit the three formal architectural gardens (knot, eighteenth-century, and topiary). Check the Web site or phone for tea dates and to make a reservation.

Turkish Kebab House, 1157 Campbell Ave., West Haven; (203) 933-0002; $. This is the third and most modest of the Turkish restaurants in the Havens. Like Saray, but unrelated to it, the Kebab House is also on Campbell Avenue and also BYO. As the name suggests, you'll find an array of sizzling hot kebabs here, along with an informal atmosphere and friendly service. Open daily from 11:00 a.m. to 11:00 p.m.

Cook's Kitchen, 620 Boston Post Rd., Guilford; (203) 533-4325; www.cooks-kitchen.com. This smart-looking cooking supply-gourmet food shop has two connecting rooms set aside for ongoing cooking programs. There are four to five classes weekly, all hands-on, limited to twelve participants each. Daytime, evening, weekend, and children's classes are available, as are private cooking class parties (a favorite with corporations). The participants work in a spacious kitchen area with the chef/instructor and then dine at the shop's refectory table, which comfortably seats twelve. Co-owner Debbie Harris, a certified sommelier, matches suitable wines to the adult meals.

Delia's Culinary Forum, 4 Laser Ln., Wallingford; (203) 303-2000, ext. 376; www.deliainc.com. Every Monday in spring and fall, from 6:30 p.m. to 8:30 p.m., chef Cristiana Chang hosts food demonstration classes that usually feature well-known Connecticut restaurant chefs. Held in a first-rate twenty-first-century facility, these seminars are typically attended by thirty to forty-five people, though Cristiana offers personal hands-on classes for smaller groups and private one-on-one lessons as well. It's best to call ahead or check the Web site for the schedule.

Fourteen Lincoln Street, 14 Lincoln St., Niantic; (860) 739-6327. This charming bed-and-breakfast is installed in a renovated nineteenth-century church that is owned by Susan and Benji Hahn.

They offer inn guests "gourmet culinary retreats," consisting of weekend cooking lessons with chef Sherry Swanson, that follow such themes as "French Classics," "Spanish Classics," and "Holiday Classics." Classes for eight to twelve are arranged in the inn's modern commercial kitchen. Check the Web site or call for details about dates and fees.

Mystic Seaport, 75 Greenmanville Ave., P.O. Box 6000, Mystic; (860) 572-5323; www.visitmysticseaport.com. I can't think of a better place for learning "Open Hearth Cooking" than in the kitchen of the Buckingham-Hall House, an authentic 1830s farmhouse in Mystic Seaport. The basic course, usually offered once in the fall and once in the spring, teaches cooking methods—baking, roasting, frying, boiling—and the specific utensils required for an open-hearth or beehive oven. An entire meal is prepared, which the class then sits down to enjoy. An advanced three-day course is often offered as well. Call for details and dates.

Learn about Wine

Mt. Carmel Wine & Spirits Co., 2977 Whitney Ave., Hamden; (203) 281-0800; www.mtcarmelwine.com. Every year since 2002, this splendid shop has been voted "Connecticut's Best Retail Wine Shop" by *Connecticut* magazine for the range of its selections from all over the world. Mt. Carmel has had plenty of time to get its act together.

When Prohibition ended in 1934, Sydney Levine devoted a corner of his family's general store to wine and spirits, which eventually took over the entire store. Descendants Ben and Bob Feinn now run the store, which is a source for rare wines, specialty wines, and "value wines" (those representing the best value for their price), taste-tested and often imported exclusively and directly from small wineries in France and elsewhere. Hard-to-find older vintages are a specialty—notably Bordeaux, red and white burgundies, Rhônes, and ports. In addition to a great depth of French wines, other parts of the world are also well represented. Mt. Carmel's Web site is a helpful source for upcoming wine events—tastings and dinners—in the area. It also lists the store's weekly wine specials, with frank appraisals of specific wines. Open Monday through Saturday from 8:00 a.m. to 8:00 p.m. Closed Sunday.

Landmark Eateries

Bentara, 76 Orange St., New Haven; (203) 562-2511; www.bentara .com; $$. Bentara ("King's highest servant" in Malay) opened in 1995 in East Haven, moved to New Haven in 1997, and has been there ever since, ensconced in this spacious restored building. With its shadow puppets, baskets, bamboo screen, and ceramic pots, the decor reminds me of many happy years spent in Asia—and so does the food, which reflects Malaysia's polyglot heritage, a mixture of Chinese, Indonesian, Indian, and Thai influences. Everything here is aromatic and tasty (and well described on the menu) and complements the cosmopolitan wine list. We're partial to the coconut curry mussels, satay, popia (spring rolls), and ikan percik (grilled marinated salmon with coconut turmeric lime sauce), among many delights. The original Bentara, by the way, is in Malaysia, operated by the chef's mother. Open daily, but on Sunday it's for dinner only, beginning at 3:00 p.m.

Bespoke, 266 College St., New Haven; (203) 562-4644; www.bespoke newhaven.com; $$$. Much of the recent restaurant buzz in New Haven has centered on Bespoke—and with good reason. Sure, the stylish black-white-and-gray decor has captured attention, and the long bar leading into a whitewashed brick, high-ceilinged dining room is certainly stunning. But it's the food that really makes this modern American place so special. Chef and co-owner Arturo Franco-Camacho is multitalented and draws on so many cuisines in his diverse, appealing cooking style that it's difficult to pigeonhole his cuisine. Here are a few examples from a menu that changes regularly: delicate house-made gnocchi in a fennel-tomato fondue, venison Wellington, braised pork shoulder in a pineapple-tomatillo mojo, pomegranate-molasses-glazed rack of lamb, two-way Mallard duck with rhubarb/celery salad/ginger, quince bread pudding and "deconstructed" almond date tart with poached plums, and ginger-honey chai gelato. Open for dinner only. In the same building as Bespoke is **Sabor** (203-562-7666; $$), which, like Chef Arturo's late, lamented Roomba, specializes in Latin American cooking. Dinner only, nightly.

Boom, 63 Pilots Point Dr., Westbrook; (860) 399-2322; www.boom restaurant.net; $$. The bad news about Boom is that the mother ship in Stonington is gone. The good news is that this Boom—and another one in Old Lyme—are thriving. The signature dish at both is razor-thin red onion rings, which are as crunchy and heavenly as ever. There are other good things to eat at Boom—duck quesadilla, ginger-marinated pork chops, and sweet potato and walnut ravioli, for instance. But no meal is complete without a side of "very thin red onion rings." Boom in Old Lyme is at 90 Halls Rd., Old Lyme Marketplace (off I-95's exit 70); (860) 434-0075; $$. Both open daily for lunch and dinner.

Café Routier, 1353 Boston Post Rd., Westbrook; (860) 399-8700; www.caferoutier.com; $$. When this French-style cafe first moved from Old Saybrook to Westbrook, some of the French village flair went missing. It's back now, and dishes like pan-roasted ginger-chamomile monkfish, braised boneless short ribs, and "camp style" grilled trout are a pleasure to behold—and devour. At the bar you'll find small plates and tapas, light meals in themselves. Dinner only. Open at 5:00 p.m. daily.

Claire's Corner Copia, 1000 Chapel St., New Haven; (203) 562-3888; www.clairescornercopia.com; $. Claire Criscuolo, chef, owner, and resident expert on vegetarian cooking, holds sway over this longtime mainstay of downtown New Haven. It opened in 1975 and loyal, longtime patrons regard the pudding-plain place almost like a

Chef Claire's Lentil Soup

This hearty soup is served at Claire's Corner Copia with the kitchen's own bread, a combination of wheat and white dough that is made fresh daily.

4 quarts water

12 ounces organic lentils, picked over for stones

1 bay leaf

5 tablespoons extra-virgin olive oil

4 large cloves garlic, finely chopped

1 medium yellow onion, finely chopped

8 ribs organic celery, cut into ½-inch slices, including leaves

6 medium organic carrots, cut into ½-inch-thick slices

1 large bulb fennel, cut into bite-size pieces

1 6-ounce can organic tomato paste

¼ cup finely chopped organic Italian flat-leaf parsley

Sea salt and pepper to taste

10-ounce container organic baby spinach

2 cups tubetti pasta, cooked according to package directions

1. Place the water, lentils, and bay leaf in a large pot. Cover and bring to a boil over high heat. Lower the heat to medium.
2. Add the oil, garlic, onion, celery, carrots, fennel, tomato paste, parsley, salt, and pepper. Stir well to mix.
3. Cover and cook at a medium-high boil (the soup will return to a boil after about 5 minutes), stirring occasionally, for about 1 hour, or until the lentils and celery are tender.
4. Add the spinach. Stir well to mix. Cover and continue cooking, stirring occasionally, for 5 minutes, or until the spinach is tender.
5. Stir in the cooked pasta. Taste for seasonings.

Serves 8.

Claire's Corner Copia
1000 Chapel St., New Haven
(203) 562-3888
www.clairescornercopia.com

private club. Claire herself is a registered nurse and knows whereof she speaks. Her vegetarian, vegan, organic, and kosher offerings, available all day long, are both imaginative and nutritious. Next door at 1006 Chapel is Claire's new restaurant, **Basta Trattoria,** drawing on Claire's Italian family traditions and recipes. It offers sustainable, organic, wild, natural food and line-caught fish and seafood. Open daily from 9:00 a.m. to 9:00 p.m.

Flanders Fish Market & Restaurant, 22 Chesterfield Rd., Route 161, East Lyme; (860) 739-8866 or (800) 242-6055 (Connecticut); www.flandersfish.com; $$. What started as a modest fish market in 1983, when Paul and Donna Formica began selling her clear clam chowder at the fish counter, little by little expanded to a restaurant with 150 seats. In 2009 Flanders celebrated its twenty-sixth year in business. On entering this modern building, which is highlighted by wraparound glass-windowed dining areas and a wooden deck with tables and sun umbrellas, you pass by the market's refrigerated display cases, often filled with cod, catfish, salmon, sea bass, fresh shad and shad roe (in season), and dozens of other deep-water delights. I especially enjoy the clam fritters, whole clam bellies, charbroiled Stonington sea scallops, shrimp scampi, and velvety lobster bisque, a signature dish. As if they weren't busy enough, Flanders also caters kids' parties and old-fashioned New England clambakes, and ships any size lobster anywhere in the country by next-day air. On Sunday there's a sumptuous seafood buffet, from 11:00 a.m. to 3:00 p.m. Open daily for lunch and dinner.

Gelston House, 8 Main St., East Haddam; (860) 873-1411; www .gelstonhouse.com; $$. The handsome Italianate Victorian building, a companion in time and architectural style to its immediate neighbor, the Goodspeed Opera House (same mid-nineteenth-century vintage) next door, has had more ups and downs than a toboggan in the Alps. Closed periodically, Gelston House is, happily, open again, serving meals in its dramatic 125-seat, slightly formal dining room with a sweeping overview of the Connecticut River below and also serving informal fare in the casual, open-sided tavern. The menu is straightforward American, with steak, seafood, and pasta the main focus. There is also a reasonable fixed-price menu for theatergoers in a hurry. Closed Monday and Tuesday.

Ibiza, 39 High St., New Haven; (203) 865-1933; www.ibizanewhaven .com; $$$. Ibiza, named for the Balearic island, began life as Pika Tapas, a tapas bar. It is now a full-fledged, first-rate restaurant, unquestionably one of the best Spanish restaurants in the entire United States. As a lifetime hispanophile, I pinch myself that we Nutmeggers are so lucky. Whether it's calamares a la plancha, braised oxtail with wild mushrooms, roasted duck breast, braised boneless short ribs, half a dozen other specialties, or the fixed-price tasting menu, I'm sure you will thoroughly enjoy Ibiza. And for tapas lovers, a nice assortment awaits you at the bar Wednesday and Thursday evenings. Open all week nights for dinner, only Friday for lunch.

Closed Sunday. Co-owner Ignacio Blanco has a new place, **Ibiza Tapas and Wine Bar,** in Hamden at 1832 Dixwell Ave.; (203) 909-6512; www.ibizatapaswinebar.com; $. Dinner only daily.

Istanbul Café, 245 Crown St., New Haven; (203) 787-3881; www .istanbulcafect.com; $$. This touch of Turkey was the first Turkish restaurant in New Haven—and remains after eleven years the one and only. In fact, Turkish cuisine is under-represented throughout Connecticut. A pity, too, given its hearty, creative, and well-seasoned nature. Amidst Turkish kilims and other Anatolian artifacts on the walls, you'll enjoy many authentic specialties, including such delights as iman bayildi (stuffed baby eggplant), ispanak ezme (pureed spinach with yogurt), patlican musakka, yaprak doner kebab, and istim kebab (broiled lamb shank). Handily located on the theater route between the Shubert and Yale Repertory Theaters, it should be a natural meal stop on the way to either one. Open daily, but only Monday and Friday for lunch as well.

Le Petit Café, 225 Montowese St., Branford; (203) 483-9791; www.lepetitcafe.net; $$. Chef-owner Roy Ip seemingly works miracles: a four-course fixed-price dinner nightly Wednesday through Sunday in cramped store-front quarters. This Hong Kong–born chef is a master of classic French cuisine, seasoned with an occasional Asian or Caribbean ingredient or two. The menu changes weekly and might include lamb and pork pâté, duck leg confit, cassoulet, or New York steak au poivre. Le Petit

Everyone's Favorite Lobster Shack

Abbott's Lobster in the Rough, 117 Pearl St., Noank; (860) 536-7719; www.abbotts-lobster.com; $, flies below the radar screen, but for more than thirty years, multitudes have braved the hairpin-twisting, convoluted shore route to find this tucked-away gem. Fortunately, the road is well signposted. Once you have arrived at this modest place, by a picture-pretty marina at Noank, facing Fishers Island Sound, the drill is simple: You order at the counter, wait briefly, then take your booty to a picnic table inside the "shack" or outside on the deck or grassy lawn. Accoutrements are basic plastic and paper, but a head-on view of the boats and water is so peaceful you might feel you are at the upper reaches of Maine. Though Abbott's has other choices, including a respectable clam chowder, Bay of Fundy steamers, or oysters on the half shell, the magnet is lobster. We prefer the lobster roll, a toasted, buttery bun piled high with luscious, tender, pure lobster meat, but lobster mavens with bigger appetites crave the whole lobster—from one-and-a-quarter-pounders up to ten-pounders—steamed and served with drawn butter, coleslaw, and potato chips. Abbott's claims a "more humane" approach to preparing its lobsters: in a cooker in which the lobster is steamed above the boiling water, not in it. Tell that to the lobster. You can also order takeout lobster bakes in a canister (with live lobsters, steamers, mussels, corn on the cob, white and sweet potatoes, all nestled in damp seaweed), all ready to pop on the stove, outdoor grill, or campfire. Open daily from June 1 through Labor Day, thereafter on three-day weekends (Friday–Sunday) through Columbus Day.

Café is a pleasant dining experience across from the Branford Green. Dinner only. Closed Monday and Tuesday.

Noah's Restaurant, 113 Water St., Stonington; (860) 535-3925; www.noahsfinefood.com; $$. In a plain frame building on the corner of Church and Water Streets, Noah's has been a mainstay of this charming seaside town for decades. Locals love the generous Sunday brunch (served from 7:45 a.m. to 3:00 p.m.), which features such dishes as Portuguese sausage and eggs, eggs Benedict, and all kinds of pancakes. Even weekday breakfasts are special, with Irish oatmeal (often polka-dotted with bananas, walnuts, or raisins), house-made granola, yogurt, muffins and scones, and a different type of pancake daily (blueberry is always on the menu). Most everything at Noah's is made from scratch, which may be why this unassuming place has earned such a loyal following—and not just for breakfast. At lunch or dinner you might encounter steamers or mussels (flavorful and briny), sautéed Stonington sea scallops, many lightly prepared fish dishes, and desserts with a mom-made flair (like blueberry crumble or blueberry bread pudding in season). Closed Monday.

Octagon, Mystic Marriott Hotel, 625 North Rd., Groton; (860) 326-0360; www. Marriott.com/gonmm; $$$. The two dining rooms here are so striking in their theatricality (wood, marble, high ceilings, floor-to-ceiling windows, provocative mural at one end) it takes awhile to concentrate on the food, primarily steak and more steak, with a bit of seafood and poultry along for the ride. Octagon is a steakhouse, with very high quality beef. Breakfast daily (because it's part of a hotel), otherwise dinner only. The Lounge at Octagon is open from 11:00 a.m. onwards, with a lighter menu.

Olio, 33 King's Hwy., Groton; (860) 445-6546; www.olioct.com; $$. Olio specializes in eclectic American fare, with elements of Italy, Mexico, Asia, and Cajun country. Smart is the operative word, both in Olio's simple good looks and medium-size menu full with a number of tempting lunch and dinner choices. We like especially the Cajun barbecued shrimp with grilled polenta (an appetizer), cheese tortellini with tomato vodka sauce, and the grilled pizzas (most notably with the grilled portobello, scallops, and Gorgonzola topping). No wonder Olio's good—the ownership's the same as Restaurant Bravo Bravo in Mystic. Open daily for dinner, every day but Sunday for lunch.

Pacifico, 220 College St., New Haven; (203) 772-4002; www.pacifico restaurants.com; $$$. When Rafael Palomino decided to venture north from his two Port Chester, New York, restaurants, his first stop was New Haven (and later Old Greenwich with Greenwich Tavern). Loosely following a Pacific theme gives him leeway to include many

Asian- and Latin American–accented dishes on his eclectic menu. This leads to such smoothly rendered dishes as tilapia on a crab-filled tortilla in a tomatillo sauce, Asian-style shrimp dumplings, empanadas, seafood paella, seared sea scallops and shrimp in a chipotle, honey chardonnay sauce with black bean ravioli and Monterey Jack, pan-seared tilapia with a yucca crust, and desserts like his velvety dulce de leche cheesecake. For theatergoers, the late-night menu (available Friday and Saturday from 11:00 p.m. to 1:00 a.m.) with a dozen tapas and a few bocadillos (bite-size sandwiches) is an excuse to morph into a night owl. The color-happy decor is as lively as the youthful clientele. Open daily for lunch and dinner.

Restaurant Bravo Bravo, 20 East Main St., Mystic; (860) 536-3228; www.bravobravocom; $$. Small, smart, and stylish, Bravo Bravo is a surprise to find in a tourist center like Mystic, where faster food is the norm. Owner Carol Kanabis's Italian-accented menu more than lives up to the urbane interior of white walls, mirrors, oak floors, and well-napped tables. The pasta dishes are most inspired, especially chicken-and-lobster ravioli (if it is on the menu when you visit) and black-pepper fettuccine tossed with grilled scallops and sun-dried tomatoes in a Gorgonzola Alfredo sauce. I am always partial to a succulent osso buco, and Bravo Bravo makes a fine one. Located in the Whaler Inn, the restaurant has an entrance directly on the street. Open Tuesday through Sunday. Closed Monday. You'll find the same ownership and efficiency at **Azu**, 32 West Main St., Mystic; (860) 536-6336, and at Olio (see above).

Restaurant L and E, 59 Main St., Chester; (860) 526-5301; www.restaurantduvillage .com; $$$. The former Restaurant du Village was recently sold to Linda and Everett Reid, who have done a make-over with many antiques. It is now Restaurant L and E, with a snappy new French 75 Bar, where small plates are the mode. You may dine on crispy Long Island Sound squid, cumin-crusted loin lamb chops, or among many creative choices. Desserts are also top-notch. Dinner only, from 5:00 p.m. on.

River Tavern, 23 Main St., Chester; (860) 526-9417; www.rivertavern chester.net; $$$. It is a surprise to find two charming restaurants in such a small town as Chester. (See Restaurant L & E above.) River Tavern, Jonathan Rapp's well-kept establishment, uses limited space to make a very strong culinary statement with its polished food and well-chosen wine list. A short eclectic menu, threaded with a touch of Asia, might include Lapsong Souchong–brined duck breast or pan-roasted flounder with chicken-of-the-woods mushrooms and lovely desserts like bittersweet chocolate soufflé, warm date pudding cake with rum caramel sauce, and almond dacquoise. Whatever you choose, the food is exemplary. Open daily for lunch and dinner.

Saigon City, 1315 Boston Post Rd., Old Saybrook; (860) 388-6888; www.saigoncityoldsaybrook.com; $$. Formerly in downtown New Haven, this Vietnamese waystation now seems firmly rooted in two

THE ODDS ARE IN YOUR FAVOR
AT THESE TWO CASINO SURE BETS

Amid scores of fast-food choices and a first-rate **Michael Jordan Steakhouse,** two acclaimed Boston chefs have given their imprimatur to the Mohegan Sun Casino's list of fine dining establishments.

Jasper White's Summer Shack, Mohegan Sun Casino, 1 Mohegan Sun Blvd., Uncasville; (860) 862-9500; www.mohegansun.com; $$. In a setting that is relatively casual, the seafood is superior, whether you head for the oyster bar or the restaurant proper. Among Chef White's winning bets: New England dishes such as chowders, Jason's garlicky clams casino, his roasted lobster and skillet-fried chicken, and his Native American–derived cuisine, most evident in the corn and crab fritters, wild rice salad, and wood-grilled venison skewers with dried cranberry compote. Open daily for lunch and dinner. Reservations recommended.

Todd English's Tuscany, Mohegan Sun Casino, 1 Mohegan Sun Blvd., Uncasville; (888) 226-7711; www.mohegansun.com; $$$. In a

dining rooms of a period clapboard house in Old Saybrook. There aren't many Vietnamese restaurants left in Connecticut (a short-lived fad that seems to have passed), but Saigon City provides an authentic taste of subtle Vietnamese cooking, with a touch of Thailand tossed in to spice things up a bit and a few French dessert accents. Red curry pork, Saigon spicy chicken or shrimp, and spicy faux rustic setting, deafened by the roar of the so-called Taughannick waterfalls, this Tuscan restaurant in the heart of casinoland is a welcome and surprising reminder of Italy's Tuscan region. The lighting isn't quite dim enough to eclipse such starters as brick-oven oysters, spicy fried calamari with Calabrese peppers, rabbit gnocchi, or baked crespelle, all delicious. Entrees of note include chicken Calabrese, wood-grilled Kurabuto pork shank, crispy-skin salmon, and veal pappardelle. Desserts are all superb, whether pecan pie crème brûlée, fallen chocolate cake, honey almond panna cotta, ricotta pie, chocolate bread pudding, or 2-inch-high lemon meringue tart. The menu changes often, but there's always something exciting to bet on. At lunch there's a generous "Tuscan Table" buffet that's both a real pleasure and a bargain. Lunch and dinner daily.

beef curry are among many worthy dishes you are likely to encounter on the menu. Dinner only; closed Monday.

Saray Turkish Restaurant, 770 Campbell Ave., West Haven; (203) 937-0707; www.saraykebab.com; $$. As far as I know, there are just three Turkish restaurants in all Connecticut and all are in the Havens.

This one, in West Haven, offers a good sampling of a tantalizing cuisine, served in a pleasant carpeted dining room surrounded by walls hung with Turkish kilims. The focus here is on a wide array of entree kebabs, unusual salads, and tempting appetizers, such as muhammara, haydari, and cumin-flecked hummus. Even the desserts are worthy, especially the baklava, kazandibi, and kadayif. Just remember, it's BYO. Open daily for lunch and dinner.

Thali Regional Cuisine of India, 4 Orange St., New Haven; (203) 777-1177; www.thali.com; $$. Thali is a mini-empire, this being the third (and some say best) of four Indian restaurants with the same name and ownership. Softly lit, with space between tables, this Thali features creative gems like jeera alu (cumin potatoes), Andhra chicken, ghosht banjara (spicy goat), Marathi ghosht (lamb stew), fish tikka, and a host of delicious breads. Other Thalis are at 87 Main St., New Canaan, (203) 972-8332; 296 Ethan Allen Hwy. (Route 7), Ridgefield, (203) 894-1080—with a fabulous Sunday buffet from noon to 2:30 p.m.; and Thali Too, 65 Broadway, New Haven, (203) 776-1600—featuring vegetarian Indian specialties. Open daily for lunch and dinner.

Union League Café, 1032 Chapel St., New Haven; (203) 562-4299; www.unionleaguecafe.com; $$$. One of the handsomest dining rooms in New Haven, this is also in one of the city's most historic structures, the Sherman Building, a brownstone erected in 1860 on the

A Trio of "Inn" Experiences

The days of "quaint"—relish trays and cottage cheese—at Connecticut country inns are long past. Now some of the loveliest modern food is served at inns whose decor is at least a century older. The following threesome, clustered together near the Connecticut River, is known even more for their food than their surroundings.

The Bee and Thistle Inn and Spa, 100 Lyme St., Old Lyme; (860) 434-1667; www.beeandthistleinn.com; $$$. A favorite romantic getaway, this vintage inn's Americana decor is as charming as the creative modern American food is delicious. The dining room has been renovated as The Chestnut Grille at The Bee and Thistle Inn. From December to mid-January an elaborate tea is served Wednesday through Saturday afternoons from noon to 4:00 p.m. Open Wednesday through Saturday for dinner only, and only by reservation.

Copper Beech Inn, 46 Main St., Ivoryton; (860) 767-0330; www.copper beechinn.com; $$$. Easily spotted by the giant copper beech tree in its front yard, this impeccably maintained inn has twenty-two exquisitely furnished rooms and suites (four in the main house, the rest in two other houses on the property). In two dining rooms elegant French food with a modern American accent is served—the likes of poached lobster, Atlantic cod, veal, and lamb dishes. The menu changes seasonally. Be sure to check out the remarkable wine list. Open daily for dinner only.

Old Lyme Inn, 85 Lyme St., Old Lyme; (860) 434-2600 or (800) 434-5352; www.oldlymeinn.com; $$$. Inside the handsome, nineteenth-century house are two dining areas. The Old Lyme Inn Grill consists of three rooms (Tap Room, Parlor, Library Bar), with a total of three fireplaces and a century-old, long oak bar, a conversation piece in itself. The Tap Room is open daily (except Monday) year-round, with a seasonal modern American menu for lunch and dinner, both casual and formal. Stonington sea scallops with saffron risotto, veal with pappardelle noodles, and yummy desserts are among many treats.

THREE ON THE ROAD, THE POST ROAD, THAT IS

When summer comes and the livin' is lazy, Nutmeggers head to the shore and the no-frills clam shacks that line US 1 for a seasonal clam-out on fried clams, scallops, and clam chowder. Here are three favorites. Two are year-round eateries, but the Clam Castle opens April through October, depending on the weather at each end.

Johnny Ad's, 910 Boston Post Rd., Old Saybrook; (860) 388-4032; $. Comfort is not an operative word here. Your mission is to eat clams, sweet, fresh delicious ones, ever-so-lightly coated and seasoned, served with fresh-tasting coleslaw. The sea scallops are almost as tasty and just as lightly breaded. Open for lunch and dinner year round.

The Clam Castle, 1324 Boston Post Rd., Madison; (203) 245-4911; $. In addition to light, sweet-tasting fried clams, cod, sea scallops, lobster rolls, and soft shell crabs, this modest little place boasts a delicious fish chowder, just the way I like it: creamy with chunks of fish, bacon, and potatoes (maybe a tad too many of the latter). I also like the light

site of Roger Sherman's home. He was New Haven's first mayor and the only man to sign all three founding documents of the fledgling United States. Stately, neoclassic, with pink-granite columns, wide windows overlooking Chapel Street, and a welcoming fireplace, the room makes a worthy stage for the polished, contemporary French-brasserie cooking of chef-owner Jean Pierre Vuillermet that follows the seasons. His moules marinières and confit de canard aux cepes are naturalness of the flour-water/evaporated-milk batter used to coat the deep-fried oysters, clams, and other denizens of the deep. You can eat indoors, outdoors at one of two picnic tables, or ferry your sea critters home. Credit cards accepted for orders of $10 or more. Closed Monday through Wednesday.

Lenny and Joe's Fish Tale, 1301 Boston Post Rd., Madison; (203) 245-7289; www.ljfishtale.com; $. As clam shacks go, this is a McMansion, with additional colonies in Westbrook and Westerly, Rhode Island. Not that Lenny and Joe's is fancy, but it is now a substantial building and full-service seafood restaurant that's open year-round—a contrast to its humble beginnings in 1979 as a real shack. The fried clams and fried scallops are still magnets, and both are delicious. The Westbrook L & J's is at 86 Boston Post Rd.; (860) 669-0767. Open daily.

mouthwatering ways to begin a meal, perhaps followed by wild striped bass or poached duck breast with parsnip puree. Other super choices are wild mushroom raviolis with chestnut fricassee, or seared New England cod. House-made ice creams or luscious pastries might complete a meal to long remember. Note: There is a less elaborate, less pricey Club Room bistro menu available on week nights. Closed Sunday.

Hunt Breakfast at "The Gris"—A Coastal Connecticut Tradition

Probably the best-known Sunday brunch in the state is the Hunt Breakfast at the historic eighteenth-century **Griswold Inn,** Main St., Essex; (860) 767-1776; www.griswoldinn .com; $$. The Hunt was supposedly started when the British commandeered the inn during the War of 1812. The fixed-price Hunt breakfast, served from 11:00 a.m. to 1:00 p.m., consists of approximately ten main dishes. "Givens" are fruitwood smoked bacon, sausages, scrambled eggs, five salads, fresh fruits, and an array of fresh-baked breads, coffee cakes, and desserts. There is an omelet station and a waffle station with fresh strawberries and chocolate sauce. There might also be such dishes as chicken français, cod with sundried tomato cream sauce or some other fish dish, roast pork loin with garlic and honey, or another meat favorite. You must reserve ahead, as the inn is a mob scene every Sunday. You are seated in one of five charming dining rooms: the Covered Bridge Room, where the buffet tables are set up; the wood-paneled Library with a fireplace; the musket-laden Gun Room; the Ward Room; and the Essex Room. The former Steamboat Room, which resembled the dining salon of an old steamboat, is now a wine bar. After a staffer takes your drinks order, feel free to meander to the buffet line, returning for seconds if you like (many people do). There is no charge for children under six years old. Consider this brunch your Sunday dinner. You won't be hungry again all day. Lunch and dinner served daily.

Zinc, 964 Chapel St., New Haven; (203) 624-0507; www.zincfood .com; $$. Not only is Zinc sophisticated in its minimalist good looks and modern American menu, but the food is executed with great panache. Chef-owner Denise Appel calls Zinc's food "market inspired and globally infused," and indeed many of the best dishes have foreign accents, mostly Asian, also Italian. Some dishes I'm addicted to are steamed pork and ginger dumplings, Korean BBQ smoked duck, grilled tamari-cured tuna, and desserts such as star anise crème brûlée and goat's milk cheesecake. The artisanal cheese plate is a beauty, too, with local and regional cheeses. Closed Sunday and Monday. Lunch is served Tuesday through Friday, dinner Saturday as well. **Kitchen Zinc,** $, formerly Chow, is Zinc's cheaper offspring next door. It too serves lunch and dinner.

Brewpubs & Microbreweries

BruRm@BAR, 254 Crown St., New Haven; (203) 495-8924; www.barnightclub.com. You don't have to be an Eli to enjoy the funky atmosphere of this multiplex, a couple of blocks from Yale University. The starting pint of this favorite watering hole for Yalies (and other thirsties) centers on attractions like Toasted Blonde, Damn Good Stout, a pleasingly bitter Pale Ale, and an Amber Ale that has overtones of caramel malts (which goes down well with the top-notch brick-oven pizza). The building began life in 1915 as an upscale auto showroom, later was empty for years. In 1991

BAR, a handsome discotheque, opened here. Five years later, BruRm ("brew room") was added, as the city's first—and only—brewpub. Currently, dinners, lunches, and those great pizzas are served daily. And at BARtropolis the Bar Night Club music rolls on daily; and each Sunday brings live music from one or more modern bands. Call for schedule and events.

Cottrell Brewing Company, 100 Mechanic St., Pawkatuck; (860) 599-8213; www.cottrellbrewing.com. In 1996 in a nineteenth-century printing press factory that belonged to his great-great-grandfather, Charles Cottrell Buffum established a microbrewery. The next year the spigots began flowing with Old Yankee Ale, a medium-bodied American amber that became an instant hit with residents along the Connecticut–Rhode Island state line. You might call the brews a two-state phenomenon as the water used in the brewing process is Westerly White Rock artisan well water, which gives a clear, crisp taste to the product. Tours are available by appointment.

New England Brewing Company, 7 Selden St., Woodbridge; (203) 387-2222; www.newenglandbrewing.com. Rob Leonard, a well-respected brewmaster in the trade, now runs the show at this microbrewery, which opened in 2001. The year-round products are a widely praised Atlantic Amber, Sea Hag IPA and Elm City lager.

Other specialty brews are made from time to time throughout the year. Open for tours Monday through Saturday, but call ahead for hours.

Race Book Bar at Mohegan Sun, 1 Mohegan Sun Blvd. at Mohegan Sun Casino, Uncasville; (860) 862-8423; www.mohegansun .com. After navigating your way through the thicket of slots, tables, aisles, falling water, and "Indian theme" decor, you may locate the Race Book Bar, a brewpub in a casino. There you can watch races on the video screen and order your brew (derived from "extract brewery" ingredients—malt-syrup concentrates that shortcut the process of full-mash brewing on-site): namely, slightly dry Sachem Ale (malty with a touch of hops), Mohegan Lager (plain and simple), Cold Moon Ale (really cold, but light), and several others. The Bar has light food, but for serious eating you can dine on the casino premises at one of more than eleven restaurants, buffets, and food courts offering gourmet, casual, or serve-yourself fare. Race Book Bar hours: daily 11:00 a.m. to race finales as late as 1:30 a.m.

SBC in Branford, Hamden, and Milford. See listing under SBC Downtown Restaurant Brewery, Stamford, page 73.

"Why does man kill? He kills for food. And not only food: frequently there must be a beverage."   —WOODY ALLEN

Connecticut Wine Trail, www.ctwine.com, offers important information about four of the state's wineries in this area, including where they're located and excellent information about each of them, for free. Included are such data as times and hours for tastings, tours, prices, nearby points of interest, and more. The wines within this region are Chamard Vineyards, Gouveia Vineyards, Jonathan Edwards Winery, and Stonington Vineyards.

Chamard Vineyards, 115 Cow Hill Rd., Clinton; (860) 664-0299; www.chamard.com. This vineyard was installed on five acres by William Chaney and family in 1984, on a grand hilltop overlooking Long Island Sound. Rich, stony soil, plus vines and a maritime microclimate, along with chardonnay, cabernet sauvignon, and pinot noir grapes, were the bases for the wines. Over time Chamard varieties have won many medals in wine competitions. Bonnie and Jonathan Rothberg are the current owners of the Chamard Vineyards, which has grown to twenty acres and includes an impressive chateau. There is also a stand-alone tasting house equipped with a small shop and an attractive lounge that boasts a stone fireplace, soaring cathedral ceiling, and exposed wood beams. Tastings and tours are available from Tuesday through Sunday, 11:00 a.m. to 5:00 p.m. year-round. There's a small fee and you may keep your wine glass.

Gouveia Vineyards, 1339 Whirlwind Hill Rd., Wallingford; (203) 265-5526. This stone and wood winery, looking over woodlands, a small lake, and rows of vines, is run by Joe and Lucy Gouveia. They're serious about wine, as was their family, who cultivated grapes here and, many years ago, back in Portugal. Joe and Lucy now work many grape strains yearly, whose varieties include pinot noir, merlot, Vignoles, and others. The results? Stone House, in both reds and whites, and two types of chardonnay, in separate classic blends and vintage aged. Others now on the list are a deep purple merlot, a Cayuga white, a fruity Seyval blanc, and a cabernet franc, Whirlwind Rose vinefera hybrid. Visiting tasters have a grand time here, picnicking at lakeside, on the terrace of the stone tasting house, inside on a couch by the fire, or at window tables overlooking fields of grapevines. There are even free snacks—cheese, dips, and salsa—for nibbling with your wine sips. The tasting room is open Friday and Saturday from 11:00 a.m. to 8:00 p.m., Sunday 11:00 a.m. to 6:00 p.m.; on Saturday there is entertainment from 4:00 to 7:00 p.m. Call for dates and details.

"During one of our trips through Afghanistan, we lost our corkscrew. We had to live on food and water for several days."
—W.C. FIELDS in *My Little Chickadee*

Jonathan Edwards Winery, 74 Chester Maine Rd., North Stonington; (860) 535-2626; www.jedwardswinery.com. It may seem ironic to be on a beautiful North Stonington hilltop sipping wines made from Napa Valley grapes, imported from California. But it's not unusual for Connecticut vintners to get their stock elsewhere. In this case, Jonathan Edwards selects, handpicks, and contracts for grapes, sending them refrigerated to his vintage (circa 1800) dairy barn. Here the grapes are crushed, blended, barrel-aged, and bottled, making his merlot, syrah, cabernet sauvignon, chardonnay, and zinfandel wine authentic Connecticut products. At the same time, the family is developing "Stonington Estate Wines," an entirely Connecticut-grown group of wines, using Riesling, gewürztraminer, and other grapes. Tastings are daily from 11:00 a.m. to 5:00 p.m. If the tasting room is not too crowded, you might snare a table and enjoy a snack of sandwich wraps, olives, and Cato Corner Farm artisanal cheeses, available for sale to eat along with your wine samplings.

Stonington Vineyards, 523 Taugwonk Rd., Stonington; (800) 421-9463 or (860) 535-1222; www.stoningtonvineyards.com. In 1987 Nick and Happy Smith bought southern-sloping Stonington uplands for their twelve-acre vineyard. Finding elements recalling Bordeaux, they focused on European-style wines and over the years have won awards for them using chardonnay, Riesling, cabernet franc, Fumé Vidal Blanc, and other French-type grapes. You'll learn how it was done and how it looks and tastes on a short wine-making tour (typically at 2:00 p.m). Otherwise, enjoy the tasting room between 11:00 a.m. and 5:00 p.m. daily. Among other events: Barrel Tasting in mid-May, a Summer Cellar-bration in mid-July, and later a festival of picking grapes/watching the crush (call for the date). Each event includes live music, food from local restaurants—and plenty of wine.

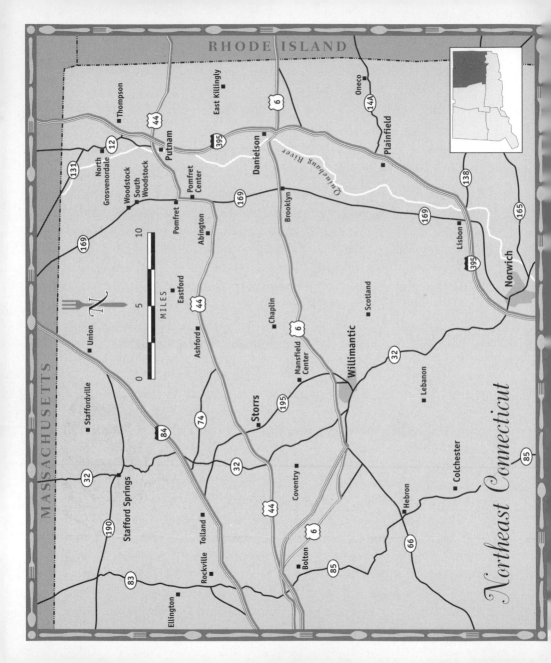

Northeast Connecticut

Connecticut is a state composed mainly of scores of small towns, small enough to have just a single zip code. This is most evident in the northeast area, sometimes called "the quiet corner." "Peaceful" or "tranquil" would be just as appropriate, for this is a terrain of rolling hills, woodlands, marshes, ponds, brooks, small streams, and clusters of state forests and state parks like Mashamoquet Brook near Pomfret. It is also a land of dairy farms, pasturelands, an abundance of apple, peach, and pear orchards, and fields and fields of strawberries and blueberries.

Such expansive farmland is punctuated by hamlets and villages whose historic names can be found on a map of the world: Lebanon, Hebron, Lisbon, Coventry, Canterbury. Yet each of these towns is quintessentially New England. Many have deep roots in American history, like Coventry, where American Revolutionary War hero Nathan Hale was born and his family farmhouse can still be visited. Also in

287

Coventry is a large herb farm, famous for its herb lunches and lectures. Norwich, on the Thames River, was the birthplace of Benedict Arnold. Norwich was also home to Colonel Christopher Leffingwell, a supplier for Washington's Continental Army; his historic home is open for viewing. The town's current claim to fame is a spa-and-inn complex, considered one of the most elegant spas in the state.

In Lebanon, with its town-long green, George Washington stabled his horse during the American Revolution. The Wadsworth stable is still there, still viewable. The state's only colonial governor, Jonathan Trumbull, lived in this town; his house, too, is open to visitors. Peaceful Canterbury has the restored home of Prudence Crandall, an intrepid Quaker who ran the first school for African-American girls in pre–Civil War America.

Quiet does not mean somnolent, as the presence here of so many farmers, dairymen, and food entrepreneurs attests. There is even a distillery in the area, dedicated to making eau-de-vie. The University of Connecticut in the bucolic hills around Storrs began life as an agricultural land-grant college; it is now a prestigious university with two famous basketball teams (male and female), but the rich homemade ice cream sold at the university's dairy bar is almost as popular in the region as the Huskies mascot.

Brooklyn and Pomfret are pastoral New England villages, whose environs now encompass vineyards, a bison farm where American buffalo roam free, maple sugarhouses, scores of orchards, and a unique restaurant in the middle of a working farm. On the Green in Woodstock is one of the most unusual historic houses in the state—the vibrant-pink Roseland Cottage, a rare example of Gothic

Revival outside and in. Its many celebrated nineteenth-century visitors included four U.S. presidents. Food lovers in Woodstock may be almost as delighted by one of the area's largest apple orchards and farm store across the Green.

Nearby Putnam, named for American Revolutionary War hero Israel Putnam, is a classic example of the Connecticut enterprising spirit. When its large textile-manufacturing companies moved out of state, Putnam didn't passively fall into decay. First it reinvented itself as a major antiques center of southern New England. When eBay undermined the antiques market, Putnam began to reinvent itself yet again—this time as a restaurant town, on a scale befitting its small size, fairly bustling with renewed Yankee spunk. In Willimantic, what was once the largest thread mill in the United States has been converted into a museum of the textile industry; of even greater interest to beer drinkers is the way the town's old post office has been recycled into a lively brewery, brewpub, and cafe.

"Quiet" in this area is no synonym for "boring," as the following pages will reveal.

Made or Grown Here

Beltane Farm, Highwater Dairy, 59 Taylor Bridge Rd., Lebanon; (860) 887-4709; www.beltanefarm.com. Paul Trubey, a former social worker in hospice care, was always interested in farming and as a kid wanted to have a goat as a pet. Now he has forty of them. They are Oberhasli (Swiss dairy goats) and La Manchas (a small-eared California breed, a cross between Swiss and Spanish goats), both known for the creamy quality of their milk. He raises them on eight acres, feeding them local hay and grass, with no prophylactic antibiotics or animal rennet. The results produce a rich, creamy chevre, which Trubey forms into four-ounce logs and rolls in various herbs. Other Beltane Farm cheeses are Danse de la Lune and a sharp feta aged in brine, plus several cheese spreads, like pumpkin chevre and chocolate chevre. Most Trubey cheeses are sold online and at twelve farmers' markets in season, Highland Park markets, Whole Foods in Hartford and Glastonbury, and Priam Winery, among other outlets. You can taste the cheeses at the farm on Sunday in the spring and fall. Check the Web site for tasting dates and for other stores that sell the cheeses.

Bibelicious Sauces, Inc., 26 Hawks Landing, Hebron; (860) 228-0745; www.bibelicious.com. Aka Frank's Marinara Sauces. Frank Parseliti has a track record in the marinara-sauce business. He developed his first commercial marinara sauce in 1993 from a recipe his father created after the latter opened Frank's restaurant in Hartford in 1944. For decades Frank's was the hangout of Hartford politicos. In 1995 the restaurant closed, and Frank Jr. began expanding his sauce line. Now there are five sauces: Marinara, Basil and Roasted Garlic, Vodka, Spicy Fra Diavolo, and New York-style Sicilian Gravy, plus Frank's Bloody Mary Mix. Several factors make his chunky, textured sauces so fresh tasting: all-natural ingredients, gluten-free, no added sugars, and the use of whole peeled tomatoes and only extra-virgin olive oil. Four of the sauces are vegan (not the Vodka). The sauces are distributed to 800 stores throughout Connecticut and in twelve states. In this area, you will find them at Stop & Shop, all Highland Park Markets, and many upscale groceries.

Birch Hills Farm, 236 Bebbington Rd., Ashford; (860) 429-8665; www.birchhillsfarm.com. What does a UPS driver do after he's retired? If he is Peter Piecyk, he buys a six-acre farm, grows fields of berries, and starts making and selling fruit syrups from his just-picked berries. Peter's fresh-tasting syrups, which come in raspberry, blueberry, and strawberry, as well as peach and maple, have intense fruit flavors and are delicious over ice cream and added to adult beverages. They are bottled in eight-ounce bottles (twelve-ounce for the maple), and he sells them at craft fairs and farmers' markets.

Bush Meadow Farm, 738 Buckley Hwy., Union; (860) 684-3089; www.bushmeadowfarm.com; $. On Nancy and Barry Kapplan's thirty-seven-acre dairy farm, you won't find cows, but you will find forty Nubian dairy goats. The Kapplans raise these frisky creatures for their milk and cheese. At the Kapplan store/cafe they sell fresh, bottled goat's milk, two kinds of goat cheese, eggs, farm-smoked pork and beef, and farm-made breads and rolls. The store/cafe seats fifteen, for breakfast and lunch. Hours are 7:00 a.m. to 1:00 p.m. Thursday and Friday, 7:00 a.m. to 4:00 p.m. Saturday and Sunday.

Cato Corner Farm, 178 Cato Corner Rd., Colchester; (860) 537-3884; www.catocornerfarm.com. Elizabeth MacAlister and her son Mark Gilman produce thirteen remarkable and quite different artisanal cheeses from the raw milk of their thirty-five-cow Jersey herd. Half of their seventy-five-acre farm is pastureland, which allows the cows an open range on which to roam. That the cows' meat is untainted by hormones, herbicides, or chemical fertilizers may explain in part why Cato Corner's cheeses are so delicious and distinctive. The operation is also fastidious. In 1997 Elizabeth built an underground cave so her raw milk cheeses could age properly at a temperature of 50°F to 55°F. Elizabeth and Mark support other area producers, by, for example, rubbing their Drunk Monk in a brown ale from the Willimantic Brewing Company, washing their Drunken Hooligan in a Priam Vineyards' red wine, and giving their Despearado a similar treatment with fermented pear mash and Pear William eau-de-vie from Westford Hill Distillers. Cato Corner's top seller is the creamy, Trappist-style Bridgid's Abbey, based on a Belgian monastery recipe. Another big hit is Bloomsday, named after Leopold Bloom in James Joyce's *Ulysses,* possibly the only cheese named after such an august literary work. Cato Cato's Hooligan, a soft, brine-washed Muenster type, recently copped a gold medal award in a competition held at the Gallo Family Vineyards, where Cato Corner Farm also won the "Never Stop Growing" award as a family-owned producer.

Other Cato Corner cheeses include Black Ledge Blue, a good-selling blue cheese; Gouda-style Dutch Farmstead; Jeremy River cheddar, aged eight months or so in the English style; Vivace

Bambino, sweet like a young provolone; and Womanchego, nutty and sharp, based on the Spanish Manchego. Open to visitors Saturday and Sunday from 10:00 a.m. to 3:00 p.m.

The cheeses are sold (with tastings) at their farm shop, which is open Saturday from 10:00 a.m. to 4:00 p.m., June through December. They are also available at farmers' markets in the area, gourmet shops (like Say Cheese! in Simsbury and Cook's Kitchen, Guilford), groceries (Highland Park Markets), restaurants (Max Downtown, Hartford, and Griswold Inn, Essex), and wineries (Priam Vineyard, Colchester) throughout Connecticut, New York, the mid-Atlantic area, and as far west as Ohio, Illinois, and California. Phone and e-mail orders are shipped via UPS with one- or two-day delivery.

Creamery Brook Bison, 19 Purvis Rd., Brooklyn; (860) 779-0837; www.creamerybrookbison.net. You may not think of Connecticut as the home where the buffalo roam, but Deborah and Austin Tanner raise bison (American buffalo) on their one-hundred-acre farm. So if you happen to be driving by and see eighty or one hundred bison grazing in a meadow, you are not hallucinating. Deborah praises buffalo as "the original health food" because the red meat is all-natural and low-fat, with fewer calories and less cholesterol than most cuts of beef, chicken, and turkey. The animals are fed only corn and grass, no growth hormones or antibiotics. The Tanners sell their meat (processed for them in Groton, Massachusetts) directly from the shop on their farm. Frozen steaks, ground meat and patties, short ribs, Texas ribs, shanks and boneless ribs, and steaks are all available. Buffalo cookouts are conducted Saturday at 11:30 a.m. to 1:00 p.m. from July to October; wagon tours of the fields to see the free-roaming bison are at 1:30 p.m. the same months. Shop hours are April through October, Monday through Friday from 2:00 to 6:00 p.m. and Saturday from 10:00 a.m. to 2:00 p.m., except the last August weekend before Labor Day, when the farm is closed. Off-season, November through March, hours are the same, but the shop is closed on Monday and Tuesday. Otherwise open by appointment.

Fish Family Farm, 20 Dimock Ln., Bolton; (860) 646-9745. Driving up to the dairy store at this beautiful 211-acre farm, you are likely to see Jersey cows grazing in the meadows. In 1981 Don and Sharon Fish bought what was then a beef cattle-raising farm and turned it into a dairy farm with a sixty-cow herd of registered Jerseys. They built a bottling plant, and they now process, pasteurize, homogenize, and bottle their own milk, which they sell in their store and also to Munson's Chocolates in Bolton, which uses the cream in chocolate making. Don Fish jokes that "our milk has been in outer space, because our astronauts made a gift of Munson's Chocolates to the Russian astronauts on the space station." Inside the spotless little store is a freezer, where the premium-quality Fish Family Farm Creamery Ice Cream is sold by the quart. There are eight rich flavors: vanilla, maple walnut, coffee, peanut butter chip,

cherry vanilla, chocolate chip, Heath bar, and chocolate. Ice cream cones are served in summer, when high
school students work the scoops. Sales the rest of the
year, including for such items as jams and jellies, eggs,
farm-fresh milk, and chocolate milk, are on the honor
system. Hours are from 8:00 a.m. to 6:00 p.m. Monday
through Saturday; summer hours are from 8:00 a.m. to
8:00 p.m., the same days. There are no organized tours of
the farm, but visitors may wander around on their own and
watch the 3:30 p.m. milking if they wish. Closed Sunday.

The Farmer's Cow, 49 Chappell Rd., Lebanon; (860) 642-4600 or
(866) 355-2697; farmers@thefarmerscow.com. This is a group of six
family-owned dairy farms in the northeast part of Connecticut that
produce and sell farm-fresh milk, free of artificial growth hormones,
from their large herds of (mostly) Holstein cows. Using state-of-
the-art milking machines and other equipment, the six are Cushman
Farms in North Franklin, Fairvue Farms in Woodstock, Fort Hill Farms
in Thompson, Graywall Farms in Lebanon, Hytone Farm in Coventry,
and Mapleleaf Farm in Hebron. Their milk is sold at markets all over
the state, including Highland Park Markets, Shaws, Stop & Shop, and
Big Y, as well as at Bishop's Orchards in Guilford.

"A gourmet is just a glutton with brains."
—PHILLIP W. HABERMAN

Meadow Stone Farm, 199 Hartford Rd., Brooklyn; (860) 617-2982; www.meadowstonefarm.com. Goats, about thirty of them—Golden Guernsey and Saanen Swiss dairy goats—dominate on the eight-acre farm of Annemarie Prause and Kristopher Noiseux. These animals supply the raw goat's milk the couple sell in their farm shop and that is used to produce cheeses like Caprino Romano, Elsa's fresh goat's milk chevre, farmstead aged and smoked raw milk cheeses, goat soaps, shampoos, crèmes, and butters. Milk from Jersey cows also goes into the farm's cheeses—Abbey, Hot Chili Moo Mama, and others. From April through the end of January, shop hours are from 1:30 to 6:30 p.m. Thursday and Saturday. Closed February and March.

We-Li-Kit Farm Ice Cream Stand, 728 Hampton Rd. (Route 97), Abington; (860) 974-1095; www.mysticcountry.com. Just opposite the milking center is the We-Li-Kit farm stand, which offers remarkably rich ice cream. Whimsical names like Ape's Delight (banana with chocolate chips and walnuts), Guernsey Cookie (coffee with Oreos), Holstein (chocolate studded with white chocolate chips and almonds), and, most popular of all, despite the disagreeable name, Road Kill (vanilla with cherry swirl, white chocolate chips, and walnuts) don't detract from the creamy ice cream's popularity. There are twenty-five flavors, about seventeen available on any given day. Maple products are another attraction, but the ice cream is the magnet for miles around. The stand is open daily from early April to the end of October.

Mary Poppins in an Herb Garden

I first met the late Adelma Grenier Simmons in the 1970s, when I was assigned by a food magazine to attend some of her herb lectures and write about her herb farm, **Caprilands** in Coventry. Short and stocky, often wearing a cape, she combined a fey pixielike charm with the "take charge" character of a governess. I half-expected her to unfurl a Mary Poppins umbrella and fly away. She was a respected herbalist, horticulturist, lecturer, and author of many books on herbs. Her lectures about the herbs in her various gardens—Silver Gardens, Shakespeare, Victorian, and Curious Knotted Garden, among others—were marked by spicy comments, a mischievous twinkle, and reams of folk wisdom. "Caraway seed," she said, "was once fed to straying husbands to get them to return home. If you don't want him back, hide the caraway." In showing silver rosemary, she observed, "It is tasty in tea, but if you don't drink tea, you can wash your hair in it." Pointing to nasturtiums in a vegetable garden, she said, "We decorate salads with them, but the real reason they're with the vegetables is to keep aphids away."

"Why the name Caprilands?" I inquired. She explained that goats were raised on the farm when her family bought it in 1929 ("capri" is the Latin root for "goat"). Her interest in herbs began as a hobby, grew into a passion, and finally into a business, which still exists, much as she left it.

Westford Hill Distillers, 196 Chatey Rd., Ashford; (860) 429-0464; www.westfordhill.com. Margaret Chatey and her husband, Louis, have gone in for "artisan distilling" on the 200-acre hilltop farm that the family has worked since 1919. They have installed a state-of-the-art distillery in their huge New England barn and produce various types of eau-de-vie—the clear, fruit-flavored brandy that is a popular tradition in Europe. "We were licensed in 1998," says Margaret, who runs the project from mashing to marketing, "and sold our first fruit spirits in 1999." The line of eaux-de-vie includes cherry (kirsch), raspberry (framboise), strawberry (fraise), and pear (Pear William), which won a gold medal in two recent competitions, plus an aged apple brandy and an elegant Poire Prisonniere (pear in a heart-shaped bottle), which won a best-of-show in package design at another. How do Bartlett pears get into the bottles? Simple, they grow there. The bottles are placed around baby pears at Holmberg Orchards in Gales Ferry, allowing the pears to mature within the bottles. Those glass containers are then scrubbed with water and filled with Westford Hill's Pear William eau-de-vie, corked, and finished. All the regular eaux-de-vie come in beautiful elongated bottles with the appropriate fruit depicted on the label. They are available in liquor stores and in many restaurants throughout the state—for example, Zinc in New Haven, Metro Bis in Simsbury, 85 Main in Putnam, and Dressing Room in Westport. Distillery visits are possible if you call ahead.

Caprilands Herb Farm, 534 Silver St., Coventry; (860) 742-7244; www.caprilands.com. This fifty-acre herb farm, with shop, gardens, greenhouse, and tearoom, was developed by the late Adelma Grenier Simmons and is still being maintained by her husband, Edward Cook. At the Gift Barn, you can buy packets of herbs grown on the grounds, Adelma's paperback cookbooks with her herb recipes, other books, and many herb-related gifts. Plants and a complete line of herbs are for sale at the Greenhouse. In warmer weather, if you have made advance reservations, you might enjoy a Caprilands high tea (soup, salad, sandwiches, and sweets) on weekends at 2:00 p.m., from May to October. Tea is served in three rooms of the eighteenth-century farmhouse, each of which is decorated with potpourris, herb bouquets, wreaths, and big wooden bowls filled with rose petals, lavender, lemon verbena, and other herbs. Call ahead for times, dates, and reservations.

Colchester Bakery, 96 Lebanon Avenue, Colchester; (860) 537-2415; www.colchesterbakery.com. Some of the area's best Jewish rye bread, Russian pumpernickel, challah, Vienna bread, rye, and babka are created every day from within the confines of a large building up a nondescript side street. Arrive there early, and you'll find the display cases in the front, which houses Colchester Bakery, overflowing with fresh fruit pies, coffee cakes, turnovers, biscotti, crispy elephant ears, assorted Danish and other pastries,

Westford Hill Distillers Savory Apple Pizza

Combining sweet and savory, this dish of Margaret Chatey's makes a great party food, appetizer, or accompaniment to a cold-weather soup.

1 12-inch prebaked pizza crust (either homemade or ready-made)

1 small onion, thinly sliced

1 tablespoon olive oil

2 medium firm apples, cored and thinly sliced (Granny Smith works well)

4 tablespoons honey (divided)

3 tablespoons Westford Hill Distillers' New World Aged Apple Brandy (divided)

¼ teaspoon garlic pepper seasoning

1 cup shredded Gruyère cheese

¼ cup chopped walnuts, lightly toasted

1. Preheat oven to 450°F. Heat pizza crust on pizza pan about 6 minutes. During this time, sauté onions in the olive oil until soft.
2. Add apples and cook about 5 minutes more. Stir in 2 tablespoons honey, 1 tablespoon apple brandy, and garlic pepper seasoning.
3. Top pizza crust with apple mixture. Add cheese and walnuts to topping.
4. Bake 5 minutes more, or until cheese is melted, and remove from oven. Mix remaining honey and apple brandy together and drizzle over pizza. Cut into squares or wedges.

Westford Hill Distillers
196 Chatey Rd., Ashford
(860) 429-0464
www.westfordhill.com

Double Chocolate Raspberry Biscotti

This yummy recipe was also provided by Margaret Chatey, proprietor of Westford Hill Distillers.

Cookie

- ½ cup butter, room temperature
- ¾ cup sugar
- 2 eggs
- 2 tablespoons Westford Hill Distillers' Framboise eau-de-vie
- 2¼ cups all purpose flour
- 1¾ teaspoons baking powder
- ⅓ cup unsweetened cocoa
- ¼ teaspoon salt
- ⅔ cup chocolate chips (for more intense raspberry flavor, use ⅓ cup raspberry flavored chips and ⅓ cup chocolate chips)
- ⅔ cup coarsely chopped walnuts, lightly toasted

Glaze

- 1½ cups confections' sugar
- 1 tablespoon cocoa powder
- 3 teaspoons Westford Hill Distillers' Framboise eau-de-vie

1. Heat oven to 325°F. In a mixing bowl cream butter and sugar until light and fluffy. Beat in eggs and the framboise eau-de-vie.
2. In a bowl combine the flour, baking powder, cocoa, and salt. Add to the creamed mixture until blended.
3. Fold in chips and nuts. Divide dough in half. (If dough is too sticky to handle, add a bit more flour.)
4. On a greased and floured cookie sheet or a cookie sheet lined with parchment paper, pat out into two logs about ½ inch high, 1½ inches wide, and 14 inches long, spacing at least 2 inches apart.
5. Bake in the middle of the oven for 25 minutes or until lightly browned. Let cool about 5 minutes. With a serrated knife slice diagonally at a 45-degree angle about ½ inch thick.
6. Separate the slices upright on the baking sheet and return to the oven for 10 more minutes to dry slightly. Let cool on a rack.

Makes 3 dozen.

black-and-whites, and éclairs, as well as yogurt and cheeses from local farms. There is a self-serve coffee bar along one side of the large shop, convenient for a drink along with a Danish. Open daily 6:00 a.m. to 6:00 p.m.

Martha's Herbary, 589 Pomfret St. (junction of Routes 44, 97, and 169), Pomfret; (860) 928-0009; www.marthasherbary.com. This unusual shop is located behind the residence where its owner, Richard Paul, lives, directly across the road from the Vanilla Bean Café. (The parking lot is behind the house, on Route 169, and leads into the shop.) Martha's carries more than eighteen types of fresh basil, tarragon, sorrel, and other herbs and herb books, along with rare teas and such nonedibles as clothes, scarves, jewelry, hats, potpourris, and other gift items. And when you are finished browsing, feel free to wander the herb gardens and sunken garden, where there's a pond with a waterfall, and a birdhouse fence. Open 10:00 a.m. to 5:00 p.m., but closed all day Monday.

Mrs. Bridge's Pantry, 292 Route 169, South Woodstock; (860) 963-7040; www.mrsbridgespantry.com. In spite of a change of ownership—Pamela Spaeth and Susan Swenson are the new proprietors—the imported British pedigree of this charming little shop remains intact. Merchandise continues to range from McVities and other biscuits, Cadbury chocolate bars (imported), Fry's chocolate, Uncle Joe's mint balls, preserves, and jams to such teas as Jackson's of Picadilly, Yorkshire, London Herb & Spice, Metropolitan, Ahmad, and Connecticut's own Harney and Sons. A freezer contains English bangers (made by an English butcher in California), sausage rolls, Cornish pasties, meat pies, steak and kidney pies, and blood sausages. There are English teapots, accessories, knitting and crochet supplies, and gift items for sale as well.

There's also an abundance of freshly prepared food for lunch, which you can enjoy at any of eight tables (seating twenty-two) in one side of the L-shaped shop (plus five tables outside in front). Lunch options include Cornish pasties, ploughman's lunch, quiches, shepherd's pie, Scotch eggs, potpies, sandwiches, and vegetable curries. Afternoon tea, a real delight, consists of crumpets, scones, clotted cream, locally made pastries, Eccles cake, tea sandwiches, and house-made strawberry jam (from the owners' own berry patch). The shop is open daily from 10:00 a.m. to 7:00 p.m., except Tuesday when it is 11:00 a.m. to 5:00 p.m. No tea served on Tuesday.

Munson's Chocolates, 174 Hop River Rd., Route 6, Bolton; (860) 649-4332 or (888) 686-7667; www.munsonschocolates.com. When Ben and Josephine Munson opened their first candy store in 1946 in Manchester, they called it the Dandy Candy Company. Ben mixed up batches of creams and caramels and hand-dipped them in chocolate; Josephine assembled and packaged them for sale. Their young business was dandy indeed and is now the largest retail chocolate manufacturer in Connecticut, run by the second and third generation of Munsons. The company employs 130 employees in ten stores (Bolton, Buckland, Farmington, Glastonbury, Mystic, Newington, Orange, West Hartford, Westport, and West Simsbury). Best sellers are almond butter crunch, pecan caramel patties (turtles), and chocolate nut bark, followed by chocolate-layered truffles and chocolate cordial cherries. There are also candy bars, four flavors of fudge, peanut brittle, boxed fruit slices, and chocolate-covered pretzel rods, with new products being taste-tested at the Bolton shop from time to time. Myriad assortments are sold via mail order, online, and in the Munson shops. If it can be found in chocolate, Munson's probably makes it. Open weekdays from 8:00 a.m. to 8:00 p.m., weekends 10:00 a.m. to 6:00 p.m.

University of Connecticut Dairy Bar, 3636 Horsebarn Rd. Extension (off Route 195, Storrs), Storrs/Mansfield; (860) 486-2634; www.canr .uconn.edu/ansci/dairybar/dbar.htm. Fans consider this the best ice cream in this part of Connecticut, which may be why the plain-as-vanilla store draws more than 200,000 visitors a year and has been a UConn icon for generations. Devotees love the ice cream for its creaminess, due in large measure to the 14 percent butterfat content. The Dairy Bar makes a total of twenty-eight flavors, of which twenty-four are available at any one

time. The most famous is Jonathan Supreme (vanilla swirled with peanut butter and chocolate-covered peanuts), named for UConn's mascot. Also popular are black raspberry, coffee espresso crunch, chocolate peanut butter swirl, and the seasonal pumpkin and peppermint stick. Open daily 11:00 a.m. to 6:00 p.m.

Willimantic Food Co-op, 91 Valley St., Willimantic; (860) 456-3611; www.willimanticfood.coop. This lively food co-op (whose motto is "member owned and operated") has been functioning since 1984, benefiting members and nonmembers alike. For an annual fee, members get discounts on the voluminous numbers of food products for sale; nonmembers pay a bit more. The co-op's emphasis is on locally grown, organic, and natural foods, which come in all shapes and sizes—fruits, vegetables, cow and goat's milk, cheeses, honey, maple syrup, bakery breads and pastries, plus health and beauty products. Open Monday through Friday 9:00 a.m. to 8:00 p.m., Saturday until 6:00 p.m., Sunday 10:00 a.m. to 5:00 p.m.

Farmers' Markets

For up-to-the-minute information about dates and times, call the Connecticut Department of Agriculture at (860) 713-2503, visit the Web site at www.state.ct.us/doag/, or e-mail ctdeptag@po.state .ct.us.

Ashford Farmers' Market, Pompey Hollow Park, across from Town Hall, Ashford. Sunday from 10:00 a.m. to 1:00 p.m., mid-June to October.

Bozrah Farmers' Market, Maple Farm Park, 45 Bozrah St., Bozrah. Friday from 4:00 to 7:00 p.m.. early July to late October.

Canterbury Farmers' Market, Josie's General Store, 189 Butts Bridge Rd., Canterbury. Last Saturday of every month from 9:00 a.m. to 2:00 p.m., late May to October.

Colchester Priam Vineyards Farmers' Market, Shailor Rd., Route 2, exit 16, Colchester. Sunday from noon to 3:00 p.m., early July to early October.

Coventry Farmers' Market, Nathan Hale Homestead, 2299 South St., Coventry. Sunday from 11:00 a.m. to 2:00 p.m., early June through October.

Danielson Farmers' Market, Killingly Memorial Library, 25 Wescott Rd. and Route 12, Danielson. Wednesday from 4:00 to 6:00 p.m. and Saturday from 9:00 a.m. to noon, mid-June through October.

Ellington Farmers' Market, Arbor Park, town center, 35 Main St., Ellington. Saturday from 9:00 a.m. to 12:30 p.m., early May to October.

Hebron Farmers' Market, Hebron Elementary School (Route 85), Hebron. Saturday 9:00 a.m. to noon, mid-June to mid-October.

Lebanon Farmers' Market, Town Hall Green, Lebanon. Saturday from 9:00 a.m. to noon, from early June to October, and Wednesday from 3:30 to 6:00 p/m, July and August.

Norwich Downtown Farmers' Market, Howard Brown Park, Chelsea Harbor Dr. (Route 2), Norwich. Wednesday from 11:00 a.m. to 1:00 p.m., mid-June through October.

Norwich Uncas Farmers' Market, Uncas on Thames, 401 W. Thomas St. (Route 32), Norwich. Monday and Friday from 10:00 a.m. to 1:00 p.m., early June through October.

Plainfield Farmers' Market, Recreation Office/Senior Center, 482 Norwich Rd. (Route 12), Plainfield. Tuesday from 4:00 to 6:00 p.m., late June through October.

Putnam Farmers' Market, 18 Kennedy Dr., Putnam. Monday and Thursday from 3:30 to 6:00 p.m., early May to November.

Scotland Farmers' Market, Scotland Green (junction of Routes 14 and 97), Scotland. Wednesday from 3:00 to 6:00 p.m., late May through October.

Somers Farmers' Market, corner of Main and Battle Streets, Somers. Saturday from 9:00 a.m. to noon, mid-June to September.

Stafford Springs Farmers' Market, Mocko's Lot (junction of Routes 32 and 190), Stafford Springs. Monday and Thursday from 11:00 a.m. to 2:00 p.m., early July through October.

Storrs Farmers' Market, Mansfield Town Hall parking lot, Storrs. Saturday from 3:00 to 6:00 p.m., early May through November.

Storrs Winter Farmers' Market, Buchanan Auditorium at the Mansfield Public Library, Storrs. Second Saturday of every month from 3:00 to 5:00 p.m.

Tolland Farmers' Market, Tolland Green, Tolland. Saturday from 9:00 a.m. to noon, first week in May through late November.

Willimantic Farmers' Market, corner of Union and Jackson Strs., under the pavilion, near the Frog Bridge, Willimantic. Saturday from 8:00 a.m. to noon, early June through October.

Bats of Bedlam Maple Syrup, 101 Bedlam Rd., on Route 198, Chaplin; (860) 455-9200; dubos@charter.net. It's not bats but maple syrup that Pat and Bob Dubos have focused on for more than thirty years on their Bedlam farm. Starting with ten acres of "sugar bush"–dedicated maple trees (usually from late February into March), they harvest buckets of top-quality maple sap. This is then boiled down into syrup and sugar for waffles, pancakes, and other tasties. As for the bats, don't worry. There's nothing batty about this operation. Their first-of-the-year run of syrup and sugar usually begins in late February and continues into March. The name refers to Bob's previous profession as vertebrate zoologist and curator of the research collection, which included bats, at the University of Connecticut. If you miss the tap/sap process, you can buy the Duboses' maple products at the sugarhouse or their own house throughout the year—such treats as maple syrup, maple cream, maple candy, maple sugar-coated nuts, maple vinegar, and maple pancake mix. But call ahead.

Blackmer Farm, 438 Quinebaug Rd., North Grosvenordale; (860) 923-2710; rblackmer@charter.net. With ten greenhouses, forty cows, forty acres of sweet corn, a roster of fresh vegetables, and a farm stand on their family farm, Myrtie and Randy Blackmer really have their hands full. Since this isn't a pick-your-own place, it's a good thing they can rely on the help of sons Tod and Mark and their nieces, too, at harvest time when the stand is stocked with fresh-picked-daily cucumbers, eggplants, broccoli, peppers, summer squash, melons, pumpkins, sweet corn, and tomatoes, as well as plants and flowers. The Blackmer farm stand is open from May through October, daily from 10:00 a.m. to 6:00 p.m. Take Route 12 north, then left on Route 131 north.

Buell's Orchard, 108 Crystal Pond Rd., Eastford; (860) 974-1150; www.buellsorchard.com. Henry Buell bought 120 acres here in 1889 and planted Rhode Island Greening apples. His great-grandchildren, Jonathan and Jeffrey Sandness, have not just followed his lead, growing twenty types of apples (Macouns are their best seller; Cameo and Honey Crisp are their newest), they've diversified. Now Buell's also grows peaches, pears, strawberries, cantaloupe, tomatoes, peppers, yellow and green squash, eggplant, pumpkins, and two acres of blueberries. All are available as pick-your-own, except the pears, which are sold (with the other produce) at the farm store on the property. Also for sale are jams, jellies, local honey, and, in fall, chrysanthemums. An additional treat is watching the candied

apple–processing machine churn through some 750,000 apples every autumn. From late August to Halloween, forty-five to fifty apples a minute enter the processor as naked, unadorned fruit, emerging seconds later rolled in cinnamon-flavored caramel with coconut topping, taffy-covered with Heath bar chunks, Jazzy (with fall sprinkles embedded all over), or covered in peanuts or sprinkles. It is a fascinating transformation to witness. The store (off Route 198 via Westford Road) is open early June until Christmas. Check for days and hours. The Web site tells you exactly when each crop is ready to pick. For examples, strawberries in June, blueberries mid-July, peaches August, apples by type (Gala from Labor Day to late September, Ida Red from early to late October, and so on).

Chase Road Growers, 174 Chase Rd., Thompson; (860) 923-9926; chaserdgrowers@aol.com. Jayne and Warren Reynolds have a nursery that specializes in flowers until fall, but it is in their big red barn that you will find fresh vegetables in season. Expect sweet corn, tomatoes, peppers, cucumbers, and other vegetables as they ripen, with pumpkins and gourds available later on. Open late July to late October from 10:00 a.m. to 5:00 or 6:00 p.m. Call ahead to confirm hours and available crops.

Fort Hill Farms, 260 Quaddick Rd., Thompson; (860) 923-3439; www.thefarmerscow.com. What was once an Indian fortress has been—for the past century—a bustling, modern dairy farm. Aside from the 400 Holstein cows that Kristin and Peter Orr raise on their 1,000-acre property, they also cultivate two acres of organic blueberries, which are pickable from early July to late August. In addition, the Orrs have planted a labyrinth with edible organic, pick-your-own lavender, which you may wander through from early June to early October. There are also sixty-six display gardens bursting with flowers in summer, and an unusually large nursery for 2,000 varieties of ornamental perennials. Flowers are for sale from May through November. Call ahead to be sure of the hours and days.

Lapsley Orchard, 403 Orchard Hill Rd. (Route 169), Pomfret Center; (860) 928-9186. John Wolchesky has been tilling his 200-acre farm for more than twenty years and can provide you with a wide variety of fruit and vegetables. He has twenty-eight types of apples, for instance, ranging from the popular McIntosh and Macouns to the newer Honeycrest and Braeburns. The prize is the century-old apple tree that still produces Gravensteins. Pick-your-own-ers are welcome to tackle the apples as soon as the earliest ones ripen— the Jerseymacs usually are first in early August—continuing into October. John also has blueberries, sixteen varieties of peaches, twelve of pears, and nectarines. His twenty acres of vegetables include sweet corn, tomatoes, and pumpkins and fresh flowers for cutting from mid-July onward. In addition to all the produce, John's farm stand carries jams, jellies, and sweet cider. Free horse-drawn hayrides are available on Sunday in September and October. Open daily, July through December, from 10:00 a.m. to 6:00 p.m.

Norman's Sugarhouse, 387 County Rd., Woodstock; (860) 974-1235; r.norman@snet.net. For more than three decades, Richard and Avis Norman have been putting 1,200 taps into the sugar maples on their fifty acres—an annual ritual of converting the sweet sap into delectable edibles. Their results can be seen, sampled, and carried home from their sugarhouse, in the form of maple syrup, granulated maple sugar, maple cream, maple jelly, and candies. Call ahead if you want to witness "the boil," which transforms maple sap into syrup; it goes on from President's Day in February for six or eight weeks. Visitors are welcome at other times of the year, but always call ahead.

Palazzi Orchard, 1393 North Rd., East Killingly; (860) 774-4363. This orchard, owned by Mark and Jean Palazzi, may be best known for its twenty varieties of pick-your-own apples, but it also yields peaches in August and, later, pumpkins and winter squash. The Palazzis offer hayride tours on weekends at harvesttime. Beyond the mouthwatering produce, you'll savor the four-state views from the hilltop; nearby is a Revolutionary War cemetery with the old Charter Oak tree. Open daily, August through December, 9:00 a.m. to 5:30 p.m.

River's Edge Sugar House, 326 Mansfield Rd. (Route 89), Ashford; (860) 429-1510; www.riversedgesugarhouse .com. Driving up a long dirt road (1.5 miles south of Route 44), you will know you have arrived at River's Edge when you see the horses in the field next to a log house and, in the parking area, a neat wooden building that is both shop and processing plant. Proprietors Bill and Amy Proulx make maple syrup there, a process you may watch in February and March. In addition to maple syrup, year-round Proulx products include honey, maple syrup, maple candy, and maple creams. Visitors are

welcome between 10:00 a.m. and 4:00 p.m. on most Saturdays and Sundays. (Call ahead about tours for schools and families.)

Wayne's Organic Garden, 1080 Plainfield Pike (Route 14A), Oneco; (860) 564-7987; www.waynesorganicgarden.com. Wayne Hansen is best known for his unusual certified organic vegetables. Fingerling-size purple Peruvian potatoes (try saying it fast), pink-outside/yellow-inside Laratte potatoes, Walla Walla onions (similar to Vidalias), Italian cipollini, Borretana onions, celeriac, and radicchio are among the specialties Wayne grows and sells at Putnam, Old Saybrook, and Danielson farmers' markets. From mid-May through early June, Wayne's heirloom tomatoes, garlic, and greenhouse vegetable plants are for sale at his Plainfield Pike farm. Call for days and times.

Winterbrook Farm, 116 Beffa Rd., Staffordville; (860) 684-2124; winterbrookfarm@cox.net. Winterbrook's big red barn and farmhouse have been on this spot on Beffa Road since the 1700s. Owners Kirby and Laura Judd haven't been raising Dorset sheep for quite that long, but their tradition of supplying Easter lambs to churches in the area and others who savor lamb does stretch back several years. Order your own Easter or freezer lamb in March to have it available for delivery the week before Easter. The Judds also make maple syrup in their sugarhouse (after March), grow rhubarb in spring, and cultivate pick-your-own-blueberries (July through September). No herbicides or pesticides used. Open mid-July through September, from 8:00 a.m. to dusk daily, but best to call ahead for specific days, hours, and crop availability.

Woodstock Orchards, 494 Route 169, Woodstock; (860) 928-225; woodstockorchards@snet.net. Woodstock Orchards's neat roadside shop, the Apple Barn, is on a road that shoots off from the Green in the center of Woodstock. That's where you'll find the fresh vegetables, blueberries, peaches, pears, and twenty-five types of apples (Ida Red, Red Delicious, Russet, Empire, McIntosh, and Cortland among them) that Harold and Doug Bishop grow on their sixty-five-acre spread. While the Apple Barn also retails preserves, corn relish, pickled mushrooms, pickled garlic buds, and other foods with the Woodstock Orchards label, as well as the farm's own sweet cider and locally made honey, maple syrup, and fresh mums, Harold seems especially proud of his Crisp-Aire apples. Crisp-Aire, you wonder? Those are apples that are stored in a climate-controlled "vault," with the atmosphere lowered to less than 5 percent oxygen, which allows the fruit to retain their crispy-fresh texture even after several months. You may also pick your own apples and blueberries in season. Open August to May from 9:00 a.m. to 6:00 p.m. daily. Call ahead for the picking schedule.

Wright's Orchards & Dried Flower Farm, 271 South River Rd., Tolland; (860) 872-1665; www.wrightsorchards.com. If you like to pick your own, you will love the dwarf and semi-dwarf apple trees that Todd and Joyclyn Wright grow here, making picking easier. Also ripe for the picking are blueberries, raspberries, peaches, and (later) pumpkins. The Wrights, who have farmed along the Willimantic River for more than twenty years, also raise tomatoes, cucumbers, squash, and other vegetables. Flower fanciers will appreciate how unusual and beautiful the Wrights' dried flowers look as they dry in the barn. The Wright farm stand, with its wide array of fruits, vegetables, flowers, fresh cider, preserves, and pies, is open from August until Christmas, 1:00 to 5:30 p.m. Thursday through Tuesday.

Food Happenings

OCTOBER

Buell's Orchard Annual Fall Festival, 108 Crystal Pond Rd., Eastford; (860) 974-1150; www.buellorchard.com. Ever since 1978 this annual harvest event has been held Saturday and Monday—but not the Sunday sandwiched in between—on Columbus Day weekend. At the festival Patty Sandness, Jeffrey's wife, dispenses free cider and doughnuts, while hot dogs, chicken barbecue, burgers, desserts, and other foods are available for sale. There are seven hayrides through the orchards to the pumpkin patch, which is open for pick-your-own, and you can watch the candied apple–processing machine, adding to a very rewarding day-at-the-farm experience for one and all. Call for days and hours.

The Downtown Country Fair, 91 Valley St., Willimantic; (860) 456-3611; www.willimanticfood.coop. This celebration of local businesses is held the first Sunday of October in the outdoor parking lot of the Willimantic Food Co-op. Local restaurants, farmers, crafts people, and musicians hold a daylong fiesta that attracts locals and visitors alike. Call to confirm the date and hours.

Nibbles

Heritage Trail Café at The Winery, 291 North Burnham Hwy., Lisbon; (860) 376-0659; www.heritagetrail.com; $$. When Laurie and Harry Schwartz bought the Heritage Trail Winery in 1996, one of their first moves was to add a cafe, which seats fifty-five indoors, an additional forty-eight outside. Laurie is the vintner, Harry the chef. He serves a number of agreeable dishes, such as starters like seafood chowder, scallop bruschetta, smoked fennel scallops, and smoked mozzarella caprice. His entrees might be smoked loin of pork, braised beef brisket, smoked chicken breast, and pizzetas. All of these are enhanced by a variety of the house wines. Open Tuesday through Sunday from 11:00 a.m. to 8:00 p.m.

Java Jive (across from Mrs. Bridge's Pantry), 283 Route 169, Woodstock; (860) 963-1241; $, is a great place for a full breakfast any time of day, as well as lunch soups, sandwiches, and wraps. Linda and Joe Surozenski open the doors of their cozy place (ten tables and a counter bar) at 6:00 a.m. every weekday and close at 3:00 p.m. Weekends there's a hearty breakfast buffet from 7:00 a.m. on Saturday and 8:00 a.m. on Sunday, and the steaming hot java is good any time, any day.

Twice each summer, usually a weekday in July and August, **Roseland Cottage** offers a fixed-price Victorian dessert tea (with scones, several desserts, fruit, and tea), from 2:00 to 4:00 p.m. The house is a rare example of a Victorian Gothic Revival (built for Woodstock native Henry Bowen) with a beautiful old-fashioned garden, at 556 Route 169, Woodstock. For information and reservations for the tea or for group tours, call (860) 928-4074 or check the Web site: www.historicnewengland.org.

Vanilla Bean Café, 450 Deerfield Rd. (intersection of Routes 169, 44, and 97), Pomfret; (860) 928-1562; www.thevanillabeancafe .com; $. Inside a big restored nineteenth-century barn at a  crossroads in the middle of nowhere is "the" gathering place—attracting Pomfret School students, faculty, and locals—for miles around. The draw is fresh-tasting, home-cooked comfort food—muffins, soups (don't miss the New England clam chowder), chili, burgers of all types, including vegetarian, other veggie specialties, and luscious pies and cakes—as well as good wine and beer lists and a laid-back atmosphere. Breakfast, lunch, and live entertainment on weekends (running the gamut from folk-music concerts and poetry readings to jam sessions and open-mike nights) are also part of the mix. "The Bean" (as everyone calls it), which siblings Barry, Brian, and Eileen Jessurun opened in 1989, had just sixteen seats at first; it is now an ever-expanding northeastern Connecticut institution. From two dining rooms, the action—from April through November—spills out to the tree-shaded brick patio. According to Brian, they use local products as much as possible, local produce exclusively during the growing season. "Our burgers are made from local free-range, grass-fed New Boston Beef," he says. He is proud of their gluten-free offerings, such as a brownie made from black beans, Ghirardelli chocolate, and espresso, and also their popular chili ("we sell eight tons of it a year"). Open daily at 8:00 a.m. Closing hours vary; it is advisable to check ahead.

Learn to Cook

Martha's Herbary, 589 Pomfret St. (junction of Routes 44, 97, and 169), Pomfret; (860) 928-0009; www.marthasherbary.com. Cooking classes are held, usually Saturday between 10:00 a.m. and 1:00 p.m. in the spring and fall. If you call the herbary and leave your e-mail address, information about the classes will be sent to you. Past classes have included soups with herbs, gifts using lavender, pie-making, appetizers, and gluten-free cooking.

Altnaveigh Inn & Restaurant, 957 Storrs Rd. (Route 195), Storrs; (860) 429-4490; www.altnaveighinn.com; $$$. A restored 1740 house, the white clapboard Altnaveigh Inn, with its three dining rooms (two of them warmed in winter by fireplaces), has been a waystation for generations of hungry UConn students and their parents. The cooking is continental, but with such starters as clams casino, Maryland crab cakes, lobster bisque, and scallops wrapped in bacon more consistent than the entrees, I'd suggest making a meal of appetizers. (That will save your wallet too, as entrees are on the pricey side.) In warm weather, you can dine outside on a pleasant patio. There are five guest rooms, so staying overnight is definitely an option, one that is more appealing since new owners Gail and Doug Parks completed extensive renovations to the inn. Closed Sunday and Monday.

85 Main, 85 Main St., Putnam; (860) 928-1660; www.85main.com; $$. When well-traveled professional chef James Martin bought The Vine Bistro in 2005, with his partners Barry and Brian Jessurun of the Vanilla Bean Café in Pomfret, the first thing he did was change the name to 85 Main. The second was to change the decor (now with earth tones and even sleeker sophistication than before) and enlarge the interior (making room for a new bar and raw bar). Then came the menu changes to modern American fusion, with emphasis on shellfish. His raw bar is a rarity in this part of the state. Vine

Bistro regulars wouldn't recognize the place. James has now added a dining patio, which jumps with activity in warm weather. Look for such dishes as mussel fritters (battered in Newcastle Brown Ale), lobster risotto, shrimp pappardelle, and maple-glazed New Bedford sea scallops. Of course, not everything at 85 Main is of the briny shell variety. Aside from wild Alaskan salmon, there's grilled house-cut Angus rib eye, orange and coriander half-chicken, and barbecue platter (with North Carolina pulled pork and pork ribs, corn bread, and seared greens), among several zesty entrees. The small wine list emphasizes California, Italian, and South American choices; note also the presence of several palate-satisfying microbrewery beers and ales. Open daily for lunch and dinner.

The Fireside Tavern at Sharpe Hill Vineyards, 108 Wade Rd., Pomfret; (860) 974-3549; www.sharpehill.com; $$. Lunch or dinner in the eighteenth-century-style Fireside Tavern evokes the past in looks and spirit, though the food—prepared on a wood-burning stove by Catherine Vollweiler, the vineyard's co-owner—is deliciously modern. The ancient-looking barn-red building dates back only to 1998, but it exemplifies Catherine's eye for American antiques and details. The cozy tavern, up a winding wooden stairway, has a double fireplace in the center of the room, ladder-back chairs, and charming murals and seats a mere forty. A single large dining table is on the ground floor near the bar for those who can't handle the stairs. A mere bunny hop from the vineyards is the spacious outdoor terrace, with four weeping cherry trees in the center, where meals are served in warm weather. Though the menu changes often, you will always find grilled dishes, such as wood-fired lamb chops with rosemary potatoes, swordfish grilled with rosemary and Vidalia onions, or wood-smoked Jamaican chicken marinated in a fiery jerk sauce. Look for an exceptionally attractive cheese platter, consisting of English, French, and other European cheeses. Served at their full ripeness, the cheeses make a fine accompaniment to the vineyard wines. Lunch and dinner are on a very limited schedule: Friday, Saturday, and Sunday, by reservation only. It is prudent to plan three weeks ahead or longer, The Fireside Tavern is *that* busy.

Golden Lamb Buttery, 299 Wolf Den Rd. (Route 169), Brooklyn; (860) 774-4423; www.goldenlamb.com; $$. This one-of-a-kind restaurant, ensconced in a big, rambling barn on a working farm of 1,000 acres, is unique in several ways. For one thing, it has been functioning as a restaurant since 1963 with the same owners (Jimmie and Bob Booth) at the same locale. The Booths, now in their late eighties, have turned management over to a granddaughter, Katie Bogert. Visitors will find things much the same. The fixed-price dinner begins with d r i n k s and a

Ellie's Linguine with Turkey (or Chicken) Sausage

Eleanor O'Neill, a creative home cook, makes this simple, hearty dish for her family. It is especially welcome on a cold Connecticut evening. Leftovers can be put in a greased casserole dish and saved or frozen, then reheated in a medium oven.

2 tablespoons olive oil
¾ pound turkey sausage, sliced in half lengthwise and then cut into small chunks
1 red bell pepper, diced
8 large mushrooms, sliced
6 green onions, thinly sliced

¾ pound linguine, freshly cooked
1 small container pesto sauce (store-bought is fine)
½ cup (or more) grated Parmesan cheese, plus extra for passing

1. Heat olive oil in heavy large skillet over medium-high heat. Add sausage, pepper, mushrooms, and onions. Stir well.
2. Sauté until vegetables are soft, about 7–10 minutes. Add cooked pasta, pesto, and 1 cup Parmesan. Toss to combine.
3. Remove from heat and season with pepper and salt to taste. Serve immediately. Pass Parmesan over the top.

Serves 4.

hayride (to live guitar accompaniment) through freshly mown fields, past the sheep, cows, horses, and donkeys grazing on the hillsides. Then guests drift into the converted barn, with its high ceilings, barn-siding walls, fireplace, and hayloft. Festooned with garden flowers, the dining room decor is best described as "sophisticated country casual." There is a choice of four entrees, accompanied by six or seven fresh garden vegetables, always prepared in interesting ways (for example, fresh peas tossed with mint, carrots in a white-grape sauce, celery braised with fennel). During dinner a guitarist strolls through the rooms, singing folk songs. Good food, a genuinely friendly staff, and the appealing country surroundings make an evening here a rare and memorable experience. The Golden Lamb is a destination in itself, one that I never tire of repeating. Dinner reservations are essential. The schedule is now limited to lunch Tuesday through Saturday, dinner Friday and Saturday only, early April through New Year's Eve.

The Harvest, 37 Putnam Rd. (Route 44), Pomfret; (860) 928-0008; www.harvestrestaurant.com; $$. Slightly more formal than most places in this area, with dark floral wallpaper and soft-lighted wall sconces, the Harvest's biggest claim to local fame is as a steak house, with five superb choices, cut to order, with one of six sauces or five stylings (Harvest, Danish, Tuscan, Française, or Montreal). The menu, while largely American, has Italian accents as well. Other commendable dishes: chicken Madrigal, sesame-seared yellowfin tuna, cedar plank–roasted salmon. Desserts not to skip: marjolaine and tiramisu. The Harvest has an admirable wine list—diverse, wide ranging, and surprisingly well priced. A relaxed Sunday brunch buffet is a treat here, too, with ten entree choices. Closed Monday.

The Inn at Woodstock Hill, 94 Plaine Hill Rd., Woodstock; (860) 928-0528; www.woodstockhill.com; $$. There aren't many Connecticut inns as entwined with the town history as this one. It was built in 1816 by William Bowen, a descendant of one of the thirteen "Goers," who founded the town in 1686. William was the grandfather of Henry Bowen, whose pink Victorian Gothic house, Roseland Cottage, is Woodstock's leading landmark. The inn, with twenty-one guest rooms, serves meals (and Sunday brunch) in several bright and pleasant dining rooms. As you feast upon rack of lamb Dijon or grilled filet mignon with Madagascar green peppercorn sauce, you may learn that most of the nearby hills and meadows still belong to the Bowen family. The inn itself, now owned by Richard Naumann, was in the Bowen family until 1981. That's continuity for you! Open nightly for dinner; closed for lunch Monday through Wednesday.

Main Street Café, 967 Main St., Willimantic; (860) 423-6777; www.willibrew.com; $. Partnered with the Willimantic Brewing Company, this pleasant cafe occupies the former workroom of an old 1909 U.S. Post Office building, vacant for almost thirty years when Cindy and David Wollner took it over. As you enjoy a casual flat-bread pizza, baked onion-ale soup, a sandwich, or a full-fledged dinner, note all the post-office memorabilia, along with a monumental 12-by-17-foot mural by Gordan MacDonald, which depicts Main Street in the 1920s. Note also that most dishes on the eclectic American menu are named after northeastern Connecticut towns, so it is possible to order by zip code, as in "I'll have an 06268" (Gurleyville garlic-walnut chicken) or "give me a 06043" (Bolton beer-battered fish-and-chips). Open daily for dinner, closed Monday for lunch.

> "God sends meat and the Devil sends cooks."
> —ENGLISH PROVERB

Still River Café, 134 Union Rd., Route 171, Eastford; (860) 974-9988; www.stillrivercafe.com; $$$. Kara and Robert Brooks have in a very short time proved that green/organic and gastronomy are not oxymorons. In a 150-year-old rusticated barn on a twenty-seven-acre farm, they turn out imaginative gourmet meals that are based primarily on locally grown green and organic ingredients from their own and neighboring farms. Their menu reads like a compendium of fresh local products: grilled Wolfe's Neck Farm hanger steak with roasted North Ashford Farm fingerlings, Ioka Farm's braised short ribs with Brogadoon Farm's Kobe beef "sliders," North Ashford Farm leek and onion risotto, a soft poached Reynolds Farm woods mushroom tart. Desserts might include Bush Meadow Farm feta, made up the road in Union; Buell Orchard's tarte tatin; North Ashford Farm poached pears with red wine; and Cato Corner Farm's Black Ledge cheese. And so it goes—superbly all the way. Open for dinner Thursday through Saturday from 6:00 p.m. to 8:00 p.m., for lunch only Sunday from noon to 1:30 p.m.

The Spa at Norwich Inn, Route 32, Norwich; (860) 886-2401; www.thespaatnorwichinn.com; $$$. In 1983 Edward J. Safdie, owner of the Sonoma Mission Inn & Spa in Sonoma, California, converted a rustic old inn in Norwich into an upscale spa and inn, with handsome public areas, rooms, villas, and grounds. The Mashantucket Pequot Tribal Nation now owns the property, but little has changed. Kensington's is the major dining room, with graceful chandeliers, carpeting, and well-spaced tables. The food is modern American, with attention paid to healthful eating. They aren't kidding about the spa: The amounts of calories, fat, protein, and carbohydrates are listed under each dish on the menu so that you can choose accordingly (or not). It is difficult to  avoid the temptation of Moulard duck breast, lobster purse, porcini-Parmesan gnocchi, and osso bucco—diet be darned! If you are on hand for lunch in temperate weather, the deck, shaded by huge trees, is a wonderfully relaxed place to eat. For a quicker, lighter meal, try **Ascot's,** a knotty-pine-paneled pub with fireplace, whose tasty items include New England clam chowder, smoked wraps, and burgers ($$). There is also casual dining poolside. Open daily for all three meals; breakfast begins at 7:00 a.m.

Trattoria de Lepri, 89 West Rd., Ellington; (860) 875-1111; ww.trattoriadalepri.com; $$. As a former chef at the late, lamented Pastis in Hartford, Frank Lepri brings valuable experience to his new and respected Italian restaurant. Located in a strip mall, seating fifty, the little trattoria dishes up Italian classics and originals, like pork saltimbocca with aged provolone polenta; three-cheese tortellini with sage sausage; shrimp and sambuca (a Lepri original); pappardelle with braised beef and wild mushrooms; and slow-roasted beef short ribs. Closed Sunday and Monday.

Traveler Restaurant: The Food & Book People, off Route 84 (exit 74), Union; (860) 684-4920; $. Situated at the Connecticut–Massachusetts line, this is one of the most unusual eateries in the state—a restaurant and bookstore combined. The plain, knotty-pine-walled dining room and glassed-in porch are awash in books—in bookcases, on ledges and counters, in fact, everywhere you turn. The books are secondhand, but the food is fresh at breakfast, lunch, and dinner. The gimmick is that with every order of food, customers can help themselves to three free books. Art and Karen Murdock, the owners, claim they give away 100,000 books a year,

Lavender Blueberry Banana Bread

Kristin Orr, of Quintessential Gardens at Fort Hill Farms in Thompson, grows edible organic lavender and shares this unusual recipe. She calls it "a good dessert for foodies."

1 stick butter

⅔ cup sugar

2 eggs

1 cup all-purpose flour

1 tablespoon organic lavender buds, finely ground in spice grinder

1 teaspoon baking soda

½ teaspoon salt

1 cup whole wheat flour

3 bananas, mashed

1¼ cup organic blueberries

½ cup walnuts, chopped

1 teaspoon vanilla extract

1. Preheat the oven to 350°F. Grease a 9 x 5-inch loaf pan. Combine butter and sugar. Beat with electric mixer until fluffy.

2. Add eggs, beat well. Sift flour, lavender, baking soda, and salt in bowl. Stir in whole wheat flour. Beat into the butter mixture.

3. Fold in bananas, blueberries, walnuts, and vanilla.

4. Pour into pan. Bake 55 minutes. Cool in pan 10 minutes.

5. Remove from pan and cool on rack.

Fort Hill Farms
260 Quaddick Rd., Thompson
(860) 923-3439
www.thefarmerscow.com

many of which they acquire through library sales. The food is hearty, generous, modestly priced, and appetizing, though in no way fancy. There is a 10 percent senior discount on Tuesday. Thursday through Saturday pizzas and grinders are added to the menu. I particularly like the fried clam strips, whole belly clams, and packed lobster roll off the lunch menu. If you sit on the glassed-in porch, you can view an enormous wooden moose "grazing" on a grassy knoll, with a small pond and Massachusetts visible just beyond. After choosing your free books, wander down a short flight of stairs to browse in Traveler's bona fide secondhand-book store (interesting tomes, but no freebies there!). Open daily; Sunday through Thursday from 7:00 a.m. to 8:00 p.m., Friday and Saturday until 9:00 p.m.

Brewpubs & Microbreweries

Willimantic Brewing Co. & Main Street Café, 967 Main St., Willimantic; (860) 423-6777; www.willibrew.com; $$. The beers at this brewery-cafe are in the town's oldest post office (a stately sandstone building, vintage 1909). They range from the light palate of Certified Gold to P.S. Pale Bock's multinational malt. Brewer and co-owner David Wollner crafts these and more (including many, many seasonals) on the premises, and from the aging tanks they move directly to the taps of the 60-foot mahogany bar that dominates the former post-office customer lobby. David's seasonal suds include Rail Mail Rye, an unfiltered rye pale ale, and AmBerlicious,

"Malt does more than Milton can to justify God's ways to man."
—A.E. HOUSMAN

an American blend with calomel. It is fun to explore all the memorabilia while sipping the house brews. David advises the first-timer to begin with a sampler of five or six tastes. The old post office's sorting room is separated by a glass partition from the dining room over which David's wife, Cindy, has presided since the Main Street Café opened in 1991. Not coincidentally, the cafe offers various beer dinner events each week. Hours: Sunday and Monday, 4:00 p.m. to midnight; Tuesday through Saturday, 11:30 a.m. to 1:00 a.m.

Wine Trail

Connecticut Wine Trail, www.ctwine.com, offers important information about three of the state's wineries in this area, including where they are located and excellent information about each of them, for free. Included are data such as times and hours for tastings, tours, prices, nearby points of interest, and more. The wineries within this region are Heritage Trail Winery, Priam Vineyards, and Sharpe Hill Vineyards.

Heritage Trail Winery and Cafe, 291 North Burnham Hwy., Lisbon; (860) 376-0659; www.heritagetrail.com. Harry and Laurie Schwartz now own this property, which has eight acres of grapes, and have expanded it from a winery to a winery-plus-cafe and gelateria. The main building is an eighteenth-century (1785) Cape Cod house, where the Schwartzes live. To the right of it in the rear

> "A man is a fool if he drinks before he reaches the age of fifty and a fool if he doesn't afterward."
>
> —FRANK LLOYD WRIGHT

of the driveway is the barn with the cafe (see under Landmark Eateries) and wine tasting room. Beyond that is the barn with renovated wine-making equipment. The vineyard plantings include chardonnay, cabernet franc, merlot, and hybrids Cayuga white and Vignoles grapes. Quinebaug White, Rochambeau Red (introduced in 2007), Sweet Reserve (which does double duty as an aperitif), Shetucket Red, and the newest label, Winthrop White, are among Heritage Trail's seven current wines. Tours and tastings are available daily from 11:00 a.m. to 8:00 p.m. Closed Monday.

Priam Vineyards, 11 Shailor Hill Rd., Colchester; (860) 267-8520; www.priamvineyards.com. This winery was started in 1998, when Gloria Priam and her husband, Gary Crump, bought twenty-seven acres of hillside, which they have since augmented with another thirteen acres. Gloria's grandfather and father were in the wine trade in Budapest in the 1890s, later in the United States, so she simply followed family tradition when she and Gary planted seyval, chardonnay, Cayuga, and other grapes and turned their property into a vineyard. In 2001 their Salmon River White won the gold in an international competition, and in 2003 they struck gold again with their Riesling and silver for their Salmon River Red. Their other wines include the crisp Barrel Select chardonnay and Westchester Red.

Priam now boasts two tasting counters (with local cheeses for sale also) and self-guided tours of the vineyard, the latter accentuated by 35-mile views from the hilltop. Open March through December, Friday to Sunday and holidays, from 11:00 a.m. to 5:00 p.m.

Sharpe Hill Vineyards, 108 Wade Rd., Pomfret; (860) 974-3549; www.sharpehill.com. The curving drive from Route 97 to Sharpe Hill Vineyards is 1.5 miles under a canopy of trees, suggesting a property far more ancient than a winery that has only been active since 1992. Young though Sharpe Hill Vineyards may be, its poetically named Ballet of Angels white wine (the state's most popular Connecticut-produced wine), late-harvest Vignoles, and three separate chardonnays have earned gold medals in international competitions. (That chardonnay and a late-harvest Vignoles have earned high praise from *Wine Spectator* magazine, too.) The one-hundred-acre property is no less poetic than the names of some of its products, with vineyards, gardens, and Grandma Moses–look-alike barn-red buildings scattered across the grounds. The rolling hills rise 700 feet above the countryside, and on a clear day you can see forever . . . well, at least into Massachusetts and Rhode Island. Owners Steven and Catherine Vollweiler have handsomely

"I like to keep a bottle of stimulant handy in case I see a snake—which I also keep handy."

—W.C. FIELDS

furnished their Tasting Room (where you may sample the range, including wines made with the vineyard's cabernet franc, St. Croix, and Carmine grapes) in eighteenth-century style, with many hand-crafted objects. It is open from 11:00 a.m. to 5:00 p.m. Friday through Sunday, year-round. The restaurant has more limited hours (see listing under Landmark Eateries). Sharpe Hill delivers to 400 package stores and restaurants in New England.

Appendix A: Food Happenings

January–February
Annual Taste of Stamford
   (Stamford), 35
Taste of Ridgefield (Ridgefield), 35
Wine on Ice (Hartford), 179

March
Maple-syrup-making Demonstrations
   (Woodbury), 108

April
Fairfield County Eats!
   (Stamford), 36
Taste of the Nation
   (New Haven), 245
Taste of the Nation (Stamford), 29

May
Dionysos Greek Festival
   (New Britain), 179
Hotter Than Heck Festival
   (Waterbury) 109
Taste of the Nation
   (New Haven), 245

June
Annual Shad Bake (Essex), 246
Branford Festival
   (Branford), 246
Connecticut Chefs Showcase,
   The, 144
Litchfield Summer Fest, The
   (Litchfield), 109

Appendix B: Wine Happenings

February

Olde Fashioned Winter Celebration, Haight Vineyard, Litchfield; (800) 577-9463. Sample prerelease wines; reservations essential.

March

Barrel Tasting, Haight Vineyard, Litchfield; (800) 577-9463. Early sampling of prerelease wines; reservations essential.

April

Barrel Tasting, Haight Vineyard, Litchfield; (800) 577-9463. Early sampling, continued; reservations essential.

May

Spring Cellar-bration & Barrel Tasting, Stonington Vineyards, Stonington; (800) 421-WINE. Savor last year's harvest, with live music and food from local restaurants.

June

Spring Fest, Jonathan Edwards Winery, North Stonington; (860) 535-0202. Wine, food, and music. Taste of Litchfield Hills, Haight Vineyard, Litchfield; (800) 577-9463. Cooling off with wine.

July

Summer Jazz series, McLaughlin Vineyards, Sandy Hook; (203) 270-8349. Live music, plus wine, of course.

Summer "Cellar-bration Clambake" in late July, Stonington Vineyards, Stonington; (800) 421-WINE. Live bands, food from nearby restaurants.

August

Summer Jazz series, McLaughlin Vineyards, Sandy Hook; (203) 270-8349. The music continues (the wine, too).

September

"Grape Stomp," DiGrazia Vineyards, Brookfield; (203) 775-1616. Third week in September. You, too, can get blue feet.

Harvest Celebration, Hopkins Vineyard, New Preston; (860) 868-7954. Midmonth event: wine tastings, meet the winemaker, live music, buffet; admission charge.

Harvest Festival, Haight Vineyard, Litchfield; (800) 577-9463. Saturday–Sunday at end of the month. Live music, artisan crafts, outdoor cafe, pony rides, hayrides, grape-stomping contests; admission charge.

October

Harvest Fest, Jonathan Edwards Winery, North Stonington; (860) 535-0202. Wine, food, and music.

Harbor Festival, Stonington Vineyards, Stonington; (800) 421-WINE. Day includes picking grapes and seeing them go through the crush; live bands; food from nearby restaurants.

Appendix C: Specialty Foods and Produce

The following businesses, farms, and shops are especially known for these items that they produce or grow.

Almonds
Dr. Lankin's Specialty Foods (Groton), 225

Apples and Cider
Beardsley's Cider Mill and Orchard (Shelton), 29

Belltown Hill Orchards (South Glastonbury), 166

Bishop's Orchards (Guilford), 237

Blue Jay Orchards (Bethel), 29

Bushy Hill Orchard & Cider Mill (Granby), 167

Ellsworth Hill Orchard & Berry Farm (Sharon), 101

Holmberg Orchards (Gales Ferry), 239

Lapsley Orchard (Pomfret Center), 312

Lyman Orchards (Middlefield), 173

March Farm (Bethel), 104

Roberts Orchard (Bristol), 105

Rogers Orchards (Southington), 175
Rose's Berry Farm (South
    Glastonbury), 175
Woodland Farm (South
    Glastonbury), 178
Woodstock Orchards
    (Woodstock), 315
Wright's Orchards (Tolland), 315

Beef and Pork Products
Bush Meadow Farm (Union), 291
Cato Corner Farm (Colchester), 292
DiBacco's Market (Hartford), 151
Dutch Epicure Shop, The
    (Litchfield), 90
Eagle Wood Farms
    (Barkhamsted), 101
Fairfield Meat Emporium
    (Fairfield), 16
Four Mile River Farm
    (Old Lyme), 238
La Molisana Italian Sausage
    (Waterbury), 94
New Pond Farm (West Redding), 11
Stone Gardens Farm (Shelton), 34
Stone Wall Dairy Farm (Cornwall
    Bridge), 106

Tulmeadow Farm Store (West
    Simsbury), 177

Breads and Bakery Goods
Bantam Bread Company
    (Bantam), 83
Beldotti Bakeries (Stamford), 3
Belltown Hill Orchards, Farm
    Market & Bakery (South
    Glastonbury), 166
Beyond Bread (Old Greenwich), 3
Billy's Bakery (Fairfield), 4
Bishop's Orchards (Guilford), 237
Chabaso (New Haven), 208
Colchester Bakery (Colchester), 300
Drawing Room, The (Cos Cob), 40
Fabled Foods (Deep River), 174, 210
4 & Twenty Blackbirds Bakeshop
    (Guilford), 213
Freund's Farm Market & Bakery
    (East Canaan), 102
Harpo's Bakery & Café (South
    Glastonbury), 184
Judies European Bakery (New
    Haven), 215
La Sorpresa (Norwalk), 42
Le Gourmet Store (Greenwich), 42

Chocolates and Other Candies

Chutneys, Relishes, Salsas and Sauces

Freund's Farm Market & Bakery
(East Canaan), 102
Giff's Original (Cheshire), 147
Gourmet Conveniences
(Litchfield), 87
Mel's Hellish Relish (Fairfield), 9
Newman's Own (Westport), 10
Nip 'N Tang (West Hartford), 147
Palmieri Food Products (New
Haven), 216
Pasta Cosi (Branford), 217
Sassy Sauces (Avon), 148
Silverman's Farm, Inc. (Easton), 33

Coffees
Arcadia Café (Old Greenwich), 38
Ashlawn Farm (Lyme), 221
Daybreak Coffee Roasters
(Glastonbury), 151
Kent Coffee & Chocolate Company,
The (Kent), 93
Omar Coffee Company
(Hartford), 154
Spic and Span Market
(Southport), 23
Willoughby's (various
locations), 351

Zumbach's (New Canaan), 24

Eggs and Poultry Products
Bush Meadow Farm (Union), 291
Flamig Farm (West Simsbury), 170
Four Mile River Farm
(Old Lyme), 238
Holbrook Farm (Bethel), 30
New Pond Farm (West
Redding), 11
Ogre Farm (Simsbury), 174
Shortt's Farm and Garden Center
(Sandy Hook), 32
Stone Wall Dairy Farm (Cornwall
Bridge), 106
Walking Wood (Woodbridge), 219
Windy Hill Farm (Goshen), 108

Fish, Fresh
Atlantic Seafood (Old
Saybrook), 222
Flanders Fish Market & Restaurant
(East Lyme), 264
Fuji Mart (Riverside), 17
Gulf Shrimp Seafood Company,
(Plantsville), 152
Star Fish Market (Guilford), 230

Italian Ices

Gelatissimo (New Canaan), 7

Gelato Guiliana (Wallingford), 214

Libby's Italian Pastry Shop (New Haven), 254

Madison Chocolates, 216

Jams and Jellies

Buell's Orchard (Eastford), 310

Freund's Farm Market & Bakery (East Canaan), 102

Hindinger Farm (Hamden), 239

March Farm (Bethel), 104

Roberts Orchard (Bristol), 105

Rose's Berry Farm (Glastonbury), 175

Silverman's Farm Inc. (Easton), 33

Starberry Farm (Washington Depot), 106

Lamb Products

Sankow's Beaver Brook Farm (Lyme), 217

Winterbrook Farm (Staffordville), 314

Maple Syrup and Other Maple Products

Arlow's Sugar Shack (Granby), 165

Bats of Bedlam Maple Syrup (Chaplin), 309

Birch Hills Farm (Ashford), 291

Lamothe's Sugar House (Burlington), 102

McLaughlin Vineyards, 79

Norman's Sugarhouse (Woodstock), 312

Pond Hill Farm (Wallingford), 243

River's Edge Sugar House (Ashford), 313

Sullivan Farm (New Milford), 107

Warrup's Farm (West Redding), 34

We-Li-Kit Farm Ice Cream Stand (Abington), 296

Willimantic Food Co-op (Willimantic), 305

Windy Hill Farm (Goshen), 108

Winterbrook Farm (Staffordville), 314

Milk

Bush Meadow Farm (Union), 291

Cato Corner Farm (Colchester), 292

Shellfish

Atlantic Seafood (Old
Saybrook), 222
Briar Patch Enterprises (Milford), 4
Gulf Shrimp Seafood Company
(Plantsville), 152
Stonington Seafood Harvesters
(Stonington), 218

Smoked Meats/Game/Fish

Bush Meadow Farm (Union), 291
Delicacy Market (West
Hartford), 156
Nodine's Smokehouse
(Goshen), 88
Scandia Food & Gifts
(Norwalk), 20
Star Fish Market (Guilford), 230

Syrups

Birch Hills Farm (Ashford), 291
Knipschildt Chocolatier (South
Norwalk), 9

Teas

A Dong Supermarket
(Hartford), 149
Asia Bazaar (Stamford), 14
Caprilands (Coventry), 297, 300
Chaiwalla (Salisbury), 111
Delicacy Market (West
Hartford), 156
Drawing Room, The (Cos Cob), 40
Harney & Sons, Fine Teas
(Salisbury), 91
Life of Riley Irish Imports, The
(Old Saybrook), 228
Martha's Herbary (Pomfret), 302
Mrs. Bridge's Pantry (South
Woodstock), 302
Oriental Food Market & Deli
(Norwalk), 19
Passiflora Tea Room (New
Hartford), 114
Simpson & Vail (Brookfield), 21
Sundial Gardens (Higganum), 257

Connecticut Eateries Index

Recipes Index

General Index

J

Jasper White's Summer Shack, 272

Java Jive, 319

J. DeFrancesco & Sons, 240

Jean Jones Cooking Classes, 50

Jerram Winery, 140

Jewett City, 233

John Bale Book Company Café,
The, 113

John Harvard's Brew House, 201

Johnny Ad's, 276

John's Café, 126

Jonathan Edwards Winery, 284

Jones Farm and Winery, 30, 31

Judies European Bakery, 215

K

Kaas & Co., 18

Karabin Farms, 172

Kent, 84, 86, 93, 98, 113,
119, 122

Kent Coffee and Chocolate
Company, The, 93

Kent Farmers' Market, 98

Kent Wine & Spirit, 119

Kitchen Zinc, 279

Knipschildt Chocolatier, 9, 39

L

Lakeville, 82, 91, 130

La Molisana Italian Sausage, 94

Lamothe's Sugar House, 102

Lao Sze Chuan, 63

Lapsley Orchard, 312

La Sorpresa, 42

Lebanon, 288, 289, 295, 307

Lebanon Farmers' Market, 234

Ledyard, 207, 234

Ledyard Farmers' Market, 306

Lee's Oriental Market, 227

Le Figaro Bistro de Paris, 63

Le Gourmet Store,42

Lenny and Joe's Fish Tale, 277

Le Petit Café, 266

L'Escale, 71

Libby's Italian Pastry Shop, 254

Life of Riley Irish Imports,
The, 228

Lisbon, 317, 331

Litchfield, 81, 87, 90, 97, 98,
109, 110, 111, 131, 132, 139

Litchfield Farmers' Market, 98, 194

Litchfield Summer Fest, The, 109

Little Thai Kitchen, 64

Liuzzi Cheese, 228

About the Author

Patricia Brooks's interest in ethnic food dates from her early adult years spent in Japan, the Philippines, and Hong Kong. She has been researching and writing about food since her first cookbook, *The Presidents' Cookbook* (with Poppy Cannon), appeared in print in 1968. Since then there have been two other cookbooks and reams of articles on food and travel for such national publications as *Bon Appetit*, *Food & Wine*, and *Travel & Leisure*. She has reported on cuisines, wines, and dining customs from Madrid to Mandalay, Ankara to Agra, Salisbury to Singapore and back. In travel guides on Spain, Portugal, Great Britain, New York state, and New England, co-authored with her late husband, Lester Brooks, she has ferreted out the best, most interesting restaurants in various milieus. Since 1977 she has been the *New York Times* Connecticut restaurant reviewer, reporting over time on more than 2,000 restaurants around the state. Among her twenty-five books are *Best Restaurants of New England*, *Country Inns of New England*, and *Connecticut's Best Dining and Wining*.